THE LIBRARIAN

THE LIBRARIAN

Allie Morgan

EBURY
PRESS

1

Ebury Press, an imprint of Ebury Publishing
20 Vauxhall Bridge Road
London SW1V 2SA

Ebury Press is part of the Penguin Random House group of companies
whose addresses can be found at global.penguinrandomhouse.com

Penguin
Random House
UK

First published by Ebury Press in 2021

www.penguin.co.uk

A CIP catalogue record for this book is available from the British Library

ISBN 9781529107425

Typeset in 11.5/16 pt ITC Galliard Pro
by Integra Software Services Pvt. Ltd, Pondicherry

Printed and bound in Great Britain by Clays Ltd, Elcograf S.p.A.

The authorised representative in the EEA is Penguin Random House Ireland,
Morrison Chambers, 32 Nassau Street, Dublin D02 YH68.

Penguin Random House is committed to a sustainable future for
our business, our readers and our planet. This book is made from
Forest Stewardship Council® certified paper.

To Mum, Dad, Hairy, my furry feline supervisors and the Twittering friends who've been there from the beginning. This is for you.

The events described in this book are based on the experiences and recollections of the author. To preserve confidentiality and the privacy of colleagues, names and other identifying features have been changed. The anecdotes described are not based on any specific individual but rather a selection of composite characters drawing on the various experiences of the author during her time working in various libraries. Any similarities between people or places are purely coincidental.

Chapter 1

The Other Kind of Magic

The day I had my interview for my library position was the day I decided that I shouldn't die. That is, I probably shouldn't die soon. Not if I could help it.

The next day, when I was informed that my interview had been unsuccessful and that I would not be working in the library, I changed my mind about that.

I'd already changed my mind more times than I can count over the previous month but this felt solid, like a plan. I have always liked a good plan. The fact that my mind hadn't changed on the subject in at least twelve hours also added to a sense of permanence. Totality. Finality.

It wasn't that I wanted to die. In fact, I really didn't like the idea of dying at all. It was just – and this all made perfectly logistical sense, I reminded myself – that I had a moral obligation to do so. I had considered merely running away, somehow extricating myself from the ever-dwindling number of bonds and ties I had to other people and things. If I could have made a clean cut from everything, I would have. Perhaps I'd go to France. France seemed nice.

The problem was that it was never really that simple. People would worry when I left and how would I even get away? I couldn't drive. I'd have to use public transport, which could be tracked, as could whatever method of payment I used and, frankly, my bank account had seen better days. If I didn't show up to my next Community Mental Health Team meeting, someone might ask questions, or at least send another stern letter about wasting precious NHS resources.

No, there was really no other option when it came down to it. I would die, a few people would mourn – my husband, my parents, my brother, perhaps some more distant relatives – and then life would go on without me. The 'going on' was the key part.

I was well aware that I had a pair of goblins living in my head. In fact, I regularly regarded myself as one third, larger goblin; a mega-goblin, if you will. I had known the first goblin for most of my life. His name was Depression. The second was a trickier, stealthy beast. Only recently had I learned that his name was Trauma and that he'd been hitchhiking in my skull since I – and presumably my skull – were around twelve years old.

I still had trouble separating the goblins from my own inner voice and it would later transpire that the Gruesome Twosome had been the ones to ignite and stoke the fire of this latest plan. I had always prided myself on being logical, cynical and intellectual. They knew that because they knew me, perhaps better than I knew myself at that point.

Ultimately the goblins had 'reminded' me that every person either makes the lives of others better or worse and, sadly, I was in the latter camp. Just a sad fact. No point in getting upset about it.

Take my poor husband, for example. He was having to support me financially and emotionally now that I'd become too sick to work. ('Or too lazy?' the goblins would often ponder aloud.) My parents, who'd worked so hard to bring me up and provide me with the opportunity to go to university, must be so terribly disappointed by this flunked-out, unemployed, mentally unstable thing I'd become. Of course, they'd never say that out loud but it was only logical, wasn't it?

Therefore, the morally correct thing to do – nay, the obligation I had – was to remove myself from those people's lives and in doing so release them from the burden of my disappointing existence.

I was about to carry on to Phase 2 aka The Planning of the Deed when my phone rang again.

The library.

Well, it couldn't be much worse, could it? Perhaps I'd left something behind, or accidentally lifted a document that wasn't meant for me. How embarrassing.

'Hello? Is that Allie?'

I nodded as I said 'yes'. I still nod when I agree with anything on the phone.

'... change of circumstances; we'd like to offer you the position after all.'

'What? I mean, sorry. Bad reception. Could you please repeat that?'

'Of course. We'd like to offer you the position at the library. Can you start next week?'

I decided, at that moment, that maybe I could delay Phase 2. After all, I'd actually achieved something today, even if by some odd twist of fate. At the very least, I could wait until my next failure (perhaps I'd burn the library down, or catch my tie in the photocopier and choke to death) before moving on to the next phase.

'Uh. Yes. Yes, I can.'

*

If you picked this book up hoping to become a librarian yourself, I'm afraid to say there's no One Right Path into libraries. We all come to this profession from different angles and quite often much of it is down to chance.

Chance, though, is actually more reliable than you'd expect. It takes a certain kind of person to be a librarian and the mere fact that you're reading this now raises the odds of you being just that kind of person.

You don't have to be mad to work here but you do have to be a little bit mad about what you do. It helps to be a little bit mad about books, too.

*

I was a blessed child. For most of my early life, I had access to a huge (and, at the time, seemingly endless) local library in the heart of my hometown. Some of my fondest memories take place amongst the towering stacks.

The library of my youth would nowadays be known as a 'cluster hub' or something equally dry and corporate, but as a child I simply knew it as The Big Library. What would go unsaid but always truly believed was that The Big Library was Magic. Not the kind of fairy-tale magic as portrayed in Disney films but the old kind of Magic: Magic with a capital M, more suited to Grimms' fairy tales and folklore shared in hushed voices on concrete playgrounds the world over.

The Big Library was a liminal space: a place between mundane reality (with all of its school uniforms and times tables and PE kit and lunchboxes) and something else, something wilder. It was a place where every tome contained a universe. One only needed to find a quiet spot (of which there were, blessedly, many) and you could be a pirate, a wizard, a dragon-tamer, a vampire and, later, a criminal detective, a street-smart forensic psychologist or a simple everyman caught up in a conspiracy that spanned continents or worlds.

The library was also a labyrinth. The shelf stacks stretched far beyond the reach of a bookish child like me. Once I'd graduated from the children's section, the entire building beckoned.

I still remember the first day I was told I could now take books from the adult section. The corridors of shelves seemed to stretch into infinity. All that choice! Books upon books upon books ... and at the centre of it all: the librarians!

I was of an age where computerised catalogues existed but were awkward and buggy. The librarians, however, seemed to traverse the serpentine racks with ease. They had their own language for subjects, seemingly random numbers that meant nothing to me but would have them click their fingers and summon forth a book on any subject: 501, philosophy; 538, magnetism; 720, architecture.

In the days before Google, these magicians were our search engines. They were the keepers of knowledge but, best of all, they were willing to share their gift with anyone who asked, for free!

Some children want to be astronauts; I wanted to be a librarian.

*

The deep-blue wallpaper was stained almost green with nicotine. Allie studied the pattern, stale smoke singeing her nostrils and clinging to her hair and clothes.

She felt sick. There was something lodged in her throat, thrumming in time with her heartbeat. It tasted like bile and rust.

A bird sang beyond the window. Blackbird. Orange beak raised to the sky. So blue. Everything was blue.

A shadow fell across her. Weight on her chest. She was trapped, crushed. Her ribs creaked and groaned as her breath came in short gasps. Somewhere, someone was whining, but a thundering roar was rising above it. Her own pulse in her ears drowned everything else out. Her eyes flicked back and forth and she struggled for a breath that wouldn't come, stale cigarette smoke singeing her nostrils ...

'Allie.' A man's voice. Not the man. A different voice. A safe voice.

Allie shuddered. The weight from her chest was gone, as was the blackbird's song and the thundering roar.

She realised that the whining was coming from her. From me. I'm Allie.

'Allie,' Graham repeated. His face swam into view, perfect tanned skin and almost blindingly white teeth. 'Allie, you're safe. You're here. You're grown up. It's Thursday.'

I shuddered again, feeling my weight in the chair (NHS standard plastic, a little bit sweaty).

'Sorry ...' I mumbled but Graham shook his head. I couldn't stop staring at his teeth. How did he get them so white? I'd heard of veneers. Was that what they looked like?

'Don't be,' he said. 'We made a lot of progress there.'

'Did we?' I asked. My throat hurt.

I wasn't supposed to fall into a full-on flashback (or, as Graham calls it, 'an episode of re-experiencing') but it's hard to tread the line. Trauma is an unpredictable little bugger and tends to prefer all or nothing; you either remember it all or you remember nothing.

Up until a few years before, my only option was nothing.

Graham was writing in his notebook. Even when I watched him scribble, I could never decipher his handwriting. Typical psychologist. I'd known plenty over the years but Graham was the first who'd been able to break through that trauma barrier, to flick the switch from not-remembering to full, technicolor memory.

If someone asked me to estimate Graham's age, I honestly wouldn't know where to begin. He was older than my 29 years but existed in that ageless place that some television personalities and presenters seem to occupy. Perfectly manicured and turned-out, I always imagined him going over his lines before I arrived. I half expected someone to call for all-quiet-on-set when our sessions began. The world's strangest sitcom, live in front of the world's quietest live audience.

We went over some grounding techniques as I returned to the present. I was no longer in my childhood body. I flexed my fingers and toes and reminded myself of that as he talked me through some breathing. He let me know that I had continued talking throughout the flashback, though I had no memory of doing so. I wondered if it was in that strange, childish voice that sometimes comes through when I dissociate, so little and contrary and alien.

I decided I'd rather not know.

'So,' he said finally as I reached for my phone to type in the date for my next appointment, 'you mentioned suicidality.'

That thing – that thrumming lump – was back in my throat. 'Uh …'

'Is that still there?'

I cleared my throat and shook my head. 'Not so much.'

He smiled and I was staring at his teeth again. Were they glowing? What did you say to the dentist to achieve that effect? Veneers? Lasers? Little LED lights?

'Good,' he said. 'So, are you looking forward to your first day in the new job?'

I shrugged. 'I think so. Maybe.'

'I really think this could be good for you, Allie.'

'I hope so.'

*

The library itself was located within a local community centre. At one time, the entire building was nothing but library: bookshelves in every direction, a children's library upstairs and space, glorious space, for activities and events, so like the magical setting of my favourite childhood memories.

These days, Colmuir Library is a shadow of its former self, almost literally. Relegated off to the back corner of the stone-and-brick building, the library is a narrow gauntlet of a room that runs from the middle of the community centre to the back, latched on like a fading parasite.

The one remaining external window provides very little light and so the flickering halogens that hang from the ceiling are on throughout the opening hours, doing little to help the overall visibility while simultaneously deepening the shadows.

The rest of the community centre was converted into a gym several decades ago, complete with a small therapeutic swimming pool. These days, the pool room is gone – the roof having collapsed some seven or eight years ago and the pool itself dried up and unusable long before then. Several 'renovations' later, there's still a lingering smell of the damp caused by the pool's final flooding, which soaked the place to the foundations.

Now, aside from the library, the Colmuir Community Centre's main function is to provide halls for rent. These spaces are used by charities and diet groups and even a local Spiritualist Church. Most of the time, however, the place lies empty.

When I first arrived, the library was locked up. I loitered in the hallway of the centre, admiring the modern fronting and the slick, automatic doors that opened without a sound. Somewhere, in one of the halls, someone was singing, slightly off-key. It echoed. The reception desk appeared to be unmanned, though I could see through to the office beyond where signs of life were scattered across surfaces: a vape pen sticking out from beneath a folder, a dirty mug with a fork in it, a pair of scuffed leather women's shoes under the desk.

I glanced again at the old wooden doors that separated the library off from the rest of the centre (paint peeling in places and scraped in others) and then back at my watch.

When the building was repurposed, nobody bothered to remove the windows that now faced into the community centre instead of out onto the street as they originally had, and so they were still covered by wrought-iron bars. I stuck my head between the bars to squint into the gloom.

The library remained stubbornly unoccupied.

Just as I was extracting my head from the window bars, a squeak and shuffle of rubber-soled shoes on tiled flooring announced the presence of my team leader and trainer for the day, Heather. She was late.

Her keys rattled on the floor as they slipped from her hand. She was juggling various folders and a mobile phone beneath an enormous padded raincoat and she only noticed me as she straightened up, the loose strands from the messy chignon at the base of her neck falling into place around her face.

'What are you doing there?' she asked sharply, her pencilled eyebrows coming together in a frown that I would come to know well. 'The library's closed.'

'I'm Allie,' I replied, 'starting today? You interviewed me last week.'

Her expression relaxed only slightly as she jabbed her ring of keys at the door to the library, scraping at the paintwork as she missed the lock several times.

I approached her cautiously and offered a hand. I was about to ask if she'd like me to take a folder or two when she shoved the lot into my arms.

'Yes. Right. Yes. Sorry. You look different today. Okay. We're running late but I'll catch you up.'

Everything she said came out in a breathless flood. I wondered if she'd been running. According to the opening times sign, the library was due to open in ten minutes.

I barely had time to look around as we stumbled inside. The first set of heavy wooden doors gave way to a second, smaller, more modern set. There were all manner of slide-locks and pad-locks and switches around the doors. It seemed to be a complex process, like entering a high-security prison.

It was an early autumn morning and so we entered in darkness. I tiptoed in to find that Heather had already somehow manoeuvred her way into the IT section, where she slapped her way through an enormous bank of light switches and began punching in the alarm code.

The lights blinked, one by one, into life.

I'd been here once before for my interview so the place wasn't entirely new to me. The reception desk faced the door, which sat at the front end of the library, next to the IT section, which was separated from the rest of the library by plastic dividers and bookshelves. The result of the shelf positioning was such that only the tiny IT section received any natural light, with the darkest area being reserved for the children's section at the back. The rest of the library revealed itself to me in stages, as each light eventually hummed into life.

'Right ... keys.'

Heather had been talking to herself the whole time. I was trying to listen in but it only came in bits and pieces. She was pulling open drawers, throwing things in cupboards and fiddling with the buttons on that enormous rain jacket.

I sat her folders down on the desk beside the staff computer and followed her at a safe distance, which was difficult because the reception area itself was clearly designed to be occupied by one person at a time.

As Heather rushed through the set-up, I took the opportunity to throw my things in the cleaning-cupboard-cum-staffroom, shaking off the morning's chill. Heather thrust a piece of paper into my hand and urged me to find a pen.

'Opening procedures,' she explained. 'Follow along and tick them off as you go. I'd like to go through them in more detail but we're running late.'

We again.

It's very simple, she explained, as she dashed around the room. Unlock the doors, turn on the lights, input the alarm code (you'll see it on your procedural documentation, there), lock the doors again, open the blinds, turn on the staff computers, turn on the public computers – oh, don't worry if the monitors are stuck; someone keeps pulling the power buttons off – sign in to the archiving software, put the padlocks in the drawer ...

I tried to jump in and ask where the padlocks came from but she was at full pelt. I tried to follow along on the list but it was some sort of corporate document and there was so much jargon between each step that I started to become a bit lost.

'—oh, and health and safety!' she announced suddenly. 'Health and safety always comes first. We're having an audit soon. Oh God, I'll have to get you to sign all of the ... never mind. Look at this.'

She stood by a half-height cupboard. It was more of a hatch than a door. She retrieved a key from her enormous jailor's set and unlocked the door.

'Always mind your head in here. I'll go in for now. You don't have your confined spaces training.'

Just the thought of confined spaces training instilled a twinge of claustrophobic anxiety in me but I simply nodded and followed along.

The hatch led to what can only be described as a crawl space within the stone walls of the building. It wasn't quite tall enough to stand in. Heather stooped inside and began going through the procedure of removing cash from the little steel safe inside the crawl space. I decided to assume that all scurrying sounds were definitely my imagination as I poked my head inside.

For some reason the phrase 'for the love of God, Montresor!' popped into my head and I struggled to shake its familiarity as Heather went on.

All in all, we were only two or three minutes late in opening the library. I was still pondering the line as Heather reopened the entrance door with a flourish.

The last time I'd worked with the public was my restaurant days. I used to do a bit of waitressing some days, a little bit of kitchen work on others. It was mostly to support my higher education.

One thing that was drummed into me from those days was timekeeping. The public does not like to be kept waiting. Not for pizza, or change; not for anything. There were days when I'd spend the entire shift simply taking names and party sizes so that we could allocate tables in the quickest possible time. We'd have secret shoppers come in and quite literally time how long it took for us to retrieve a drink from the bar and bring it to a customer's table. It was in that industry that I picked up my habit of power-walking whenever I'm on the clock.

There were no queues for this library. The doors swung open to reveal an empty hallway.

'Right then,' Heather said briskly, finally slowing down enough to look at me. 'Let's begin your training.'

The Cask of Amontillado, I recalled as she sat behind the desk; I felt almost triumphant. *That's* where the line was from. 'For the love of God, Montresor!'

Library assistant training, it turned out, mostly consisted of lists. In fact, most of the role itself was list-based.

Having worked in archiving previously, I found that the software used for issuing and returning books was fairly familiar. It didn't take me long to get to grips with the barcode scanner and till, either.

But oh, the lists.

We tracked footfall, Heather explained. There was a laser sensor on the door. Every time the beam was broken, the counter went up. The higher the number, the better. Library funding (and therefore staffing and opening times) was allocated based on footfall. It didn't matter whether Mr Smith wandered in and out several times a day and didn't take anything. It didn't matter if we failed to loan out a single book; so long as the counter's number remained high, everything would be fine.

I wondered why nobody just waved their hand in front of the thing to put the numbers up. Maybe they did.

Next, the stock. At this library, physical book stock took up, at most, one quarter to one-third of floor space. The vast majority of stock movement happened within the children's section. The large print moved with the regulars. Crime did okay. Everything else? Well … it sat and gathered dust.

IT was where most of the foot traffic came from. Computers filled every surface wherever possible. Those were the money-makers. Surfing the internet was free, so long as you were a library member. Most people came in to do their job search. Prints were 15p a sheet. That's where the majority of the library's income was generated.

I found my eyes glazing over as Heather went over the IT service in more detail. The computers were old, running on a version of Windows I hadn't seen in years. The keyboards were sticky and the monitors were in 4:3 format. The standard council disclaimer that popped up after login was entirely in bold, itali-cised Comic Sans.

If despair were somehow made physical, it would be a council-run IT service.

The laser printer reeked of spilt toner. Heather was showing me how to replace the paper in it and clear a paper jam. 'It only works in black and white, you see …'

I struggled to contain my disappointment, which was a sur-prise. It's not that I expected more from a library, it was just so … quiet. Gloomy. Run-down.

Even the books seemed sad in their dusty, standard-issue plastic jackets. They were supposed to be in alphabetical order and for the most part they were but very little care or attention had been paid to how they'd been put back on the shelf. Novels were shoved and crammed into spaces that didn't really exist, resulting in a haphazard mess of upside-down books and squashed jackets, peeled covers and curled edges.

'Of course, you'll need to sign through your shelving procedural documents. Then the IT ones. Then the Digital Privacy ...'

Heather was flicking through the ring binders on the reception desk. It slowly began to dawn on me that she expected me to read and sign everything she'd brought with her.

'Um ... why are the hardbacks separate?' I asked, taking a rare pause in her commentary to speak at last.

'Hmm?'

'In the romance section. There are romance paperbacks and romance hardbacks.'

'It's better that way.'

I bit my lip. I couldn't imagine why. Did people care about the format of their book? Even if they did, in a place this size, with so few books, did they really care that much? The paperbacks were on a plastic turnstile, all out of order and crumpled.

'I like it that way,' Heather said. She eyed me suspiciously.

I cleared my throat and gestured to the nearest form on the desk, helpfully entitled SOP 297-A: chemical storage.

'So, um ... I need to sign this too?'

The suspicion was gone. Heather was back on script. She nodded. 'Yes, yes. We're having an audit, you see. You need to be signed off on these things.'

'And uh ... this one?' SOP 306: Swimming Pool Decontamination. 'Is that important?'

Heather looked at me as though I'd grown a second head and I silently cursed myself. She was joking! Of course, she was joking. There was no way a library assistant would ever need to decontaminate a swimming pool. She'd brought these folders here with all of the random procedural documentation the council had and wanted to see how far along I'd go with the charade before saying something.

'I guess the pool's in the staffroom, right?'

I laughed but she didn't laugh with me. Her eyebrows were together again, her mouth a perfect, thin line.

'We're having an audit,' she repeated. 'You need to be trained and signed off on all of these procedures.'

I blinked. She wasn't bluffing. There was no sparkle of a hidden joke in her eye. She was serious.

I opened the first ring binder, pulled out the first procedure sheet (SOP 100: Lightning Strikes and First Aid) and started to read.

*

It went like this for the first few weeks: I showed up, I was let in by a more experienced member of staff. I read forms. I signed forms. I read lists. I signed lists. I made lists. I photocopied lists. I printed lists from emails.

When Heather wasn't there (she was the team leader for several branches in the area), I was joined by Ruth, a septuagenarian with sparkling blue eyes, a gentle, fairy-godmother voice and little-to-no sense of hearing.

Ruth mostly got on with the day-to-day running of the library and I shadowed her as she scanned in returned books, dusted shelves and assigned computers to the regulars with a sort of exhausted resignation. She was long past retirement age, she admitted: 'Library work just isn't what it used to be.'

It quickly became clear that the branch had become little more than an IT suite for most users. I watched over the top of my latest stack of forms every time the library door creaked open, only to feel a little dip of disappointment when the library user requested access to a computer.

Eventually, however, we started to receive visits from the Readers.

Readers are not just people who read. They are the vivacious library users who devour every new book as it comes in. They are the ones on 100-people strong reservation waiting lists. They are Readers-with-a-capital-R: the ones who still use the library's magic.

Each Reader tends to fall into one of two camps: the first is the young parents. Children's books are expensive, especially when babies and toddlers grow out of one style and into another in mere weeks. The library had a good stock of nursery books (kept in an enormous wooden box in no particular order) and they moved well.

The second – and largest – group of Reader is the elderly user. These (mostly women) are a force to be reckoned with. My first interaction with an elderly Reader involved a Mrs Callaghan – a tiny octogenarian in a twin-piece – shuffling through the door with a trolley stocked full of books.

'Second time this week!' she announced with a grin as she began the arduous task of decanting her finished books onto the desk. She had a laugh like a fairy godmother, musical and a little bit mad-sounding.

Ruth scanned them one by one at an equally leisurely (or perhaps a little less than leisurely) pace. I found myself counting them as they were passed from walker to desk, to shelving-trolley.

Sixteen books. Twice a week. Thirty-two books a week.

'Didn't like that one,' Mrs Callaghan said, gesturing to one of the larger hardbacks. 'Too silly. Not enough grit.'

'I've kept some aside for you,' Ruth replied, 'from our delivery yesterday.'

Thirty-two books a week. That was, what, well over a thousand a year? Surely not. Surely she had to take breaks. The maths of it all bothered me. Were there even that many books in the library?

With hindsight, I no longer doubt the numbers behind that first, startling revelation. Capital-R Readers are something quite incredible.

Once Mrs Callaghan had left (with another sixteen books), Ruth explained that Mrs Callaghan had, like many of our elderly readers, read everything in the library. Ruth had to keep new titles aside for her. She ordered in books from other branches for many of the elderly Readers. Anything with a grisly murder or gruesome discovery would keep Mrs Callaghan happy.

I was suddenly in awe of this tiny, magical woman.

'Can you make me a list?' I asked.

'Of books?'

'Of regulars. What they like. I could order some in for them.'

Ruth beamed a smile worthy of a Werther's Original advert. 'That's a good idea.'

She let me serve at the desk for a while. Soon, I'd be able to do this unsupervised. I looked forward to getting stuck into tidying the stacks (I'd already cleared the crime shelves of more than one cobwebbed crisp packet) and creating displays.

*

It had taken me less time than I'd expected to have the opening and closing procedures down to a fine art and soon I found myself expertly locating the alarm panel and bank of light switches in the dark, ducking into the crawl space for the safe without hitting my head and even answering enquiries from members of the public with a relative degree of certainty.

As autumn brought with it longer nights and a chill in the air, it was not uncommon to find several poor souls huddled in the hallway of the Colmuir Community Centre up to an hour before opening time. Over time, I got to know these gaunt, poverty-stricken men and women (often young, always polite) as the residents of the local tenement flats who had had their heating cut off due to lack of payment or neglectful landlords.

I was shocked by the depths of poverty I came to see in that time. I was born to a working-class family and while we did have our share of difficult times there was nothing that could have prepared me for the daily realities that some of the users of that little library and community centre experienced.

One of them, a young man called Aaron, was an ex-heroin addict who spent every minute of the library opening hours within its walls, either using a computer or thumbing through a novel.

Some days, Aaron was the only person in the library with me, which quickly created a sense of familiarity between us. We'd chat about the status of his job search (useless, nobody wanted to hire an ex-addict) and his plans for lunch that day. (Nothing today so that he could have chips for dinner. Some days I'd see the poor boy with a loaf, just eating slices of plain bread to stave off the hunger.)

Poverty was awful but boredom, he said, was the killer. Nothing will turn an ex-addict back into a full-blown user like boredom. He couldn't afford to go shopping or travel, so he came to the library. He tried to read (he'd dropped out of school early to feed his habit so his reading was almost entirely self-taught), played games on the computer, searched for jobs and watched endless documentary videos on YouTube. His hearing was poor after repeated ear infections, so even with his headphones in I could always tell what he was learning about each day.

Aaron quickly became part of the furnishings of Colmuir Library. I could usually smell him before I entered. The boiler in his flat was never working and so he couldn't shower. Instead, he'd douse himself in the cheap deodorant left for public use in the community centre's toilets. He didn't have a phone (and his electricity was regularly cut off anyway) so he would rely on his social worker and anyone else seeking to contact him calling the library instead.

Occasionally I would – much to Heather's disapproval – allow Aaron to meet with his social worker in an unused meeting room upstairs. The room was musky, damp and not intended for public use but at least it was private and afforded the lad some sense of dignity.

At the weekends, children from the local primary school would shuffle in with their parents or guardians to take out books on their history research topics for the year: usually Vikings, Romans, Ancient Greeks or World War II.

Only one child came in alone. She must have been around seven or eight, chubby in the way that children who are about to have a growth spurt are. She had bright-red hair, which was always pulled up into a ratty pastel-blue scrunchie, and she would simply stare, one finger absently poking at the freckled dimple in her cheek, at the rainbow parade of children's books.

For the first few weeks, I'd ask if she would like some help, to which she'd shake her head and run outside.

'Funny wee lassie, that,' Aaron would comment. 'I used to know her da.'

After three weeks of the same routine, I became determined to connect with this red-haired, wide-eyed girl. I recognised the uncertainty in her stare. I knew the anxiety in her fidgeting hands. I recognised myself in that little girl, all alone in a place that could be a haven if she just took the next step.

The next time she appeared, I was flicking through Roald Dahl's *Matilda* at the front desk. She hesitated upon seeing me and I took my chance.

'This one's my favourite,' I said, holding it up. 'Have you ever read it?'

She shook her head.

'Oh, it's great! It's about a girl with magic powers! She uses them to beat her big bully of a headteacher.'

The girl dropped her hand from her face. 'What sort of powers?'

I held the book out to her. 'She can move stuff with her mind. She's super smart, smarter than everyone she knows.'

The girl took the book from me and examined it. I'd had a feeling the first time I saw her. The way she studied the books suggested that she wanted to be a reader, maybe even was one already. What was holding her back from the library was the fear of strangers.

Silently, the girl took the book to the children's section, sat on one of the plastic seats and began to read.

Aaron made a 'huh' sound and returned to his documentary. (*Battleships of World War II.*)

The next day, the girl – who I'd come to learn was named Rebecca – returned but this time she wasn't alone.

'Th-this is my dad,' she whispered, clutching the large man's hand.

Rebecca's father wasn't particularly tall, but he was wider than the doorframe, all of it muscle. Even in his shapeless t-shirt it was clear that he not only spent a lot of time working out but getting into fights – or possibly wrestling alligators. His face and arms were pitted and scarred. His teeth were cracked and uneven and he appeared to have several amateur-job tattoos on his neck and hands.

''S'cuse me,' he said in a voice that seemed disproportionately soft for the form from which it came, 'I uh … lost some books a while back. Other lass that worked here said I had to bring them in. Thing is, they're baby books for the wean and I've been, uh … in the jail.'

Rebecca nodded. 'The other lady said I can't get books because the card is blocked.'

I could picture Heather lecturing the child on the importance of paying fines and returning library books. I could see her pointing out SOP one-hundred-and-whatever 'Fines and Lost Item Procedure' at length to this little girl who so clearly wanted to just sit in a corner and read. No wonder the wee girl had been so nervous.

'Do you have your card with you?' I asked.

The man shook his head. 'Er … nah … it all went. When I was in the jail. She usually looks me up by my name. Craig Young, that is.'

I turned to Rebecca. 'That's okay! You go and pick some books and I'll sort this out with Dad.'

Her eyes lit up. 'Can I take them home?'

I nodded and she ran off wordlessly, almost tripping over herself on the way to the children's section.

'All right, Mr Young, I'm going to look up your account and you're going to tell me that you've just had an extended stay in the hospital, okay?'

'Uh … what will I say I was there for?'

'That's a private matter and absolutely none of my – *or any other staff member's* – business,' I emphasised. 'Maybe we should sign Rebecca up for a card of her own, too.'

'They have books about WITCHES!' Rebecca called from behind the stacks.

Mr Young mouthed a 'thanks' at me and left to join his daughter in the children's section.

'Do you want your own card?' he asked.

From behind a display about local wildlife, Rebecca shrieked with excitement.

Perhaps there was still some Magic here after all.

Somewhere outside, something went bang, followed by the shriek of a car alarm.

Chapter 2

Conflict Management

Visitors Daily (average) September: 55
Enquiries Daily (average) September: 8
Printed Pages Daily (average) September: 36
Violent Incidents September: 5

It quickly became clear to me that Heather wielded her authority over library users at any given opportunity. Despite the fact that I had barely crossed paths with her since that first flurry of a day, evidence of her strict enforcement of 'the rules' was everywhere.

From the children who – like Rebecca – clearly wanted to borrow books but dared not ask, to adults who would apologise profusely before I even scanned their card, the fear Heather inspired in these people hung over the place like a storm cloud.

All of this fear seemed to revolve around fines.

Several times a day I'd find myself comforting a library user after pointing out a fine on their account because they were convinced that they'd be unable to access the library services any more. Some appeared to visibly flinch as I turned the computer monitor to show them the message that popped up on their account, detailing the cause and cost of the fine.

Twenty pence per day was the going rate for late returns, up to a maximum of three pounds per item. While this could

certainly pile up, the entire exercise struck me as counterpro-
ductive, especially when coupled with Heather's overzealous
enforcement.

The vast majority of people with fines were regular users
who'd had an issue crop up, usually health-related, sometimes a
simple misreading of a due date. The problem was that Colmuir's
locals were, by and large, dirt poor and several pounds' worth
of fines could be the difference between a meal that day and
going without.

I spent the first few days working alone waiving fines left,
right and centre. It struck me as profoundly unfair (and still
does) to punish someone for being sick, for missing a bus, for
being caught out with childcare or anything else life throws
at us. Not only do financial penalties disproportionately punish the very poorest for their financial situation, but they
compound the problem. Someone who is only just scraping
by is already likely to be juggling a whole host of responsibilities and is, therefore, less likely to have the time (or a
reliable means of transport) to get to the library and return
borrowed books.

Of course, there will always be those who simply do not
return books on time out of laziness. Of course, there are those
who will be more motivated to return the books on time due to
the threat of fines but, in my experience, as it was in those first
few weeks, fines actually deter people from using the library *at
all*, especially those who need the library most.

Technically, any account that had several lost items or had
accrued more than fifteen pounds in fines was blocked from
accessing all library facilities, including computers. Heather
had informed me that she believed the fifteen-pound threshold was far too lenient and I began to encounter users who

would beg and plead for the use of a computer, even though they had only accrued two or three pounds' worth of fines on their account. Clearly, Heather had her own, much lower, limit.

I was quite honestly astonished by either her ignorance or her cruelty. Surely she knew that a great many of these users required access to the computers to apply for welfare, for financial help, to pay bills and to keep themselves from becoming homeless? I honestly don't know if it crossed her mind.

Obviously, I did not enforce Heather's rule when it came to fines and usage of the computers. In fact, I'd allow anyone, so long as they weren't barred for non-financial reasons (which would be flagged up on their account) to use the computers. What was the point in refusing? They wouldn't suddenly become un-poor, producing some previously unavailable money from a pocket they'd forgotten about.

It took only a week of this, along with the waiving of any fines I perceived as unfair or likely to dissuade the user from returning (after all, weren't we funded on footfall alone?), before I received an email from Heather. In it, she claimed that my staff login had been flagged for 'excessive fine waiving', a claim which I, even now, do not believe. In truth, I believe that she was merely keeping an eye on the newcomer's financial transactions and didn't like the look of what she saw.

Who was I to argue? I hadn't been in the job long enough to make any kind of moral stand. Still, the petty enforcement didn't sit right with me.

The first time a library user burst into tears – a young woman who needed access to the computer to apply for jobs and receive her unemployment benefits – and offered me the change she needed to get the bus home, just so she could pay off some of the paltry fine she'd accrued from a slightly overdue book for her baby, I knew I couldn't work this way.

'Keep your money,' I said. 'Here's the staff guest login. I didn't give you this. How long will you be?'

'Ten minutes tops. I promise,' she replied.

'Okay. Don't tell Heather.'

That became a bit of a catchphrase of mine for a while. 'Don't tell Heather.'

The thing is, that young woman came back a week later and she did pay off her fines. As far as I know, she never borrowed a book again, though. It angered me to think that her baby boy would miss out on his first books because the library held his mother's access to her benefits to ransom.

Many people have disagreed with me about library fines over the years. If you work in a library, you'll know all about the debates that rage on the secret chat groups, forums and Facebook groups about it. There have been countless articles and posts made about the matter and I know that there's no One Right Answer.

I can only speak from experience and my experience is that fines don't help anyone. They're too small to be of any actual benefit to the branch and they're too easily exploited by power-hungry jobsworths.

If our goal is to have as many people accessing the library as possible and bridge the gap between rich and poor when it comes to access to information, then fines are antithetical to that aim. The rich shrug them off and the vulnerable, the anxious and the poor are put off returning to a place that – by all rights – is already paid for in their taxes.

Yes, books go missing. The majority of the time those books will never be seen again and certainly never replaced by the user. Those who use the library regularly and properly are not in the habit of losing books, unless by genuine mistake. (More than once I've left a book on a chair in an airport, or a hotel room, or even a café table. It happens to us all.) The people who keep books and never return them are the people who visit the library once and never come back. No amount of fines or restrictions on access to services will change that.

If we must have fines, then let us also have regular amnesties. Let us have weeks when books can quietly make their way back into stock without fuss and any fines accrued, struck off. Let us re-welcome those potential readers who were made to feel anxious and judged.

In the meantime, I came up with a compromise: I would not enforce the restriction of services below the fifteen-pound fine mark. I'd still waive fines accrued for hospital stays and other life-or-death situations but I'd have to be more selective.

After a bit of back-and-forth with Heather, she agreed that those above the fifteen-pound threshold could make use of computers if they paid something towards the fine each time. That could be a pound, ten pence, whatever.

What she didn't know was that I would secretly gather any dropped change during the day and put it in a drawer. Any time someone told me to keep the change from buying old stock or paying for prints, it, too, would go in the drawer. Then, when a fifteen-pound-plus member desperately needed to use a computer and didn't happen to have any change to hand, I'd use the secret drawer change.

Did some people take advantage of my kindness? Probably. Frankly, I don't care. Ultimately, I didn't ever want to be the cause of someone going without food for the week. If that makes me a mug, then so be it.

Until you see the kind of poverty that exists in places like Colmuir, you cannot conceive of the difference a few pence can make to someone.

Working alone also gave me the freedom to take the initiative when it came to library maintenance. It allowed me to come in early and pull the racks apart to give them a good clean. Even during opening hours, if I suspected that the shift would be a quiet one (as most of them were), there was nobody to keep me from hauling the books off entire shelves, wiping them down and repairing stretched covers or torn pages to the best of my ability.

The work was meditative and I spent many an hour on these simple, repetitive tasks.

With the freedom that lone-working brought came a downside, one that began as a mild annoyance and quickly became all-consuming, engulfing every other responsibility and ambition I had for the place.

Working alone meant that I was vulnerable and unsupported. The library being open to anyone meant just that: we were open to *anyone*.

It was one of those early, optimistic days at the beginning of my time at Colmuir that taught me the dark side of lone library work.

I had come in early to tidy the shelves. They looked ... well, the books had seen better days but they were all in proper order now, no upside-down novels or hardbacks stuffed down the backs of displays. Speaking of displays, I spent ten minutes swapping out books for the upcoming autumn season. The work was soothing, almost hypnotic.

I gave the computer mouse a quick shake as I sat down. The cataloguing system interface blinked into existence. The accessions list was empty, like a blank page. The cursor blinked, waiting for a barcode.

The library door swung open with a heave and a creak that I'd later come to hear in my dreams at night. A large figure filled the gloomy doorway for a moment before staggering into the jaundiced light.

I smelled him first. It was the sweet smell of overripe fruit, slightly vinegary. The sour smell of dried sweat tickled my throat as the man appeared in a cloud of old cigarette smoke. He was almost as tall as the doorway, completely shaven head pitted with dents and scars. His round chin was covered in patchy stubble and he wore paint-splattered overalls, a sports jacket and a spaced-out, sleepy expression.

My dad has a phrase that always pops into my head when I see someone in what I assume is this state of inebriation: 'One eye going into the shop, the other coming out with the change'. It refers to the way that a drunkard's eyes seem to move and blink independently of one another. This bloke had the tell-tale wandering squint.

Something was off, though. I'd seen people on drugs. I'd seen junkies in the depths of a fix and teenagers tripping off their heads. This wasn't that, exactly, though the sour, rotten smell did remind me of when I used to work in a distillery.

''S'cuse me, hen,' he slurred and my chest tightened.

Not just drunk. Or high. He was staggering towards me, one eye fixed on me briefly before his eyelids fluttered and I could see only whites.

I instinctively stood, putting my chair and the desk between us. Still, I was the new face. This was my job. I was the keeper of the information, the book magician. I helped everyone.

'Hi,' I managed.

He appeared not to notice my movement. Instead, he leaned forward until both palms were flat on the desk, dented and scruffy head bobbing just above the computer monitor.

I swallowed the bile that rose in my throat as his smell hit me full-on. It reminded me of meat that had been left out too long to defrost. Grey mince.

'Have you got any horror?' he asked. 'Any horror books? Stephen King n'that?'

A nervous laugh burst from me before I could stop myself. *Of course*, I thought, *I'm in one. I'm in a Stephen King novel.* This man was about to transform into a monster. Maybe something would burst from his chest.

'Horror?' I repeated. 'Oh, yeah, sure. We have horror. Just over—'

I was about to point out our modest (okay, tiny) horror section when he lurched back, straightening and almost falling backwards. His head tilted back and for a moment he looked every bit the B-movie zombie, right down to the crusted spit at the corners of his gaping mouth.

'Th'thing is,' he said, fidgeting with his jacket sleeve, rolling it back. His fingers slipped and fumbled with it. 'I had a wee accident las' week. At the work, y'see. I'm a roofer. I dae the roofs. Hit the scaffolding. Cut my arm.'

Oh God, I realised, *he's going to show me*. What did this have to do with books? Did he think I could help?

My back was against the wall. He leaned forward once more, sweat beading on his pale head as he worked at the sleeve. The smell of rot was stronger now.

I was, suddenly, acutely aware of my isolation in the otherwise empty library. I was viewing the situation as though from above – a passive audience to the beginnings of a horror scene, unable to change the circumstances as they unfolded.

'An' I never got it looked at,' the swaying man continued, as though I had asked. 'Been feeling a bit under th'weather.'

He peeled back his sleeve and with it, several dried scabs cracked and fell to the desk like tiny feathers. The smell hit me and I suppressed a gag as his butchered arm was revealed: puss-covered and scabbed and so infected it was almost green.

'D'you think this is why I feel this way?'

Later, I wondered if I should have called an ambulance. I went over the interaction in my head as I scanned books and re-shelved DVDs. Should I have phoned 999? What could they have done? Was that sepsis? I'd never seen anything like it.

I barely heard Mrs Collins, another elderly reader, as she told me all about her colon. It was perforated or irritated or some-thing. She got cramps, you see. Her daughter had the same thing. She took these pills. Now, what were they called again? She'd check her bag . . .

I nodded and umm'ed and I see'ed, but all I could think about was that monstrous arm. Every time I got a whiff of the bleach I'd used to wipe down the desk and clear away the – ugh, no, I couldn't think about it – I wondered if I'd made the right call in directing him to the GP's surgery down the road. What if he was lying in a gutter now? What if he'd got lost? Was it drugs? Could drugs do that?

'—it's the cramps, though, hen,' Mrs Collins continued. 'You've got to get on top of those or you won't be sleeping at all. That's why I'm up so early. Are you okay?'

I blinked and her withered little face beneath glorious, slightly purple blue-rinse curls came into focus.

'Hmm? Oh. Yes. I get IBS so I know about cramps,' I said quickly. A side effect of this infuriatingly constant anxiety, ever since the breakdown.

She nodded approvingly, as though we shared membership of a secret club. She smiled. 'Then you'll know all about it, hen. Hellish, innit? You take care of yourself, sweetheart.'

I returned her library card and she swept the counter with her hand, an unconscious mannerism.

I hoped I cleaned it thoroughly enough.

This wouldn't be my last frightening encounter. Nor, sadly, would it be the worst. Over the weeks I'd had to log a few disturbing sights and experiences: a scuffle outside the library, petty vandalism, drug-takings and even a suspected overdose in the community centre. Still, the violence had never been directed at me. Not until the day the snow began.

The cold weather came in very early that year and so the day came quickly when the falling flakes first settled on the ground. That was when I learned my next lesson in library violence. By the time I reached the library that day, the snow was lying a couple of inches thick on the road.

I had expected the building to be empty when I arrived, so I was surprised to find the door unlocked and the lights on.

A tall woman hunched over the photocopier. She glanced up as I entered. She wore the same awful council uniform as me, though hers seemed better fitted than mine.

'Um. Hi,' I said as I brushed the snow off my shoulders and dropped my keys on the desk. 'I'm Allie.'

She looked me up and down, appraising me openly. I felt vulnerable under her stare. Judged. For some reason, I had a sudden and desperate need for her to approve of me.

'Phoebe,' she said finally, pointing to her name badge.

The photocopier whirred as she continued to deftly work it, paper fluttering in her hands. I had no idea whether or not I'd passed her judgement. She looked as though she was mentally filing away every aspect of my appearance.

'Oh, I didn't realise—'

Phoebe cut in, 'It's snowing. We're to go to our nearest branch. This is mine.'

'Ah,' I replied quietly. 'Well … I'm here now. Suppose I should probably do some work.'

She smirked and I found some of the tension dissipating slightly. I fumbled with my gloves.

'If you like.'

It was quiet but by midday there were more people in the library than one might expect on a snowy day. Rain or shine, most unemployed people must come and do their job search. I'd been chatting with one young man in particular. He told me that he was training to become a primary school teacher but they'd put recruitment on hold, so he had to find something temporary in the meantime.

Phoebe knew him. He was a neighbour. He was softly spoken and looked tired. He'd been studying all last week and had exams soon. They began to chat and turned away just as the library door slammed open with a reverberating thud.

I felt myself go into fight or flight mode. I could hear my therapist's voice reeling off flashback symptoms. Hyperawareness. Checking exits. Muscular tension …

I forced my shoulders down as a group of teenagers entered the library, each a good foot taller than me. They were loud, guffawing at something the tallest of the group was saying. They seemed familiar.

'Boys,' Phoebe warned, 'keep it down, people are working.'

One of them did a quiet, sarcastic impression of her, but the rest quietened down. Snickering, they retreated to the children's section. I assumed that they were here to escape the snow, like many of the other users. The children's section was quiet at this time of day but it was also hidden from view of the rest of the library by a half-height shelf. Only the tops of their heads were visible.

I thought I'd had some problems with a couple of these boys before but I wasn't entirely sure. We'd had a few incidents of antisocial behaviour, mostly teenagers showing off to their friends between classes or at lunchtimes. I resolved to keep a wary eye on them. They were quiet now.

I had returned to my shelving duties (picking gum off the spines of one of the romance books), satisfied that any potential situation had been diffused, when it happened.

'There he is. That POOF. Hey! POOFTER!'

My heart leapt into my throat. I thought about throwing myself under the desk and was annoyed by the impulse. I never used to be this anxious!

'*Coward*,' hissed one of the goblins in my head.

I was on my feet. Phoebe had turned but the boys were on the move, marching towards the young man at the computer. His face was red, fists shaking.

'Don't – you don't get to call people that!' he stammered. Now he was on his feet too.

My heart beat a frantic tattoo as I moved to the centre of the room to block the progress of the teens. Phoebe held the young jobseeker back and the teenagers hissed curses and slurs at me. At that moment, they seemed more animal than human. Feral.

Every inch of me wanted to run. For a moment, I wasn't in the room any more. I was in another place, the place that my therapist took me to in our sessions. I was little and alone and in pain and I was scared.

'No!'

The teens paused. The room was silent. I realised that I was the one shouting.

'No, you don't! Not in the library! You get out of here now! Go! I'm calling the police!'

The largest one leaned in, putting his face close to mine. He was at least a foot taller than me, reeking of cheap deodorant. His face kept changing from that of a teenage boy to someone else, the face I saw in the nightmares that left me screaming and wrestling my bedsheets.

'What are you gonna do about it?'

'Get the FUCK out of here!'

Again, a stranger's words in my own voice. I wasn't all me. In a moment of clarity, I shoved my hands in my pockets because they were making fists and my flight instinct was rapidly becoming a fight instinct. Oh, to break that leering face into a thousand pieces . . .

Phoebe stepped forward. 'You heard her. Get out. Now.'

The boy immediately backed off. Phoebe was six foot something to my five foot two. She was ex-military and it showed in her stance.

That's when his friend picked up the chair . . .

Later, as I inspected the damaged chair with trembling hands, I glanced at Phoebe.

'Still no police,' I commented. 'We called over an hour and a half ago.'

'They won't come,' she grunted. 'You may as well go home. Police don't come here.'

I glanced at the young man who wanted to be a primary school teacher. 'We'll go out together.'

I'd fixed the chair but the dent in the wall would probably never get filled in.

The lesson I had learned that day: **The public is an unpredictable beast. Never turn your back on it. Violence is mindless and it can come from anywhere. Be prepared**.

Still want to work in a library? Remember that lesson. Make it a rule. I learned the hard way so that you don't have to.

A secondary lesson from that experience was this: **fill out the paperwork**. Yes, even if your hands are shaking and you just want to go home. (*Especially* if your hands are shaking and you just want to go home.)

That day I spent some time after closing filling out the Violent Incident Report Forms as I'd been shown by Heather. Phoebe muttered something to the effect of there being no point but eventually consented to sign off as a witness.

I scanned in the forms and sent them off to Heather just as SOP one-hundred and … something specified, locked up, and headed home for some junk TV, an entire pot of tea and – hopefully – a night of unwinding.

The next day (my day off), I received a phone call from Heather. After clarifying some of the details of the incident, she offered me a place on the local authority's 'Conflict Management' course.

'It might help,' she said. 'I've been and I found the instructor very good. There's another block scheduled next month.'

Having spent the day obsessively replaying the moment the chair had been launched at my head all day, the suggestion was genuinely welcome. I had never heard of conflict management before then but it sounded like exactly what I needed.

'Sign me up!' I said.

After that conversation, the dread that had begun to fester in me calmed to a quiet simmer. All I had to do, I figured, was keep my head down until I could access the training course. So long as between now and then I didn't end up in another violent situation I'd be fine, right? The magic of the library would keep me afloat.

It may sound like a cliché, but the joy of interacting with Capital-R Readers and chipping away at the reorganisation of the place really did keep me going. It was great to see people reacting to the updated displays or commenting on the ease with which they found their desired author amongst the newly reorganised shelves.

I began to greet each library user with a sense of pride. *Welcome to Colmuir, under renovation.*

*

Three days before I was due to go on the Conflict Management course, I was assaulted by a library user.

Every week, Colmuir Library played host to Bookbug. This was an hour-long session in which Lisa, our children's assistant, led babies, toddlers and their carers in a singalong and then read a story to them from one of our nursery books. It was an opportunity for carers of young children to get together, chat about parenthood/grandparenthood and learn some techniques for structured play with their little ones.

Or at least it would have been if anyone had ever actually attended.

Over the weeks, Bookbug had become less a time for singing and learning and more a block in Lisa's diary that she could use to catch up on paperwork and emails.

I'd stopped being disappointed by the lack of attendance, though something niggled at the back of my mind. We were in a socially and financially deprived area with plenty of single young parents. I saw them out and about pushing buggies all day. Hell, they often popped into the library to make use of the computers. So why wasn't anyone making use of this particular free service?

It played on my mind as Lisa sat at one of the public computers and pottered about on a spreadsheet. She seemed pleasant enough, perhaps a little stern in a school-teacher kind of way, but there was certainly nothing off-putting about her. She knew her stuff when it came to childcare, at least as far as I could tell from the few brief conversations we've had. She, too, used to be disappointed by the lack of attendance at the Colmuir Bookbug sessions. Now she seemed determined to make use of the time in other ways.

Lisa was in her mid-forties with beautiful thick black hair that fell about her shoulders. She scraped it into a messy bun whenever Bookbug time arrived, on the off chance that she might get to interact with some young children. She was well-spoken, a little prim and proper but always thanked me for offering to provide teas and coffees, should any parents show up.

Other than this weekly hour at the computer I rarely saw her, but I had a feeling that today something was different. She was antsy.

The morning was quiet and after assigning some computer logins and reshelving a fresh delivery of rotated stock, I approached her at the computer and cleared my throat.

'Are you okay?'

'Hmm?' She looked up at me. 'Did you know that Iris is coming in soon?'

Iris. The cluster manager. I'd only met her a few times. She had conducted my interview alongside Heather and I always suspected that she was far less keen on my employment with the library than Heather. She was in charge of several library branches in the local area, hence the cluster.

Iris was a misnomer. She was grey. It's not just that her hair was grey. It was everything: her pale skin, her choice of clothing, her accessories, even her voice was somehow grey. It rasped like she was gargling sand yet was also flat and faint, like she was speaking from the bottom of a well. No matter how quiet the library was, I always had to lean in to make out her words.

For some reason, she terrified people. I'd never understood it; I still don't.

Lisa was frowning at her spreadsheets and I left her to it just as a troupe of teenage boys pushed their way into the library. These were the same boys who had accompanied the one who'd left the dent in the wall, though he was conspicuously absent.

That day they were relatively quiet and I ignored the fact that they had clearly skipped school to be here. Instead, I simply kept an eye on them as they dropped their bags and bodies into scattered sitting positions in the tiny children's area at the back of the room.

'Hey, guys,' I called over, 'we might have some children's activities on, so if that happens I might need to ask you to move.'

The boys nodded and shrugged but one of them – the tallest, a mop of dark hair and wearing designer clothing – just stared at me. I held his gaze. I knew the look of defiance but I really needed to hold the authority here. He eventually looked away. They returned to their chatting and whatever else teenagers do when they're skipping class.

Lisa was sitting almost right beside me and I knew that between the two of us we could keep this lot under control if they started mucking about. Still, the memory of that last lesson was fresh: *even if you're not working alone, the public is an unpredictable beast.*

I try not to regard all teens with suspicion. They're just as entitled to use the library as anyone else. God knows I spent plenty of my teenage years with my head buried in a book. The library was a haven for me then. It still is. Unfortunately, the vast majority of violent incidents I've experienced in this line of work have involved teenage boys, so I do tend to get a bit more vigilant around teenagers. Sorry, teens.

Iris appeared almost silently. Somehow, she could open the door in a way that didn't cause the usual creak. I almost had a heart attack when she stepped around behind the desk beside me. I'm still not entirely convinced she didn't just materialise from the dust between the stacks.

'Allie,' she croaked, a hand on the back of my chair.

'Hello,' I replied awkwardly. There was something incorrect and unsettling about this interaction. The pauses between each participant speaking were too long. She was too quiet and I was speaking loudly to make up for it.

'I'm just here to collect your – *huhuhuh* – latest batch of SOP 420s.'

Everything about the sentence, from the refusal to refer to the violent incident forms by their names, to the strange little breathless laugh in the middle, grated on me.

Latest batch indeed.

'No problem!' I said cheerily and, again, far too loudly. I had to balance that grey with a splash of colour before it devoured me.

Over in the children's section, the boys' conversation was picking up volume. One of them laughed and another threw something. I didn't catch what it was but I was watching them now, even as I listened to Iris.

'Are they the revision 5s, like Heather asked?' Iris continued, her own grey gaze falling limply upon the boys.

I was distracted now. The boys were tossing a packet of crisps at each other, hard. One of them fell over trying to catch it. He hit the shelf behind him and a couple of books fell off the end.

'*Boys*,' I snapped. 'Come on, this is a library. People are working.'

I turned back to Iris, who had been speaking to me in her whispery, ghostly voice this entire time.

'Sorry, Iris, what were you saying?'

I was distracted for a second time by a loud bang and a shower of laughter from the boys. I got to my feet. The tallest boy stood too, chin jutting out, awaiting confrontation. My heart sank a little. I really didn't want to have to throw these kids out. I hated throwing people out at the best of times. I'm no bouncer.

'—got the forms,' Iris continued as I moved around from behind the desk to approach the boys.

My chest was tight with that familiar bloody anxiety, but my hands were out, palms offered to the boys in a peace offering. I had my best 'let's be reasonable' face on. God, I wish they had just come in and read or chatted quietly. I really wouldn't have minded.

'Look, guys, you can't just—' I stopped as I realised that one of the boys was now quite deliberately pouring crisps from the burst bag into the box of nursery books. Something red-hot shot from my gut to the back of my throat and settled in my cheeks. He turned to fix me with a smug grin.

You horrible little …

'Well, I can see you're busy,' Iris called over. For once her voice actually carried and I turned, incredulously, to watch her gather up her paperwork and all but flee towards the door.

'Iris,' I called. I didn't know what I was going to say. Maybe I'd tell her to stay put. I wanted to tell her to keep her cowardly arse in a chair and witness this.

None of that mattered because, pretending not to hear me, Iris quite literally ran from the library.

Lisa was still at the computer beside me. She shrank down in her chair, avoiding eye contact. So much for backup.

The boys laughed. They were all on their feet now. One of them looked me in the eye and knocked more books from the shelf, in much the same way a particularly mischievous cat might but smugger, stupider and more brazen.

I shoved my clenched fists in my pockets. They all towered over me but I was blazing with the fury of a thousand suns. It was all I could do not to grab the lad by the collar and shake him.

'This is the CHILDREN'S LIBRARY. You are ruining books FOR CHILDREN. You need to leave, now.'

'Or what?' the crisp-scatterer drawled, finished with his task. He dropped the packet on the floor and crunched it into the carpet with the heel of his shoe. I imagined doing the same with his throat.

'Or I'll call the police, right now,' I replied. I met his eye. I meant it. We stared at each other for what felt like hours – my anxiety being replaced by that fiery anger – until finally, thankfully, he looked away.

'Guys, don't make me force you,' I continued. My voice shook with anger.

Why wasn't Lisa doing something? I was trying to subtly gesture for her to get the phone, but she was very deliberately looking at her screen, even as I knew she was listening. I turned away from the boys to look directly at her. I was about to tell her to do it, call the police right now, when I heard the tallest pipe up.

'*Guys, don't make me force you,*' he repeated mockingly and then there was the stomach churning-sound of hacking, then a spit.

Something struck the back of my head. Something wet and heavy. It bounced off the back of my hair and I spun on the spot, wide-eyed.

'Did you just SPIT ON ME?'

All pretence of professionalism was gone at that moment. The smirk on the lad's face flickered and I knew that he realised he'd crossed an invisible line from which there was no return. My fists fought against my pockets and my nails cut into my palms.

'GET. OUT. NOW.'

The spitter's friends were quiet. I could hear my own pulse.

'DID I STUTTER?' It was my own voice but the words were all goblin.

The friends were scrambling for their things, throwing coats and backpacks on as they hurried to leave, murmuring half-apologies as they passed me.

Finally, the spitter straightened, his backpack on. I stared him down. It took every ounce of self-control I had not to physically grab him.

'Get. Out. Now.'

'Fine,' he huffed, as though coming to the decision on his own. 'I'm going.'

I could *see* my pulse on the edges of my vision as he approached me. I stood my ground. That's when it happened. His shoulder collided with mine. I'd been tensing but he struck me with enough force to send me reeling until I collided with the bookshelves behind me. Something in me screamed with white-hot anger and if he hadn't run off at that moment I honestly don't know what I would have done.

I still think about that moment, how much worse it might have turned out, had the boy not fled. Would I have retaliated physically? I certainly believe it's a possibility.

As the door slammed shut behind him, I reached down for the thing that was spat at my head. I turned to Lisa and showed her the glistening wad of chewing gum, my stomach turning.

'He just spat this at my head,' I said dumbly, still torn between disbelief and blind rage.

She didn't look up from the computer. 'That's disgusting. You should write that up. There's an SOP for it.'

I called the police. They didn't show up.

*

Training day.

I crushed a frost-crispened leaf under my shoe as I folded my arms to my chest. I was waiting for someone to open the heavy double-doors that led into the main foyer of an enormous country house.

I'd been told that this was only part of the original castle that once stood on these grounds and I was sure it was all very grand and impressive but I'd been waiting in the chill autumnal air for over three-quarters of an hour and had started to wonder if the training seminar had been cancelled without my knowledge.

I wasn't alone. There were four of us, all stamping and shivering and huffing out clouds of hot breath like impatient horses.

Finally, a side door opened and a stout, balding man grunted, 'You're late! C'mon!' He softened the command with an insincere smile and stood, taking up two-thirds of the doorway, gesturing for us to enter. We squeezed past.

Overthinking as always, I noted that we were all women and wondered if he'd have left more room for a man to pass him.

Inside, five people in various council uniforms sat around a long dinner table, which had been turned into a conference desk. I presumed that they had been given the message about the side entrance.

The stout man sat at a separate table at the back and immediately began tapping away on his laptop. I realised that I recognised him as the head of Health and Safety for the entire local authority.

A man with a crew cut in a brown polo neck stood beside a projection screen. He was middle-aged with the kind of build that might have once suggested strength and muscle but now leaned more towards a few too many complimentary seminar buffets. He grunted as we entered and called out a number between one and three for each of us. I was assigned a three. He told us to memorise our number.

I spotted a familiar face at the table. She was tall, her face a permanent scowl of bony disapproval. She sat rigidly straight, long, dark hair scraped into an immaculately crafted bun. She nodded with a slight smirk when she saw me and I took that as an invitation to sit beside her.

'Miss the side door?' she muttered.

'Yeah,' I replied sheepishly as she handed me a plain white sticker and a marker to write my name and assigned number.

She was already wearing hers: 'Phoebe – 1'

'Have you done this before?' she asked.

'No, you?'

She nodded, the smirk more pronounced. 'You're a three? Interesting.'

I was about to ask what that meant when the man with the crew cut called for our attention. He pointed to the projector screen, which showed various corporate logos above the heading 'CONFLICT MANAGEMENT – 2 DAY SESSION'.

'Ignore the title, folks,' Mr Crew Cut said. 'We're only here for the day so we'll be moving fast. I'm Charlie.'

He listed off a spiel of military ranks and roles that he had presumably held throughout his career, ending triumphantly with 'and ... special-forces'.

There was a pause as he glanced from participant to participant like an eager retriever. I think we were supposed to be impressed. Rain began to tap at the windows. I scratched the back of my hand, an awkward compulsion.

'Ooh, wow,' one of the women finally muttered compliantly.

Charlie cleared his throat and clicked to the next slide.

'You're all here because you have experienced – or witnessed – conflict in the workplace, am I right?'

Phoebe and I shared a knowing look as Charlie continued, heading straight into the first section: points of escalation.

*

'Of course, if it reaches the point of violence, that's when you call the police,' Charlie stressed. He drew a circle around the word POLICE. 'Never worry about wasting police time. Your safety comes first. That goes doubly for you, ladies. Tell the police you're a woman on your own. They'll come quicker.'

I shared another sceptical glance with Phoebe.

'Now, let's talk about body language. When you got here, I assigned you all a number and asked you to write it on your name tag. We're going to talk about that.'

At last, I thought, *I'm about to find out what's so interesting about number three.*

Charlie clicked over to the next slide. It displayed the number one surrounded by words like *closed, distant, walls up, unapproachable*.

'Some of you,' he said, 'will be a number one. You may find that you experience a different kind of conflict to those who are number two. You may have been described in the past as "unapproachable" or "closed-off". Am I ringing any bells?'

Phoebe was nodding furiously. Was it a scale? Was I some sort of overly welcoming weirdo? How did he get that from me? I was analysing everything I did as I entered the room earlier. I was flushed from the sudden transition from cold to heat, wrestling with my coat. I think I nodded at everyone. Was that it? Was that too friendly? Should I have scowled? Hissed? Bared my teeth?

'Now I'm not saying that this is necessarily a bad thing. It will depend on your role. Obviously, your bosses might like you to be more approachable if you're working in a public-facing role ...'

I remembered the permanent scowl with which Phoebe 'greeted' the world.

We'd been given a script to recite when we answered the phone: *Good morning/afternoon/evening, X Library, Y speaking. How can I help?*

Phoebe didn't use the script. There was no warmth in her voice. She barked, she grunted. Yes, 'unapproachable' was definitely the term.

We were on the slide for the twos now. A huge, red number two was surrounded by words like *open, approachable, friendly.*

Well, shit, I thought. Now I really didn't know what to expect. If one was closed and two was open, what was three? Was I creating some sort of gravitational pull?

Charlie pulled a chair out from under the desk. He straddled it, cowboy style, and rested his arms on the back support like a youth counsellor at a fictional American summer camp. I half expected him to pull out a guitar.

'Now, folks. Let's talk about you twos.'

Jesus, said a little voice in the back of my mind, suspiciously goblin-esque, *he thinks this looks natural. He's a behaviour expert and he thinks this is a good way to address a group of grown adults. Look at him.*

I busied myself with scribbling 'notes' in my notebook. I drew a number two and copied some of the phrases from the slides. I could feel my ears burning. I always get this way with people putting on an obvious persona, like a failing comedian begging for audience participation in a pretend, nonchalant way. My entire soul cringes.

'Twos, you're the ones more likely to get harassment, I'm afraid. You're warm. You're welcoming. You probably work in a public-facing job and even when you're not feeling your best, you try to put a friendly face on things. That's good! Nobody's saying that it isn't. Unfortunately, you probably need this workshop a little bit more than the ones.'

I recalled the incident with the teens, the way the chair was definitely aimed at my head and not Phoebe's. Except I was also thinking about therapy. I was thinking about the mantras that Graham and I went over almost every session.

What happened is not my fault. I did not invite this trauma. I am a good person.

Charlie was talking but mentally I was back in that little NHS treatment room, on those sticky plastic chairs. Graham was tapping the back of my hand.

Allie. Allie, come back. You're safe. It's okay. You're here. It's Thursday and you're grown up and you're safe.

But I was never safe, was I? Not if I was this great big wide-open conflict-magnet. No wonder the violence was always aimed at me. No wonder people got so aggressive around me. It was in my nature, wasn't it? My behaviour. I am a number three. Come and hit me. What a shit thing to say. Victim blaming. Stupid Charlie. Stupid Charlie with his stupid numbers.

'As for threes, well...' He stood, turning the chair back around. It was the end of heart-to-heart time with the twos, I presumed. He almost tripped as he straightened up. I think I hated him.

'I don't think I rated any of you with a three, did I? Weirdos, mostly.' He chuckled, stroking his stubbly chin. 'IT people. Nerds. It's not PC but ... a bit on the spectrum, you might say.'

Yes. I definitely hated this bloated man-baby with his silly crew cut and his beer gut and his false tan and his stupid credentials and his *I'm just telling it like it is* Commander Riker bloody chair pose.

'So, focusing on ones and twos. Here's the thing: When I say that twos are more likely to experience harassment, I mean that more people are likely to interact with you. They'll walk into a room full of ones and twos and, without meaning it, gravitate towards the twos if they've got a question. Do you see? It's a matter of numbers.'

Phoebe nodded. In fact, many of the group were nodding. One of the guys, a young man who also worked in libraries, was sitting, starry-eyed. He was drinking this in as though his entire worldview had been turned upside-down.

Gosh, introverts, extroverts and weirdos, what a useful way of categorising the world. For once, I was glad that the goblin had turned its snark on someone else. I felt almost empowered in our agreement.

Another, much quieter voice whispered, *He's right, you know. Weirdo. You shouldn't even be here. Why are you still alive?*

My face burned.

'So it's on a scale, like everything,' Charlie continued. 'Let me tell you a little something about number ones, though. You're more likely to have experienced conflict in the past. Before we finish up for lunch, I'd like to tell you a little story.'

He reached for the chair once more and, yep, he straddled it again. Mr Camp Counsellor, all earnest. There was a tiny stain on the collar of his shirt. Mustard, maybe.

'I was running this course a few years back and we were working on personal space, just like I'll be doing with you lot later. So I've got this one woman. Beautiful young lady. Quietly spoken and polite. Just beautiful.'

Tell me some more about how beautiful she is.

I had to roll my eyes. My God, I had to roll my eyes or I'd vomit.

'... still, she's a number one and I'll tell you why: she's closed-off. She doesn't make much eye contact. Keeps her arms crossed most of the time. Very on-guard.'

If Phoebe nodded any harder her smirk might have fallen off.

'So we do this exercise. I approach her, she puts her hand up when she feels I've come too close. We start and she puts her hand up right away. Big personal space. Strong boundaries. Some of you will have a bigger bubble than others and that's fine, but when she does this exercise, she bursts into tears. All of a sudden. Everyone is stunned. I'm stunned.'

I wrote 'stunned' on my notepad and underlined it twice. I don't know why.

He'd paused for effect but all I could hear was something jingling on Phoebe's person as she nodded.

Charlie lowered his voice further. 'Now, between us, this bright young lady approached me after the exercise. I wanted to make sure she was okay. Well, it turns out she's been abused. Sexually abused … as a child.'

He said it like he was spreading office gossip and I stopped scribbling. That thing that thrums in my throat was back.

'Her dad, you see. Shame. Real shame. Beautiful woman.'

I didn't dare to look up. It felt like he was talking to me specifically. I had this horrible image, suddenly, of looking up from my notepad to find everyone in the room looking at me. It was so horrendously vivid that I had to close my eyes for a moment to shake it off. It probably looked as though I was moved by the story.

Maybe I was.

'Now, ones, I'm not saying you're all damaged but I'll say this: the more of an archetypal one you are, the more likely you are to have experienced trauma.'

Damaged.

I looked up and, fucking hell, he was smirking. Not at me, just indulging in his tale, lounging in the sound of his own voice like a pig in shit. His eyes met mine as he looked around before moving on. *Ugh! I'll show you 'damaged'.*

'I'm no shrink but I can tell you the people who've been abused. My system never fails. You'll rarely find a two – or a three for that matter – who's been sexually abused.'

A bark-like laugh rang out. My eye twitched and I looked around. My horrific vision manifested itself as everyone in the room turned to look at me. Their combined gaze was somehow hot and cold at once.

My hand darted to my mouth but not quickly enough to stifle a second laugh.

Allie. It's okay. Allie, you're safe. Come back to the room. It's Thursday. You're grown up and you're safe.

'Sorry,' I muttered. 'Nervous habit.'

Wanker.

It was time for lunch, Charlie announced, his eyes still on me. Nobody argued.

*

I was poking at a truly enormous baked potato when Phoebe sat beside me. The café at the old castle was surprisingly good and I was wondering why I'd never eaten here before when she brought her sandwich to her lips.

'What do you think?' she grunted with a mouth full of crust.

I stopped poking at the potato. There was no point. I'd never had much of an appetite to begin with.

'About the course?' I asked, reaching into my bag.

She nodded, putting the sandwich back on the plate. She gave it an inspection highly reminiscent of the one applied to me when we first met. Her fingers moved between the layers and she began to pick out slices of cucumber with precise dexterity.

'It's all right,' I say noncommittally.

She grunted in agreement as I found what I was looking for in my bag. I quickly popped a pill from its packaging, slipped it into my mouth and washed it down with my can of Coke in a practised motion.

A long finger jabbed my elbow as I was fastening my bag and I looked up. Phoebe was no longer dissecting her sandwich. Instead, her attention was focused on my bag. She gestured to it.

'What's that?'

'What's what?'

'The pill.' She paused as I took a moment to process what she was asking. Her tone softened. 'I mean, you can tell me to fuck off. Just wondering. What's the medication for?'

150mg of extended-release Venlafaxine. It's an SNRI antide-pressant. I take it twice a day. I used to take it in one huge 300mg pill but the side effects were awful. A split dosage makes it slightly more tolerable. If I miss a dose, I'm punished with blinding migraines for the next twelve hours. It's supposedly one of the few things keeping me this side of sane. I'm never entirely sure.

'It's uh ... medication,' I said.

I was actually about to open my mouth and tell her exactly what kind of medication it was when I caught myself. Her abrupt-ness had, once again, caught me entirely off guard. The intensity of her stare had me rummaging around in the back of my brain for more vocabulary and maybe a good lie or two.

'Pain medication,' I added finally. 'Sore head.'

She huffed, apparently satisfied. I was annoyed with myself. I kept telling myself that I was going to be honest with everyone this time around. No more acting like nothing's wrong. So much for that resolution.

Except ... it really was none of her business. I wish I'd had the guts to tell her to piss off but the truth is she scared me a lit-tle bit. She was tall and sharp and swung so rapidly between detached amusement and pure, concentrated intensity that I struggled to know where I stood with her. I felt judged in her presence. I felt unsafe.

'These pills,' she went on, 'I don't like them. Just paracetamol for me. Everything else is poison. You know, these antidepressants and so on. Addictive.'

She wasn't looking at me any more. She was back to peeling cucumber from her sandwich. I was honestly too exhausted to even mentally rebut her. She was one of *those* people. She wasn't the first I'd encountered and certainly wouldn't be the last.

My own mother was a pill-shamer. Those words could very well have come from her at one point. 'Don't get hooked on those pills. Your body doesn't need them.'

Ever since her cancer (thankfully, she's fully recovered) and then my breakdown (my recovery is ... debatable), that changed.

Phoebe clearly had a prepared speech, because for the next five minutes as she fingered her sandwich and I poked at my potato, she gave me 'real statistics' about people who'd overdosed on psychiatric medication and what the Big Pharma companies made and why they profited from keeping us all doped-up and 'did you see that documentary? It's on YouTube. We don't even need medication. There are plants that do the same thing, but better. Alternative medicine is the way forward.'

I almost interjected with the jibe that alternative medicine is what they call medicine that doesn't work but I was so damn drained then. I wondered if I had a cold.

Finally, lecture complete, she resumed her lunch. I heaved a sigh of relief and was about to make my excuses and spend the rest of the lunch break in the toilet when she spoke again.

'So you're at Colmuir?'

'Hmm? Yeah.'

'Full-time?'

'Part-time.'

'So you know Heather.'

I knew Heather. I knew that messy bun and the dark, pencilled eyebrows and the paperwork, dear God the paperwork.

Phoebe was clearly waiting to see how I responded. Her tiny eyes were boring into mine. I hesitated. I suspected that she disliked Heather but I also didn't want to offend her, lest she dissect me with the same detachment she did the sandwich.

'She's ... all right,' I said in almost exactly the same tone I used to describe the course. 'She's a bit ... anxious.'

Phoebe laughed suddenly. I actually drew back because it was so unexpected. She didn't seem to notice. Instead, she clapped her hands as she laughed, drawing the attention of the people at nearby tables.

'Mad! She's mad, isn't she? I'm glad you said it!' Phoebe cackled.

I'm fairly certain that at no point did I describe Heather as 'mad' but at this point I'd say whatever it took to get away from this cackling, clapping woman.

'Oh, she's terrible,' Phoebe gushed. 'Has she got you signing all those forms? And counting things?'

I nodded. Admittedly yes, 'signing forms and counting things' was about 80 per cent of my job at that moment.

'Has she been emailing you?'

Again, I nodded. I couldn't deny that Heather had, indeed, been emailing me. At all hours. In distinctive ALL-CAPITAL TRANSMISSIONS that seemed to consist mostly of her demanding that I count more things and sign more forms.

'I'm at Roscree,' Phoebe explained finally, 'the sister branch. She manages them both. Oh, you're in for a nightmare!'

She seemed altogether far too happy about the prospect.

I finally took the chance to make my excuses and dashed off to the bathroom.

*

We stood in a semi-circle. The tables and chairs had been pushed off to one side and Charlie stood in the centre of the room, looking like a politician at a press conference. He had that mock-sincere, saintly expression on as he surveyed the room.

'Right,' he said finally, as though deciding that we were worthy of his next nugget of wisdom, 'we've established that everyone has a different personal bubble. Some of you are more comfortable with strangers getting close than others. That's fine. Now I want to talk about the factors that influence your personal bubble on a day-to-day basis.'

The word bubble had lost all meaning to me. Earlier, we'd performed an exercise where we paired off and stood face-to-face or, in the case of Phoebe and myself, face-to-chest. I'd craned my neck to look up at her as we had a pretend conversation, then we'd tried the exercise again, this time at an angle of forty-five degrees to each other. The conversation, though still awkward, had gone much more smoothly.

To give Charlie his due, the physical exercises were interesting. He went over the conflict arc: an imaginary ninety-degree arc in front of a person where conflict was more likely to become physical. It's all about arm's reach, he said, and the perception of standing face-on.

It bothered me that what he said made sense. It bothered me that I was beginning to regard him as less of a pompous idiot and more of a pompous ... well, expert.

It bothered me that my body language was responding exactly as he predicted, even as I fought it. I wanted him to be wrong, useless even; I needed it for the sake of my sanity.

'Appearance will affect your comfort. If someone approaches you in a state of inebriation you're not going to let them as close as you would a sober person, right?'

He was making an alarming amount of sense.

'You certainly wouldn't be comfortable being alone with someone who's off their face, not without something between you. Maybe a desk or a chair. Trust your gut instinct.'

*

We huddled around the enormous tea and coffee flasks like cavemen around a campfire. The council had really gone all out on this one with the biscuits. I counted three different kinds of shortbread as I refilled my mug with watery black tea.

I'm not sure how I felt right then. I wanted to dismiss everything Charlie had taught us thus far as easily as I had dismissed his observations about Ones and Twos earlier but in playing the various conflict scenarios I'd experienced in the library over in my head, I found that – for the most part – he was right about body language. He was right about the posturing that precludes an attack and the fighting arc and the voice shifts and the neck-scratching.

My cycle of self-doubt was broken when George, the portly head of Health and Safety, asked me to pass him a teaspoon. I realised that this was my opportunity to address some of the concerns I'd had over the past six months at Colmuir.

As I passed him the teaspoon I blurted, 'Uh hi. I'm Allie. I don't know if you know. I work at Colmuir. We've had some violent incidents.'

George looked around, muttered, 'not here,' and gestured me back into the meeting room with a knowing look. I followed. He sighed and wordlessly signed for me to take a seat. I suddenly felt like I'd been called into a meeting and instantly regretted my request. Was I about to get a dressing-down for bringing up the subject in a relatively public setting?

George looked tired. He scratched at his bald spot as he unlocked his laptop.

I blew on my tea and waited. He stretched.

'I'm the one who asked that you be put on this course,' he said finally. His voice was gravelly, like he'd been up all night shouting. Maybe he smoked.

'Oh,' I said and then added, 'uh, thanks.'

He sipped his black coffee without flinching despite the fact that I could see it steaming. What a pro.

'I've got some of your incident reports here, in fact. Let's just say that I've been aware of the situation at Colmuir for a while.'

The situation. The series of escalating incidents, culminating in assaults, chairs being thrown at heads, drug deals (ironically in the crime section), not to mention the man who was found not once but twice in the toilets, passed out with a needle in his arm. All of this in the six months I'd been there. Did six months count as 'a while' or had this, as I suspected, been going on far longer?

When he looked up from his screen, I no longer saw the corporate professional who had been working away in the background of our training session. He wasn't just tired. He looked worn out, emotionally. There was five o'clock stubble on his chin and rings under his eyes. This was a man who was fighting a battle.

Welcome to the club, I thought.

'Between you and me, I've been pushing for more budget on this. You can't tell anyone about this but I can help put your mind at ease. I've come up with a solution to our antisocial behaviour problems at your branch.'

He told me this like he was presenting me with an incredible gift, and, for the first time in a while, I actually felt something akin to hope. This guy gets it. This guy has been listening and now something will be done. I won't have to watch my back every night as I lock the side gate after closing. I won't have to pretend to be on my phone every night as I walk to the train station and pray that I'm not being followed.

Maybe, just maybe, I'd stop holding my breath every time the library door opened.

He saw my expression and smiled. 'I think you'll like this. Again, you can't tell anyone yet, okay?'

I nodded, leaning in. What had he made the budget for? A security guard? A second staff member? Someone to help me close up at night? Better lighting? Pepper spray?

'We're going to install CCTV in the library.'

I waited for the 'and' ... but none came.

'Oh,' I said, trying and failing to mask my disappointment. I hid behind my mug of tea and allowed my glasses to become fogged with steam. 'That's ... cool.'

That was most definitely *not* cool.

*

'Self-defence!' Charlie announced.

He'd acquired a laser pointer. Had he had a laser pointer this whole time? No, he'd found it. Maybe he'd lost it before now.

Maybe he'd just remembered that he had it this whole time. I'd tuned him out and was getting caught in another thought-spiral about the laser pointer.

'—legalities and, of course, what we mean by reasonable force,' he concluded.

I flipped my notebook to a fresh page and wrote reasonable force. I added a question mark for good measure.

Charlie clicked the end of the pointer and the slideshow moved on. Now I was wondering how he'd changed slides before. Was George doing it for him back there? Maybe he'd had a different clicker for the presentation. Maybe it was the same one but he'd only just remembered that it had a laser on the end.

'—injuries, many of which are listed here.'

A close-up picture of a bloody, bruised face appeared. Many of us at the table winced. The eyes were swollen. Another click. It faded into a blurred background and a list appeared, one bullet point at a time. Broken bones. Cuts. Bruising. Short- and long-term damage.

Charlie was speaking over the top but I was still thinking about that bloody face and the one incident I hadn't recorded in an SOP 420. I had managed to blank it from my mind until the moment I saw that slide with the bloody face on it.

*

Vicky was a regular. She was a poor soul. She wore the same outfit for days, maybe longer. She always had the same tatty cream coat over the top.

Vicky was one of our job-searchers. Every weekday, she came to the library with her friend and they'd use one of the computers to look for employment.

I had a soft spot for her. She clearly didn't have anything going for her. She tried, she really did. She dragged herself into the library and applied for just about any job going. I think part of her knew the reason she never made it to the interview stage: she had no experience, no qualifications. Still, she wanted to work.

Her friend's name was Stephanie. Stephanie was also dirt poor. She was tall, broad and extremely muscular. She had a deep voice and huge hands.

(The first time I saw Stephanie, I had to step outside for some air. She smoked the same cigarettes as the person in my dreams.)

Stephanie wore the same uniform every day: a baby-blue tracksuit. She had no teeth. She was loud and prone to big gestures. Vicky flinched whenever Stephanie shouted. Stephanie shouted a lot.

Every day, I signed them on to a computer and they performed their mandated job search.

Today was different. Today the library door creaked open at their usual time but only one of them entered.

Vicky shuffled in, her hair obscuring her face. There were more stains on her cream coat than usual. It was torn in patches. Her hair was matted and there was something stuck in it. The stains on her coat were rusty red-brown.

She limped to the reception desk and I saw her face.

No, I saw what was left of her face.

There's no other way to put it: Vicky's face was broken. Her jaw was swollen shut. Her eyes were two slits within twin, orange-sized swellings. Both of her lips were split and there was a boot-shaped bruise down the side of her cheek.

'C-computer, p-pleashe.'

She was crying. Her tears were pink.

I leapt to my feet, stepping around to her side of the desk. I grabbed her elbow as she swayed and she flinched, pulling away. She was hunched over, breathing hard through her slit of a mouth. I suspected that her nose was also broken.

'Jesus Christ, Vicky! What happened? Do you need an ambulance? Police?'

'HhhNO!' she cried and I pulled away.

She shook her head and whined in pain.

'No police,' she coughed, 'no ambulanshe.'

'Okay,' I said, moving away, 'but are you okay?'

She shook, one hand clutching her ribs and the other steadying her against the pillar beside the desk. After a moment I realised that she was sobbing.

'You want a glass of water?'

'J-jusht a c-computer,' she hissed through clenched teeth. Her jaw was definitely broken.

I ran to the water cooler, afraid to leave her alone in case she passed out. By the time I got back, she was no longer shaking but the tears were flowing freely.

'Sh-she was supposed t-to be my f-friend ...' she huffed, lowering her jaw with what was clearly a monumental effort.

I placed the cup on the desk in front of her. 'Who? The person who did this?'

'Y-yeah.' She reached for the cup with a broken, bloody hand. 'Some friend, eh? All over twenty quid. I owed her twenty fucking quid. Look at me now.'

I've seen some messed-up things. You don't end up in and out of the NHS psychiatric system without seeing some strange and awful sights. I mean, I've been in some states myself, but I had never, ever seen anything like this. If I had seen her in a film,

I'd have assumed that the special effects artists had gone over-board with the injury make-up.

I could smell her blood. I realised that I'd never smelled blood like this before. I could taste it on the back of my throat, metallic and meaty.

'Vicky, you really need to see a doctor ...'

'No doctors. No hospital. No police. She'll know.'

'Okay,' I relented. 'Can I at least give you the number for Victim Support? It's confidential.'

She appeared to consider the offer and I took the opportunity to scribble the number down on a scrap of paper.

'Use the library phone if you need,' I told her.

Two of her fingers wrapped around the piece of paper. Tears stained it slightly pink.

'Thanksh,' she said.

Later that day, she returned to the library. This time with Stephanie. The sight of that woman after seeing evidence of the violence she was capable of made me feel physically sick. I actually felt my stomach cramp in anticipation of further violence.

'Two computers,' Stephanie said. 'One for me and one for my *friend*.'

Vicky gave a watery, swollen smile.

*

As Charlie was packing away the projector, I felt my phone vibrate in my pocket. I stepped out into the cold.

Despite not having the caller saved as a contact, the smart ID on my phone picked up an official number and displayed the name:

Police Scotland.

I frowned and put the phone to my ear.

'Hello?'

'Hello? Is that Ms Morgan? Librarian at Colmuir Library?'

'Uh, yes?'

'Hi Ms Morgan, I'm calling with regards to an ongoing investigation into a suspected assault at the library. I believe you called us to report that you'd been spat on by a youth.'

'Oh! Yes.'

'We've taken some statements from the witnesses whose details you provided, including your er—' I heard papers shuffling '—the children's assistant, Lisa.'

My heart leapt. Were they taking this seriously? Finally! And what timing!

'Unfortunately we can no longer proceed to arrest at this stage, Ms Morgan.'

I stared out into the dark estate grounds. A bat swooped around a lamppost above my head, its clicking making the hairs on the back of my neck stand on end. Somewhere, a sheep bleated sleepily.

'Ms Morgan?'

'Can I ask why not?'

'I'm afraid we've received a conflicting statement. That's all I can say at this stage. Your witness claims that nothing of the sort occurred. If you had CCTV ...' He sounded almost as frustrated as I was. 'I'm ... I'm sorry. I really wanted to catch this little ... I'm sorry.'

For a moment, I was genuinely touched. I realised that I'd spoken to this particular officer before. He was young, new to the area. He'd popped in once or twice to have a look around the library. Once or twice he'd been out of uniform.

'Me too,' I replied. 'Thanks for letting me know.'

*

'Dissociation' is a psychiatric term. It's not a syndrome or ill-ness in and of itself but rather a symptom. To dissociate is to disconnect from reality. Unlike psychosis, dissociation does not usually come with hallucinations or unusual beliefs. Instead, the sufferer experiences a sort of distance, as though watching themselves in a dream. They become an observer of their own life. It's a common symptom of trauma and can last anywhere from minutes to weeks. It's particularly dangerous in situations where the sufferer needs to concentrate, like driving or operat-ing heavy machinery.

I am no stranger to dissociation.

The next month passed in a sort of haze. I was robotic at the desk, no longer going out of my way to answer enquiries.

Scan books in. Scan books out. Scan computer logins out. Scan computer logins in.

The shelves were starting to look messy again. My displays went out of date. I stopped updating the 'coming soon' list.

Stephanie began to show up on her own. She began asking around about my shift pattern. More than once, she waited for me at opening time and lurked around at closing. Every now and then she'd look as though she was out for blood. *My blood*. Some nights I'd vomit before locking up for the night. It passed like an endless bad dream.

'C'mere,' she'd say from a darkened corner of the library.

'Not right now,' I'd reply in a monotone. I wasn't even afraid any more. I was somewhere else, watching this poor, doomed person delay the inevitable. 'After I put this book away.'

Every time, she accepted the excuse.

'Later, then,' she replied.

We both knew what she meant by that.

After all, I knew what she did to Vicky.

*

Graham was worried. We made very little progress in our sessions. Finally, after a particularly frustrating non-starter of a therapy session, he threw his hands down and growled in frustration.

'I can't treat this.'

I was shaken out of my reverie. 'What?'

'I can't treat your trauma if the trauma is ongoing, Allie. You're just going to get worse.'

'You mean the library stuff?' I asked.

I'm slower on therapy days. I don't eat before I start so that I don't vomit during a session. My stomach grumbled.

'Yes,' he said, 'the library stuff. The violence. The ongoing danger. You can't treat a soldier while they're still in combat. You have to get out of there.'

I found myself nodding, not fully present. 'I know,' I heard myself say. 'I just hoped ...'

'There will be something else.'

'Maybe. I really loved libraries ...'

'There will be something else. I promise.'

The next day, I prepared my notice letter.

*

It was nearly the end of a late shift. My husband had just phoned, a little strained. He was on his way to pick me up.

'I have a meeting then I'm done,' I replied. 'Are you okay?'

I may not care much about my own well-being but his was another matter. I love him so much it makes my chest hurt sometimes. I'm not sure if that's normal.

'Yeah,' he replied. 'Well, I think so. Just bumped into some of your regulars from the library, I think.'

Bile hit the back of my throat and I swallowed hard. The library was empty but I ducked behind a pillar all the same.

'What happened? Are you okay? Who was it? Did they hurt you? I'll fucking kill them—'

'No, no! I'm fine!' He laughed. 'I'm out for a walk. A young boy looked hurt. He must have been scared because he approached me. Me, Allie.'

My husband is a good foot taller than me. His hair is longer than mine. His beard is, too. He's very much the stereotypical heavy metaller. He's slender but wiry and tends to wear bulky clothing that makes him look more muscular. All in all, he can look fairly intimidating at times. Only I know that he's a total pacifist. I'm definitely the temper of the two of us.

'Some older kids had beat him up. We found his house. He doesn't live far from the park. When I was coming back, I bumped into the boys who'd done it. Teenagers, beating on a wee kid! They were all smug about it. Anyway, it's fine. They asked about you. Seemed to know you worked at the library. I don't think they knew that I'd helped the boy get home.'

No, I thought. *No, they knew. They know who you are because they know me. I know exactly who they are.*

'They said they were Stephanie's friends or something. Said you'd know. Anyway, they seem like right charmers. Don't blame you for quitting.'

'I haven't ... uh ... actually quit yet.'

'What?'

'Iris is on her way here. I'm going to tell her as soon as she gets here. Then I'm out.'

'Okay. I'll see you soon.'

'Be careful.'

As he hung up, something wailed. I glanced out of the front window and the wail became a scream: a long, drawn-out, primal scream.

Three figures collided: a young couple and someone older, hidden beneath a hooded coat. They'd been scuffling already and the couple were running from the one in the coat, straight into the community centre.

The door to the library swung open and by the time I glanced back outside, the hooded figure was gone.

The couple staggered in, clutching each other. They were young, maybe late teens. The girl was screeching, the boy silent, mouth agape. His face was white as chalk. I recognised shock at work.

The girl sobbed. 'Call a taxi!' she shrieked. 'Please, God! Please! Call us a taxi! We have to get out of here!'

I didn't offer to call the police. Instead, I picked up the phone and called in a taxi, as instructed. My movements were robotic but my hands were shaking.

Here we go again.

The girl had the boy's face in her hands.

'Kev, Kev. Look at me, Kev. It's okay. He's gone. We're getting out of here. We're getting a taxi. He's gone.'

'Kev' was nodding but wasn't fully there. He was dissociating, just like me.

I offered them water. They declined. I told them to wait there for the taxi.

The girl continued to sob. I tried not to listen. Knowledge was dangerous around this place and I wouldn't be around for much longer.

'He-he could've killed you,' Kev stuttered.

'No. No, baby, no. He was going for you. I just scared him away. He's gone. I'm okay.'

I closed my eyes and prayed for Iris to appear soon.

*

The couple asked me to accompany them to the taxi. As I stood outside, Iris arrived.

'Why are you outside?' she asked, ignoring the sobbing girl and the shell-shocked boy.

'Long story,' I replied. 'I can't do this any more.'

I handed her my notice letter and with that, my library career ended.

*

I sat with Iris. The library was closed. She clicked her pen against the tabletop arrhythmically. The most annoying sound in the world.

'It's not just the violent incidents,' I said, 'it's my family, now. They're contacting my husband. They know I'm in contact with the police ...'

She nodded in what I assumed she thought was a sympathetic way. She looked more confused than anything else.

'Well ... how about this?' she droned nasally. 'We have a small opening at Roscree. Why don't you transfer to a different branch for a while?'

I swallowed. Tears pricked at the corners of my eyes and I silently cursed them.

This bloody anxiety.

'I-I don't know. If it's more of the same—'

Iris shook her head. 'It's a two-man branch. Not as bad an area. There are always at least two members of staff on at all times. It's bigger. More activities. More . . . life.'

'Can I think it over?'

'Call me tomorrow.'

I nodded.

*

'When do you start in the new branch?' Graham asked as I finished saving the date of our next appointment in the calendar on my phone.

'Tomorrow,' I replied.

'Remember, you don't have to stick around if it's just as bad.'

I nodded and he leaned in the doorway.

'There will be better. I mean it,' he repeated. 'You'll find something safer.'

I wanted to believe him but I shrugged.

'See you in a couple of weeks,' he said.

As I waved him goodbye, my phone buzzed in my pocket. I pulled it out and checked the caller ID.

Police Scotland.

'Hello?'

'Ms Morgan? I'm calling with regards to an incident that we believe you witnessed last week, around 5pm . Did you call a taxi firm for a couple of teenagers?'

Chapter 3

Not All Libraries Are Made Equal

Visitors Daily (average) October: 60
Enquiries Daily (average) October: 10
Printed Pages Daily (average) October: 49
Violent Incidents October: 0
Children's Event Attendance: 75%

The very first library I ever encountered was a modest affair: each classroom in my primary school had a turnstile or two of age-appropriate books. These were, collectively, referred to as 'the library'.

Access to 'the library' was a reward reserved only for those who had completed their tasks for the afternoon. To browse those little stalls, to make them creak and groan on their wobbly stands as one stood on tiptoes to inspect the books was to announce success. To sit with a reading book in front of you at your desk was a signal that you were a quick learner and an even faster worker.

For a primary school child with little sense of humility and an almost crushing need to impress the adults in my life, the ritual of book selection and the triumphant return to my desk was *everything*. The reading itself was, of course, merely secondary.

That is until I discovered the very first book with which I ever fell in love.

The book itself was a battered, green hardback copy of *The Secret Garden* by Frances Hodgson Burnett. By the time I got my hands on it, it had definitely seen better days. It was, however, the only hardback in our little assortment of fiction and the decorative, embossed cover caught my eye immediately.

Once in my hands, the book felt important. It felt grown-up. Until that point, most of our reading material had been encased in plastic sleeves over wrinkled cardboard covers. The pages themselves were almost rice-paper thin and stained from years of sticky fingers. The typeset was less rounded than I was used to, reminiscent of the lettering produced by the school's one and only printer made available to students: a decrepit dot-matrix hooked up to a BBC computer.

The language itself was new to me, too. Most books I'd read before that point had used language more similar to my own, spoken tongue. This was floral and theatrical, descriptive and dramatic. This was how I, at the age of seven or so, imagined royalty spoke.

I devoured that book in a few sittings and then, having finished, went back to the beginning and read it over again.

I had a vague sense that there was more to the tale than merely what was being described. Like the eponymous garden, I sensed hidden importance beneath all that delicious prose and, being a stubborn child with an insatiable appetite for knowledge, I became determined to find that hidden meaning. I was vaguely aware that we'd learned a term for things-which-mean-other-things, too; my teacher had called it *metaphor*.

By the end of the year, I must have read the book at least a dozen times. I remember at one point my teacher poking her head up from a pile of coursework during a silent reading session to enquire, 'Haven't you read that book before?'

'Six times, yes.'

'Aren't you bored with it?'

'Not really.'

To this day I often find myself chasing the high of that first love and while I've since found other books that have invited me to read and re-read until the words are as warm and familiar as hot buttered toast, I will always have a special place in my heart for the garden, Mary, Dickon, Colin and Misselthwaite Manor.

*

The relatively nondescript sandstone building that houses Roscree Library initially began life as a school for the children of Roscree: a small yet steadily growing town centred around the locally famous textile factory and colliery. As the town grew, the one-school-fits-all model became increasingly impractical until the local authorities approved the construction of separate Primary, Boys Secondary and Girls Secondary schools.

Since then, the building has been home to a tax centre, a Jobcentre, various textile shops and even a nightclub at one point. The building has been divided and subdivided, extended and had sections demolished. Externally, little sandstone remains. In fact, I often wonder if anything of the original building exists at all. Still, the land on which the building sits remains at the heart of the Roscree community. As housing has sprung up and stretched out, it has extended from this point like petals from a central pistil.

Now, the building houses a discount supermarket, a handful of charity shops and, right at the very back, the library itself.

Despite having been installed some thirty-odd years ago, locals still refer to the current iteration of Roscree Library as 'the new library'. It's a multi-levelled, open and yet oddly shaped space, owing to the countless additions and removals that have been applied to the structure over the decades.

To me, on that first shift, it was like finding a secret garden – something beautiful, which had existed this entire time without my knowledge – or, it would turn out, the knowledge of many of the younger locals.

With a high ceiling and enormous windows dominating both of the external walls, the library was awash with daylight, even in the early hours of sunrise. The shelves were relatively low, allowing the glorious daylight to reach almost every part of the building and highlight the beautiful mess of colour.

The children's section was a riot of shapes and slogans, of characters and art. Children's paintings were strung between pillars on washing line and held on with bright-pink clothes pegs. Posters encouraging attendance at the regular classes and clubs were lovingly crafted and attached to rainbow, textured card. Nursery books were arranged in playfully designed boxes at just the right height for babies and toddlers to rummage through with their guardians.

And oh, the displays!

Dotted around the library were purpose-made display units, bedecked with books on various themes and decorated with vibrant signage indicating the author of the month, or the seasonal theme ('Spring into Reading').

At the time, I didn't pick up on some of the less-impressive details, like the stains on the seats, or the fact that a spring-themed display was still set up in October. Had I looked closer at those posters, I'd have noticed that they were for events that had occurred months ago.

I was too busy admiring the enormous reception desk at the back of the library to notice that the calendars were out of date, or that the pillars in the area were plastered with posters advising that the branch took a 'zero tolerance' approach to aggression. I was more concerned with the fact that the posters were *in colour*, having been used to a branch that only contained a black and white printer.

Most importantly, I wouldn't be working alone. Roscree Library was a two-person branch, a far cry from the claustrophobic isolation of Colmuir.

What I didn't know and wouldn't know until much later was that the branch had previously been classified as a three-person branch until declining footfall had caused it to be declassified. Would it have changed the way I felt about the place on that first day? Probably not. The contrast between this and the dank darkness of Colmuir was too great.

I marvelled at the place as I moved through it, shadowing Phoebe as she went through the setup procedure. We were to host a Bookbug session today. The children's assistant would be arriving shortly to set up the children's area.

I'd never seen a Bookbug session in action. At Colmuir, the attendance had dropped to zero long before I began.

We had barely lifted the shutters and started the automatic doors (one rotating, one wheelchair-accessible to the side) when Bookbuggers – as I would come to mentally, if not verbally, call them – began to trickle in.

Back at Colmuir, it wasn't unusual to have one or two regulars (at most) waiting at the front door for opening time. They were usually the jobseekers who wanted to come in, log on and get their daily search done as quickly as possible so that they could have the rest of the day to themselves.

Bookbug is a class or event run in libraries all over the UK. It has a flexible structure and usually lasts around half an hour. It's very often the first experience a child will have in the library and is key for getting potential new readers used to books, reading and the general practice of coming to the library.

Often the children's assistant or library worker will lead the carers, toddlers and babies in a singalong. Mums, dads and other carers will perform actions with their little ones and encourage them to sing along. After songs comes story time, during which the Bookbug Host will read a nursery book to the assembled tots, giving the parents and carers a chance to relax, so long as their child can sit and pay attention without causing a fuss.

At least, that's the theory.

On my first shift, our Bookbug group consisted of around twenty or so tots, along with similar numbers of carers. Many of the tots had only just learned how to crawl and so a thorough inspection of the library from floor-level seemed far more interesting to them than any singing or reading.

Susan, the children's assistant, was no stranger to herding little ones. Being a seasoned veteran of Bookbug, she set up 'gates' (large, painted boards affixed to the shelf stacks) around each of the possible exits from the children's section as the parents and guardians found parking spots for their buggies and prams.

Between the buggy barricades, cheerfully decorated board-gates and the inattention of the wandering, noisy children, the library seemed host to the world's cutest and tiniest prison riot.

'The Wheels on the Bus' proved a crowd-pleaser and, for a while, Phoebe and I stood on the sidelines, watching babies gurgle and toddlers giggle in time to the chant. However, when story time came around, the collective attention waned again.

One little girl threw a beanbag at a baby. A completely unrelated toddler began to shriek and tug on his sister's pigtails. Another baby began the low, slow build-up to a proper cry. A two-year-old, who I can only assume was feeling particularly empathetic, dropped her trousers in solidarity with the crying baby and wailed. Beanbags sailed over heads and books were knocked from shelves. Chaos reigned. It was wonderful.

Phoebe and I retreated to the safety of the standing-height reception desk. We both sat. She, a good foot-and-a-half taller than me, continued to observe the bedlam in the children's section with a wince every time a particularly discordant shriek cut through the general anarchic din. I turned to my computer, realised that the desk height made it almost unusable from a sitting position and stood up, just as a group of adults (blissfully unaccompanied by children) made their way in to begin the day's job search.

And so began the complaints.

'Bit noisy in here, eh?'

'That young Susan has a lot on her hands.'

'In my day, libraries were supposed to be quiet places.'

It's true. Anyone of my generation or older will most likely recall being 'shhh'ed by a librarian at some point or another. I, personally, used to live in fear of a specific elderly matriarch of the local branch who had, on more than one occasion, scolded me for chuckling too loudly at a comic book.

What I quickly learned (and what any regular visitor of modern libraries can tell you) is that libraries haven't been a place of quiet study and reflection in quite some time. Even when the commotion of Bookbug doesn't reign supreme, there are often events running that require speech, or song, or various other forms of verbal communication.

Many libraries have been redesigned into open-plan spaces. This serves the dual purpose of making the place feel more modern and airy, while allowing for reduced staff numbers as assistants no longer have to patrol labyrinthine shelf stacks like Dewey-Decimal obsessed Minotaurs. One can, in theory (so long as you're over five-and-a-half feet tall, unlike most female librarians), monitor most of the library from a standing position.

A side effect of this redesign is that noise carries. Without tall, dense shelf-stacks to muffle it, even the chug-chug of a busy copy machine or the steady swish-swish of rotating doors carries right across the library.

It's simply not practical to police the sound levels in a library any more. Quite frankly, an ordinary conversation between users is the least of your worries when a single session of *Rock and Read* (a class for preschool children, where they dance and mime along with musical stories) will generate enough noise to shake the windows at times.

All of this isn't to say that every library is a cacophony of sound at all times. Some branches are lucky enough to have separate rooms for children's activities (and noisier adult activities). Academic libraries, particularly those attached to university campuses or businesses, often have separate 'loud' and 'quiet' zones where conversations are allowed and disallowed respectively. Some have meeting rooms that can be rented for the express purpose of discussion out of earshot of other library users.

Every branch has its own way of balancing the needs of the noisy users and activities against the needs of those who require silence but ultimately it boils down to three things: building layout, available resources and profitability. Yes, even in previously silent libraries, money (quite literally) talks. After all, noisy events like competitions and children's learning sessions often require a ticket, and tickets cost money. Silent study is, for now, free.

One of the ways in which the assistants at the Roscree Library attempt to create harmony between the noisy/quiet users is by helpfully informing users, including those without children, of the children's activities timetable. Most regulars by now know that a Wednesday morning is not the best time to, say, sit and relax with the day's crossword or compose an essay as this is when the first of the twice-weekly Bookbug sessions dominate.

That first Bookbug session was my introduction to the wealth and class gap that exists in Roscree. The parade of various parents, guardians and their associated children, along with the accoutrement that comes with taking any baby or toddler out of the house, served as a perfect demonstration of all the difference poverty makes.

First through the doors were the Colliesh Mums, sometimes referred to as 'the WAGs' aka wives-and-girlfriends. It's a slightly derogatory (or at the very least patronising) term used in the UK for the partners and spouses of sports stars, particularly those of footballers. The term conjures images of fake tans, false nails, designer clothing and expensive cars, and, while it may be a somewhat misogynistic descriptor, the connotations aren't too far off the truth.

Colliesh itself is a wealthy, somewhat gated town adjacent to Roscree. Populated with the kinds of people who have a Maserati as a daily car because the Lamborghini is strictly for play, it's a source of much resentment for the people of Roscree. However, our library Bookbug times just so happen to be more convenient for many of the Colliesh-ians and so, twice a week, the Colliesh Mums grace us with their presence.

They tend to arrive in groups of five or six, in a cloud of perfume, with designer prams in tight formation and leave together in much the same way.

It would be easy to dislike these women. For one thing, they tend to float into the library and group together as though to prevent being picked off by our poorer regulars. For another, they are ostentatious. Childcare is a competition for them and accessories are everything. They're forever preening and poking at the latest buggy-mobile, designer rattle or high-tech bottle-warmer. Nothing draws more cooing and 'ahh'ing than a bedazzled dummy or colour-coordinated nappy changing kit.

As I have said, it would be easy to dislike these women, especially – I imagine – if one were a struggling single mother relying on a pittance from the government to get by each month. Still, there was something entrancing about the Colliesh Mums whenever they entered the library. I couldn't quite put my finger on it that first day, but I struggled to take my eyes off them.

Speaking of parents in poverty, we had one or two more obvious cases at that first Bookbug session. They also have been, over time, the largest-growing group of adults we see at our free children's sessions.

It's hard to describe the markers of obvious poverty without coming across as snobbish but the fact is that there comes a degree of utter destitution that cannot be concealed. Most of these parents are single mums, a large number of whom are disabled or chronically ill. Some have quite obvious learning disabilities and mental health issues and those are just the ones whose conditions are more apparent to the untrained eye.

These adults come in alone with their children, quite often late due to reliance on sparse and unreliable public transport. Very often we will see the same women (as they are, for the most part, women) in the same outfit for two or even three days running. Their buggies and prams are second-hand, never designer, and usually showing signs of long-term wear-and-tear.

There is no other way to put it: very many of these parents smell. However, only a truly ignorant or cold-hearted person could see them week-in, week-out and not feel some degree of compassion, if not outright awe. How on earth these people juggle chronic illness, debt, caring duties, Department for Work and Pensions harassment, part-time work and God-knows-what-else with the full-time role of parent I honestly have no idea. Something has to give. Quite often, the first sign is personal hygiene. I can't imagine I would be any different in the same situation.

The contrast between those two groups on my first day was staggering. I was aware of the degrees of wealth inequality in our local area but nothing prepared me for that. I often wish I could drag every blustering politician who is responsible for our current economic and benefit systems to a Bookbug session. Talk to me about 'scroungers' and 'social mobility' after you've watched a sick, starving girl struggle to wheel her child into the library just so that the tot can experience something other than the four walls of their tiny, cold flat.

The third, smallest group of adults at the Bookbug session were the grandparents who were acting as babysitters so that their adult children could go to work. It's quite something to watch an elderly couple using a buggy as a shared mobility aid. Again, these people filled me only with compassion and admiration. It may sound patronising but, again, I honestly don't know how an elderly person with their own health issues could possibly summon the energy to run around after a hyperactive toddler or take care of a baby. I'm aware that they do this out of financial necessity but, my God, what kind of country do we live in when this is what we expect from people who should, by all rights, be enjoying their retirement years?

A sombre chorus of 'Goodbye, Everyone' heralded the end of the Bookbug session and the tension seemed to dissipate from the room. Though the children continued to coo and gabble and even cry and howl, there was a sense of movement. Parents and guardians began packing prams and tying the laces of tiny shoes until, one by one, they began to leave.

Blessed quiet began to descend upon the library. Had it really only been half an hour of Bookbug? I felt as though I'd aged a decade.

I hopped over a baby gate and helped Susan with the clearing-up process. Props from the singalong lay scattered: beanbags and cuddly spiders (for 'Incy Wincy Spider', of course) lay strewn amongst discarded baby wipes and abandoned dummies.

I hadn't realised how much my hearing had adapted to the racket until I became aware of a low sobbing sound in the after-math. I paused, tossing a beanbag in the toy box as I looked around to locate the source.

After a bit of careful manoeuvring around debris, I turned the corner at a taller stack and almost walked into one of the Bookbug parents. She straightened abruptly as she spotted me, hurriedly wiping mascara-streak tears from her cheeks.

I recognised her immediately as one of the Colliesh Mums. Beside her, one of the grandmothers held a perfectly manicured hand in her own wrinkled pair, clearly providing comfort to the woman who, as I approached, I realised was actually a lot younger than I'd initially assumed.

There was no point in pretending I hadn't seen the tears. Instead, I ducked down (as though I were visible over the stacks anyway) and shuffled over.

Two babies slept soundly in prams and it was only when I reached the mother and grandmother that I realised that I still had a cuddly spider in my hand. I hid it behind my back as though it might offend the pair.

'Hey,' I said quietly, 'are you okay?'

'She's fine,' answered the grandmother sharply.

I moved to hold my hands out in what I hoped was a surrendering gesture, but instead ended up just sort of ... thrusting a spider toy towards them.

'Er ... sorry. I just wanted to see if you needed anything. I'll go grab a box of tissues.'

The offering of tissues seemed to placate both mother and grandmother alike and I was informed in hushed tones that their names were Sophie and Margaret respectively. Sophie's baby was only a few weeks old but she'd brought the little one here as an excuse to get out of the house.

'I'm just so exhausted,' she confessed, 'but it's driving me mad. My boyfriend's away with work all the time it's just ... you know.'

I nodded and Margaret gave her hand a squeeze.

'It's lonely,' said Margaret, 'being a mum when they're wee. I thought I was going to lose the plot when I had mine. You need adult conversation but you're knackered all the time.'

Sophie nodded and I pulled out a couple of chairs for them to sit. I was out of my depth here, having never had children of my own. At this point, I felt the most helpful thing I could do was offer a seat and hold the tissues.

Margaret cleared her throat and gestured to the baby beside her.

'This one's my daughter's. Six months. Wee Cameron.' She said the name fondly but there was a hesitation.

As Sophie took another tissue I realised that were I not wearing the library uniform, these women would probably never have opened up to me. It's a powerful thing, a library uniform. It puts you in a position of trust and responsibility. It's a signal of safety but it's also an invitation.

'How long are you looking after him for?' I asked.

Margaret's voice cracked. 'All day. Every day. While *she's* at work. I love him and I love my daughter but ...'

It was my turn to take Margaret's hand and, to my great shame, I realised that there were tears prickling at the back of my own eyes, too. A strange, intimate moment passed between the three of us. Three unrelated women in our own little world at our own little table amongst the bookshelves, just propping each other up.

'It has to be hard work,' I suggested.

'It's not fair,' Sophie offered, 'asking all that of you.'

'Och, no,' Margaret snapped. The moment shattered. I withdrew my hand. 'No,' she continued. 'Have you seen the cost of babysitters? I don't mind. I don't mind.'

She shook her head but I could tell she was no longer really talking to us. Her gaze was elsewhere. She paused and her shoulders slumped.

'Stacey and Rob. Stacey's my daughter. They're talking about having another one.'

I bit my lip as she turned to me. Her eyes were wide, suddenly, and searching. There was something sharp in her expression, something that had clearly been boiling away beneath for some time.

'If she has another one it'll be the death of me,' Margaret said, finally. Tears began to form in the corners of her eyes.

Sophie looked at me and then back to Margaret.

'I feel like a baby-making factory,' Sophie confessed in a low voice. 'Stuck in the house, making babies. While he gets to go out.'

I pushed the box of tissues into the centre of the table, speechless. I hadn't asked for these revelations and I had no idea what to do with them but both women seemed almost lighter for the release of it. They looked to one another with a warmth that to this day I can't quite put into words. I felt like an intruder on their suffering, but maybe I was the neutral party they needed present to reveal their struggles.

'I'm sorry,' I said to both of them.

Sophie began to get to her feet. 'I really should go, Bookbug is over—'

'It's a library,' I said, 'stay as long as you like. Keep the tissues. Read a book if you want.'

I gestured to the stacks and gave an awkward laugh that Sophie mirrored. She turned to Margaret.

'You should tell Stacey if she can't afford a babysitter she shouldn't have another one.'

'Oh, I don't know ...'

'Definitely! You're allowed a life!'

Margaret nodded thoughtfully and I gave them both an awkward smile before turning away, cuddly spider in hand. Sophie sat back down and I returned to the reception desk.

Phoebe looked up. 'Where did you get to?'

'Just tidying,' I replied with a shrug.

'Messy wee shits,' she grunted. 'We should make the parents clean up after them. It's not *our* job.'

I thought about Margaret, struggling to lift baby Cameron into his pushchair, wincing every time he looked as though he might be stirring from sleep, exhaustion etched into her wrinkled face. I thought about Sophie, cooped up in her beautiful Colliesh home without a single soul to talk to except a babbling baby. I thought about the poor disabled parents managing nappy changes and bottle feeds around chronic pain and hunger.

'Eh,' I replied noncommittally. 'I don't mind.'

'Hello again!' a voice called cheerily. 'How are the cramps?'

Mrs Collins shuffled up to the reception desk. It seemed that she was a regular at Roscree, too.

*

A memory that stands out for me from that first shift at Roscree is sitting on the low sandstone wall that separated the library car park from the 'main road'.

Having grown up in the city of Glasgow, I felt it was a push to call the little road outside the library the 'main road', but that was how all the locals knew it.

One of the conditions of my 'release' from the Community Mental Health team's clutches was that I didn't travel anywhere unfamiliar on my own for a while. It had been a little while since I'd been passed into the hands of Psychological Services and into Graham's care but my husband – whom I love deeply, I promise – was being infuriatingly stringent in adhering to this condition and had insisted that he would pick me up from the library on his way home from work.

Phoebe had pulled her own car out of the car park at exactly 5pm on the dot and, to her credit, had offered me a lift home, which I'd turned down.

As I sat, swinging my legs, backside going numb on the cold stone wall, I spotted a young crow awkwardly dragging its broken wing as it moved across the car park. It seemed to have emerged from the unkempt bushes outside the abandoned building across the street.

According to the locals, the building had been a private residential care home up until six months or so previously, when the foreign company (the 'foreign' usually emphasised with an eyebrow lift as if to say – *you know how those foreign companies are*) who owned the place went bust. Until that point, the place had seemed rather nice, though the residents tended to hail from rather more prosperous areas like Colliesh. None of the Roscree locals could have afforded the exorbitant costs to have a loved one stay there.

Now, the building was yet another boarded-up face on the Roscree main road.

The crow and I made eye contact for a brief moment and I became still. The poor thing was clearly malnourished and struggling and of course I, forever laden with emergency snacks and an absolute hypocrite of an omnivore who had a soft spot for all creatures broken and struggling, fished a slightly crushed peanut flapjack bar from my coat pocket.

The crow, clearly used to living off the generosity or littering of humans, made a distorted, gurgling sound that immediately reminded me of the discordant grunts and grumbles of the Bookbug babies, the kind that heralded a full cry.

The reason I'd been forbidden from travelling alone was that certain symptoms of my Big Breakdown had been exacerbated by movement and unfamiliar surroundings.

At that moment I wholly and utterly resented my brain goblins. I'd managed a whole day in a new library! What manner of failed adult was I, sitting here, waiting for a lift home like a schoolchild?

I tossed the flapjack bits towards the crow, which continued to gurgle, even as it hopped/dragged itself closer.

I'd headed up acquisition meetings. I'd designed user interfaces for some of the biggest names in the industry. I'd presented portfolios and earned awards and yet, here I was, swinging my legs on a cold stone wall because I couldn't be trusted to take a bloody bus home.

Why had I ended up so utterly broken and useless?

Before I realised it, I'd thrown the whole damn flapjack down for this bird. I stuffed the wrapper, slightly sticky, back in my pocket and licked my fingers.

The crow gurgled and chattered away happily before heading off, managing a few short, wobbly, almost ground-level flights back towards its bushy hiding place.

'Yeah, enjoy it, mate,' I grumbled. 'Looks like we're both grounded for a while.'

Chapter 4

The Rules

Visitors Daily (average) November: 57
Enquiries Daily (average) November: 12
Printed Pages Daily (average) November: 52
Violent Incidents November: 0
Children's Event Attendance: 77%
Photocopies Daily (average) November: 22

I have friends who love to run. They'll take part in 5ks, 10ks, marathons, triathlons. They wake up early each morning, pull on their running shoes and hit the tarmac before sane individuals like you or I have even had our first coffee.

I once asked one of these mad runner friends what drove them to get out of bed on a miserable autumn morning and head out into the pissing rain and fog, just to travel in various iterations of a rough circle and return right back where they began, sweatier than before.

They said that it was a habit, just like any other. Some (like me) might call it an addiction. Whenever a change in routine caused them to have to skip their morning gallop, they'd find themselves twitching like an unwalked dog for the rest of the day, knees bouncing under their work desk, eyes perpetually drawn to the nearest window.

Reading for pleasure is like running. If you haven't had a good read in a while, the effort required to get back into the habit of picking up a book can seem enormous. The energy required to actually stick with the book to the end can seem unattainable, especially if the book is long or the writer particularly verbose.

Many people give up at this stage. I've done it myself. For years, I stopped reading for pleasure because I was already reading textbooks for my studies and the mere thought of yet *more* work felt like something only a masochist would seek out.

My mind was out of shape.

The thing is, equating reading for work or study with reading for pleasure is like avoiding a bouncy castle because you've spent your day lifting weights. Yes, some of the same muscles are involved but the intensity and direction are all different.

There is no one-size-fits-all approach to reading for pleasure, just as there is no one technique for getting into the habit of exercising. However, I have my own version of the couch-to-5k for the mind that tends to reignite the spark of sheer pleasure from reading that perhaps had dwindled since their school years:

Read what you love first, not what you feel you *should* **read.**

I mean this in as literal a sense as possible. No matter how busy you are, every human being in the world has something that helps them ground and centre themselves, whether it's the soap opera the busy mother watches after putting her children to bed, or the children's films that the teenage student secretly watches to de-stress after a long day at school, there's always something.

I often have parents bringing their teenagers to the library in the hopes of having them return to reading, which feels a little bit like dragging someone to a random museum and demanding that they appreciate the art. They might indeed connect with the art on display but it's equally likely that they'll resent you for forcing them to visit a place they had no intention of visiting and into an activity in which they had no intention of participating.

Worse still are the parents who then heap upon their 'moody' teen the books of *their* childhood, or the 'classics' (don't get me started on those) purely because they feel that these books are something their child *ought* to be reading.

Nothing will kill a hobby quicker than assigning it as homework.

To these parents, to their teens and to you I would say: don't read what you feel that you *should*. That way lies boredom and disappointment.

Think of the thing that you love. That cheesy soap opera? The writers may have serialised some of the storylines in the romance section, or maybe they started off writing books. The film you went to see about the wars in space? I guarantee that there is something *strikingly* similar in the science fiction section. Love dusty old westerns? Oh boy, have I got good news for you.

What about those who are too busy?

That's fine. Try a quick read or a magazine. Read a blog. Read a newspaper. Read some tweets.

You wouldn't push a novice runner to enter a marathon, so why do we do it with readers?

The same goes doubly, or maybe even triply, for young readers. So what if your autistic son doesn't enjoy the book about wizards that everyone's raving about. What are his special interests? Does he like computer games? We have books about computer games! Yes, even those specific ones with the blocks!

What about the dyslexic kid who prefers sports to being stuck in a classroom? Dyslexia-friendly books exist! They're shorter and often illustrated. Do you think they seem too 'babyish' for your daughter? Why? Who cares if she's reading below the 'expected' age? She'll be getting plenty of pressure in school already, so why don't we just let her power through a book with fewer pages so that she can get a sense of the satisfaction just *finishing* a book can bring? We have books about football, hockey, every sport you can imagine.

I have spent time researching and requesting books about specific makes of trains from specific countries and specific time periods after having a chat with an autistic child who *loves* those kinds of trains. Yes, she could probably tell me every fact about them already but knowing that she could come into the library and look at pictures of them and, better yet, chat with an *adult* about why she loves those trains so much? That's priceless.

The point is, there's no such thing as a book that's too low-brow, too young, too simple or trashy or short when it comes to reading for pleasure. Nobody in the library is going to ask you for a book report. Nobody is going to judge you, I promise. We're probably going to assume that the adult taking home an armful of children's books is a parent but, ultimately, we're just happy to see the books moving and I am just glad to know that they're being enjoyed.

Besides, have you read a children's book recently? They're a lot better than you remember, I promise. I can personally recommend some wonderful modern children's and young adult books that grapple with themes like bereavement and sexuality far better than many adult fiction authors could ever manage.

Read what you love if you want to love reading.

This is what I was trying to explain to the horrified-looking woman who was clutching a copy of *Pride and Prejudice* as I scanned out a vampire-romance novella for her teenage daughter. The girl was smiling for the first time since she'd entered the library, or rather, had been shoved pointedly into the library and towards the Classics section.

We'd discussed the bands she liked as her mother plucked Jane Austen and Brontë-sisters titles from the shelf.

The girl's name was Olivia and she liked vampires, werewolves, music about dead lovers and actors who generally played brooding supernatural entities in love with mortal girls who tended to look and dress like, well, Olivia.

So I'd introduced her to paranormal romance books. (They all have titles like *Clawed* or *Dark Fangs* or *Wolf Passion*. You can spot them from a mile off.) When I explained that most of her favourite TV shows had started as books and that we could order in an entire series at a time for her, Olivia practically glowed with excitement.

'Do you get many people taking out those . . . kinds of books?' her mother asked, regarding the dark paperbacks with disdain.

'Quite a few, yeah. They're mostly aimed at young adults and a lot of them don't know that they're here until we point them out.'

Olivia asked, 'So how much will they cost to borrow?'

Now it was her mother's turn to laugh. 'It's a library!'

Olivia chewed on one of her black nails. 'So . . .?'

'So,' I cut in, 'it's free. It's always free to take books out, as long as you have a card.'

The teen's eyes widened. 'What, everything? Everything in here is free? Any book?'

'Yep,' I confirmed as I stamped the due date on the date slip. 'Everything's free.'

'*Olivia*,' her mother reprimanded, 'we told you all this when you were little! You used to come here all the time!'

Olivia blushed and shrugged, her fringe falling across her face. 'I forgot.'

'Well, now you can tell your friends,' I said, 'and they can get free books too.'

*

It didn't take long to get used to the routine of the library. All libraries have a rhythm to them: a weekly schedule, a daily pattern. A library is dependable, official. Its users rely on the predictability; from the jobseekers who must sign on every weekday to apply for employment, to the parents who bring their children to the weekly events and classes, to the pensioners who get the bus at the same time every Wednesday to exchange their towering stack of read books for a fresh, unread stack; the library really is the beating heart of a community.

At Roscree, the weekly flow was dictated by the children's events. It was clear that Susan's activities were the main draw for footfall to the library. Bookbug, Rattle and Read, coding classes, Lego club and after-school homework clubs drew children of all ages and often brought their carers in too. I marvelled at her ability to switch from reading a story to toddlers, to teaching coding to high schoolers, to setting up a teddy bears' picnic in the children's section for primary school children and their parents.

The high attendance and frequency of activities for children were twin sources of ire for Phoebe who, it quickly became clear, simply wanted a quiet life. She'd grumble throughout Bookbug sessions, quietly curse the school visits and feign headaches so that she could go for a 'walk' in the car park whenever children and carers began toddling in for the next event.

I came to associate the draught from the open staff entrance door with children's events. She'd hunch in the doorway as I ran around handing out juice cartons, herding stragglers from breached baby gates and taking payments and bookings. I didn't resent the work. On the contrary, having so many things to do and people to interact with was a joy, especially in comparison to the dragging, lonely shifts at Colmuir.

Roscree had a relatively large bank of computers for use by the public. The IT section was, second to the children's library, the busiest section of the branch. This was yet another source of displeasure for Phoebe. (After all, wasn't the point of a library to lend books? At least according to Phoebe this was so.)

I took a more practical approach to the provision of computer and internet access. Instead of mirroring Phoebe by smirking (always bloody smirking) and muttering something about 'not being an office assistant', I'd routinely pick my way between computers, looking for anyone who might need a bit of help. Having come from a relatively computer-based career, I thought I might be of some use to anyone having trouble with the complexities of technology usage.

In hindsight, I can't help but laugh at my naivety.

Without wishing to sound like a snob, the simple fact is that until you have worked with the public, you will have absolutely no idea how technology-illiterate they can be. This is something on which all library workers (and I'm sure other IT workers) can agree and another rule of public library work:

Never, ever assume a level of familiarity with technology. Don't assume that the person you're helping has ever even *seen* a keyboard. Don't assume anything.

Instead, take notes. Take notes because you will be asked the same things over and over again. Take notes because sometimes you will forget that vital first rule. Keep your notes to hand and go back to them from time to time. Here's an actual transcript of some of the notes I took in those first few weeks at Roscree:

Where is the internet? – User was looking for the browser icon. (Solved, 1 min.)

Why is my email asking me for a password? – User has password saved on own device. Tried to explain that public computers did not save passwords because this would be a security issue. Tried to help with resetting password. (Unsolved, 45 mins.)

Why is the screen dark? – The user hadn't moved the mouse in over five minutes. (Solved, <1 min.)

The internet looks wrong. – User was used to mobile browser. Tried to explain this. Failed. (Unsolved, 15 mins.)

I'm left-handed. – Tried to explain that mouse could be moved to other side. Demonstrated. (Solved, 5 mins.)

My email is broken. – Emails in browser look different from those on phone app. (Solved, 5 mins.)

I've lost the internet. – First user again. Pointed out browser icon. (Solved, 1 min.)

Where are the numbers? – User thought the computer was a fax machine. (Unsolved, 25 mins.)

Where are all my things? – User inadvertently opened a new tab in browser. Took a while to communicate this. (Solved, 25 mins.)

I need a letter. – User wanted to use Microsoft Word to type up a letter. (Solved, 10 mins.)

I need letters. I need to send the letters to my son. – User needed to access their emails. Did not know password. (Unsolved, 30 mins.)

Where is the Google? – User couldn't remember the URL for Google.com (Solved, 3 mins.)

Where do I put the money? Where does the copy come out? – User asked for computer access but actually required a photocopier. Requested that user did not insert money into the computer or photocopier. (Solved, 45 mins.)

As ridiculous as these requests may seem (and trust me, I've had far stranger and more vague over the years so I try not to judge), they do highlight something important about the kinds of people who use a library and the enormous disadvantage that the technology illiterate often have.

As with those poor Bookbug mums, the people who come to me and other library workers for help with computing tasks are some of the most vulnerable people in society. They're most likely poor, elderly and/or disabled. The vague and seemingly nonsensical queries aren't a result of stupidity or a desire to be awkward, they come from unfamiliarity.

Here is where an important rule comes in: **Patience is everything. You never know what someone is going through.**

*

Chloe was the first regular I got to know at Roscree. She visited the branch almost every single day, walking from a supported living complex for young disabled people at the top of the main road through Roscree.

Chloe had a number of learning disabilities, though I've never asked what they were specifically. Some days, she would visit with a group of other disabled teens and their carers. Other days, she'd arrive by herself. She must have been around eighteen or nineteen and always wore the same red coat, rain or shine.

My first encounter with Chloe was when she approached the desk during one of my early shifts with Phoebe. She walked past the queue (though those waiting seemed to be used to her presence, some even saying hello to her) and put her hands on the desk in front of me.

'Okay?' I asked.

She seemed agitated. She was clearly trying to get Phoebe's attention.

'Can I help?' I continued. I'd never really worked with anyone with learning disabilities before and to be honest, I was worried I'd done something to cause her agitation.

'Phoebe!' she shouted.

I winced. At that point I struggled with loud, sudden noises. It was something we had been working on in my therapy but my reaction was so mortifying I could feel my ears burn.

I turned to Phoebe.

'Uh … this young lady would like to—'

Before I could finish, Chloe rattled off a series of words and numbers at Phoebe.

'Crime, two-hundred-and-twenty-three. Science fiction, forty-seven. Romance, ninety-eight …'

I slowly came to realise that she was listing off the number of books we held in each section of the library. I stared in amazement.

'Did you count all of those?' I asked before I could stop myself.

Chloe nodded.

'Thank you, Chloe,' Phoebe said dryly, which appeared to be the girl's signal to leave.

She hovered, fidgeting for a moment in front of me.

'I said *thank you, Chloe*,' Phoebe repeated. 'Goodbye.'

Chloe nodded and began to step away from the desk. She paused, biting her lip as though she wanted to say something else. I wanted to ask her when she'd had time to count all of the books, or why she'd done it, or even how she'd managed to remember all of the specific numbers but I just waved awkwardly at her before greeting the next person in the queue.

In the years since that first meeting, I've spoken to library workers all over the country and even the world. It seems that many branches have their own Chloe: someone who enjoys or finds comfort in counting the books. I can't help but wonder if there's something appealing in the sensory aspect of it: libraries are structured spaces that thrive on precise numbers and data.

I certainly find tidying and restocking shelves a somewhat mindful experience when I'm left to it. It's easy to become lost in a reverie of spine labels and careful shuffling, so I think I can understand why so many people out there enjoy counting the things.

Chloe's agitation bothered me and I couldn't quite figure out why.

As soon as we'd served everyone at the reception desk, Phoebe turned to me, expression sour.

'Now you've met Chloe.'

'Does she do that a lot?' I asked.

Phoebe smirked. 'Every bloody day. If she gets interrupted, she'll start again. Pain in the arse. You just need to smile and say "thank you" or she'll keep at it all day.'

I hadn't recalled Phoebe smiling at the time and I didn't like the way she spoke about Chloe but what did I know? I could imagine the shouting becoming disruptive for other library users, especially if she cut in front of other people often.

Still, it seemed as though most of the regulars knew her and I couldn't see any harm in it. Frankly I was amazed at her ability to retain the information.

It took a few weeks of visits from Chloe – some accompanied, others solo – for her to feel comfortable enough presenting the numbers to me instead of Phoebe. Heeding Phoebe's advice, I'd always make a big show of thanking her for it (which in retrospect I realise was incredibly patronising), though it didn't seem to ease her agitation.

One day, more out of curiosity than anything else, I grabbed a pen and paper and jotted down the sections and Chloe's counts as she reported them to me. Truthfully, I wanted to do my own count because I just could not conceive of anyone being able to remember that many precise numbers like that. I'd taken to thinking about her counts in my spare time. Some days I'd watch her move around the room, wordlessly pointing at each shelf as she made her lap of the branch.

Chloe seemed to light up as I put pen to paper. Gone were the nervous fidgets. She delivered the day's count with greater confidence than I'd ever heard from her.

When I was finished scribbling, I glanced at her. She was watching my hand on the paper.

'Um. Thanks, Chloe.'

'You're welcome.'

She turned away without hesitation and returned to her companions. A tall boy with glasses gave her a thumbs-up.

I looked at my notes, then up at Chloe and her friends' retreating backs.

Was this what she had wanted all those previous times? Had she been telling us so that we might take note? Her speech had always seemed so urgent, previously. Perhaps she knew that we didn't share her ability to memorise those numbers and needed to know that her report wouldn't simply be lost on us.

Later that afternoon, I counted off the science fiction books. Our science fiction section was small and tended not to move very much.

Chloe's numbers were correct.

I've since realised that what Chloe wanted was no different to what many, if not most, library users want: to know that she was being listened to.

I may never understand why she feels compelled to count all of the books in our branch and I don't need to. What's important is that I acknowledge the count and let her know that I have the information.

Nowadays I usually print out a table for Chloe's counts as it can be rather useful to track the busier and quieter genres and sections of the library. I've taped it to the wall behind the reception desk and add a new row every time she visits.

*

'Can I help you with anything?' I asked the well-dressed woman sitting by herself at the window.

The branch was especially quiet that day. There were no children's events or activities and even the IT section was empty. Maybe it was the weather.

Puddles glinted in the sunlight outside.

I'd been watching the woman, who must have been in her early fifties, for a little while now. She hadn't browsed the books, nor was she glancing at the newspaper in front of her. Something about her posture and expression seemed downcast.

'Are you busy?' she asked in a small voice. Her mouth trembled.

I looked around at the empty library and chuckled. 'Not today.'

'Could you ... could you just sit with me for a while?'

I glanced at her, surprised.

'Uh, sure. I mean, of course.'

Phoebe was reading a newspaper of her own at the reception desk, so I pulled up a chair and had a seat.

'Is everything okay?' I asked.

I got the same feeling of unspoken desperation from this wee woman that I'd sensed in Sophie, the Colliesh mum. She clutched an old-fashioned handkerchief in her slender fingers, her long scarlet nails worrying at the edges of it.

'I'm sorry, sweetheart,' she said. 'I just had to get out of the house. It's so quiet since ...'

She trailed off and waved the handkerchief as though reprimanding herself. She dabbed at her eyes.

I pulled my chair in closer and tried to look less stiff. I was now overly aware of my posture. I wanted to seem understanding and informal. I put my elbows on the table and then awkwardly withdrew them.

She gave a bitter, quiet laugh.

'Oh, listen to me. You must think I'm so silly. My husband is at work and my boys have both left for university. You'd think I'd be enjoying the quiet!'

I released my breath. I'd been expecting a tale of bereavement and her explanation punctured the tension.

'My mum said the same thing,' I commented. 'When my brother and I moved out. She even had plans for our old bedrooms but I think she was surprised by how much she missed us.'

The woman smiled.

'I bet she was,' she said softly. 'Allie, is it?'

She gestured to my name tag and I nodded.

'Jennifer,' she said, offering me the hand that wasn't clutching the handkerchief.

We shook.

'What are your boys studying at university?' I asked.

Jennifer and I spent the next twenty minutes or so getting to know each other. Her husband worked full-time as a pharmacist. She had been an office manager in a legal firm but had gone part-time when the boys had started high school. Now that they'd grown up and left the nest, she was at a bit of a loose end. It had only been a week since her youngest had moved out but she was already sick of the quiet in her home where once there had been, from the sounds of it, organised chaos.

'I've done all of the laundry!' She laughed. 'When you have two boys, the laundry is never done!'

I chuckled. 'I bet.'

'Football kits, school uniforms, you name it. I hated it all but … I can't believe I'm saying this … I miss it.'

'It's a big change.'

She nodded.

'So what are your plans for your spare time now?' I asked.

She looked down at the handkerchief. 'Oh, I don't know. I hadn't really thought about it. I suppose I thought that I'd keep myself busy.'

'Give me a sec,' I said, getting up from the table.

I walked back to the reception desk, where Phoebe was hard at work filling out the sudoku challenge in the local paper. She didn't register my presence as I grabbed one of the leaflets from the display and headed back to where Jennifer was sitting by the window.

I popped the leaflet down on the table and pulled up a chair again. Jennifer seemed surprised at my return. I think she had the impression that I'd been looking for an excuse to get away.

'These are all of our adult groups and activities,' I said. 'It's not a huge amount but there's a list of classes at the local college, too.'

I pointed to the back of the leaflet.

'Some of them are free, it just depends on what you're looking for. The book club here is pretty good. It's mostly crime and thriller at the moment, if that's something you're interested in.'

Jennifer turned the leaflet over in her hands.

'Do I have to be a library member?' she asked.

I shook my head. 'Not for most of them, though if you've got some ID, I can get you signed up in a couple of minutes.'

'Can I keep this?'

'Sure! I know it's not the biggest list but we're always looking for new clubs and groups to run here.'

Jennifer folded the leaflet and carefully deposited it in her handbag. She smiled.

I leaned in. 'Look, I know how it is. I was stuck at home sick for a long time while my husband was working. I wouldn't wish that kind of quiet on anyone. His was the only face I'd see for weeks. You end up going to the shops just to meet someone new.'

Jennifer put a hand on my arm and I felt a rush of affection towards this woman. She reminded me of my mum in some ways, myself in others. It was obvious that she loved her boys dearly and worried about them a lot. So much so, in fact, that she'd forgotten to take time for herself over the years and now she was out of practice. I could relate to that.

'Thank you for sitting with me,' she said.

'Any time,' I replied. 'Well . . . as long as we're quiet like this. I'd probably get the sack for letting a queue go unattended.'

I stood.

'Y'know, if you take a look at our children's activities time-table, you'll see a few days which don't have events on. Those are the best days for a chat. We have a few people who just pop in to read the paper. Retirees, students, mums who've dropped the kids off at school. They're good people. I wouldn't recommend the days with kids' classes on. It gets loud.'

'Thanks, Allie.'

There's something about a library that attracts people going through transition in their lives. I suspect it's the familiarity. Even if you've never visited a particular branch, you know the basics of what to expect at it. There's a comfort in regularity, especially when it's free.

I learned quickly not to underestimate the comfort that Roscree Library brought to its residents. It's easy to take it for granted when you work in the place but for people like Chloe and Jennifer it can be a true lifeline.

*

Every weekday, Mr Taylor would arrive at the library almost bent double with pain. Amongst other conditions, he suffered terribly with arthritis. On the coldest days, he would be so buckled that he appeared to be inspecting the carpet, or ducking under a low rafter, as he approached the desk. It took immense effort for him to slide the library card across the counter and yet he would, without fail, attend the library at 10.30am precisely every single weekday.

In a previous life, he'd worked in construction and then had gone on to teach apprenticeships in metalwork. He'd remained in this role for decades, dividing his time between the local vocational college and various local worksites, where he could teach on the job until a series of health complications had led to him being unable to lift and manipulate the tools of his trade and forced him to leave the role at sixty.

To qualify for unemployment allowance, Mr Taylor would drag himself out of bed every weekday, get dressed (and he was always impeccably turned out, shirt and tie and everything) and catch the bus to the library, where he'd wince, slide his card across the desk and politely ask for computer access.

Once seated at a computer, he'd check his Universal Credit account. He'd check the journal for messages from his 'job coach', a semi-anonymous someone who could be 1,000 miles away for all he knew. They'd let him know whether or not his progress with job applications thus far was to their satisfaction, would perhaps advise him of some more websites to try and whether or not they had any additional tasks for him, such as a CV update.

Then began the arduous slog of The Search. The search itself would take up the rest of the morning and some of the afternoon for Mr Taylor. He would go to the suggested websites, search for jobs in his area and painstakingly type out applications for whatever arbitrary number of jobs the DWP had decided that week. He would do so in the full knowledge that he would never even make it to an interview and, if he did, would be dismissed out of hand due to his various ailments.

Mr Taylor was too sick to work and everyone but the DWP seemed to know it.

Still, this was the ritual required of him to access his benefits, the money that would keep him from losing his home, paid for most of his food and kept his house heated (at least for most of the month, if he was careful).

Ritual complete, sufficiently humiliated, he would log out, take a moment to prepare himself, then rise from his chair with a wince and begin the long shuffle back to the bus stop. Sometimes, later in the month, he would shuffle all the way home to save money.

Once, when signing him up to a computer, Phoebe – with all her trademark tact – bluntly enquired as to why Mr Taylor had never signed up for disability payments.

I'd never seen him look as flustered as he did at that moment. He puffed, wheezed and gripped the counter for support. I was genuinely worried that she'd finished him off. The poor man gathered himself and shook his head.

'I did. Couple of times.'

Phoebe opened her mouth as though to enquire further but I cut in. 'You're on computer six, Mr Taylor.'

He gave me a look that suggested gratitude before shuffling off to his computer. As he made his way, Phoebe turned to me, crossing her arms.

'If he applied, why's he not getting it?' she grunted.

I could have told her that I'd been through the assessment process myself. I could have told her that it was the most humiliating experience of my life. I could have told her that, after being made to fill out a truly enormous stack of forms discussing, in detail, what I was rendered incapable of doing by my illness (*can't travel alone, can't be left alone with knives, high suicide risk, can't manage medication alone – see section 8C 'medication and talking therapy'*), I was summoned to be inspected by . . . someone. It was never specified. Just an assessor.

I could have told Phoebe that, despite the apologies from the assessor, nothing had prepared me for her looking me in the eye and saying, 'Now, I have to ask this . . . what is keeping you from killing yourself right now?'

I could have told Phoebe that I'd actually managed to qualify for Personal Independence Payment for a while, that it had been a pittance and hardly worth the toll on my health the assessment had taken.

I could have told her that, just six months later, I received a letter from the DWP summoning me to a 'routine reassessment', that my husband had shredded the letter after agreeing that another round of questioning like that could very well be what pushed me over the edge to sectioning or worse.

Instead, I watched Mr Taylor pause halfway to the IT section to take a break against a pillar and said, 'I don't know.'

My train of thought having threatened a line-change at Depression West (at which two very eager goblins prepared to join my travel), I was grateful for being spared ruminations by the noisy arrival of Heather.

As well as being line manager for Colmuir, Heather was the acting team leader at Roscree. As always, she appeared in a flurry of files, folders, jangling keys and plastic bags, many of which she proceeded to drop en route to the management office.

I didn't notice the air shift until I'd picked up the first folder and handed it to her (receiving a breathless 'ta' in return). I glanced up to catch Phoebe staring in my direction, looking like she'd just swallowed a pint of hot piss. The expression itself was startling enough but the absence of the ever-present smirk made it all the more alarming. She was unblinking, unflinching and made absolutely no effort to conceal it.

I couldn't tell if her undisguised disgust was directed at myself, Heather or both of us. It took me several moments to realise that Heather had been speaking to me the entire time.

'—training on closing procedures here. I've got the Standard Operating Procedures for the till here, much the same as Colmuir—'

Phoebe was *still staring*. I'd never encountered a grown adult who didn't at least blink when caught staring. I could feel sweat beading on my scalp. I wanted to scratch my face, or cover it somehow. For one mad, dizzying moment I saw myself moving to firmly press the cover of the ring binder in my hands against her face, just to break that stare. I could almost see the twin lasers of her gaze burning holes in the plastic cover.

'—oh, and you'll meet the part-timers, Emily and Claire. I have paperwork for them. I don't suppose you could ... no, I'll give them the forms. Anyway, *Phoebe*!'

Phoebe turned her glare, as blazing as the sun, to direct it entirely on Heather. I almost expected to smell burning flesh.

'What?' she grunted. I cringed internally, dipped my head and continued picking up Heather's debris.

Heather nudged the office door open with her hip.

'Have you looked at updating the displays? Could you do that, please?'

Phoebe grunted noncommittally. Heather disappeared into the office and dropped her baggage on the desk noisily.

Phoebe's gaze softened as soon as Heather was gone, yet I felt a degree of trepidation as I returned to the reception desk. No sooner had I taken my position at my computer than Phoebe started clicking her teeth, tutting and huffing like an agitated bear.

I kept staring at my computer screen. I'd already had enough of the theatrics and the tantrums. A cruel little part of me wanted to wait until she directly sought my attention like a grown adult.

Phoebe gave an exaggerated sigh. I closed my eyes, inhaled and then turned to her.

'All right?' I asked in a forced chipper tone.

She smirked as though she hadn't just spent a solid minute huffing and puffing like a fairy-tale wolf. 'So you've met Heather.'

'Yeah. She showed me the ropes at Colmuir, remember?'

'Hmm.' She unfolded herself into a standing position and leaned against the desk.

I paused. She seemed to expect more from me, so I added, 'She uh ... interviewed me.'

'Well,' Phoebe said, the smirk deepening, 'displays are *my* remit. It's my choice if they change and I'm not going to do it just because *she* says so.'

It all began to click into place: the dated posters, the obsolete display topics, the messy shelves. The children's library was a place of colour and joy but here, in the adult's section, the library was a battleground between Heather and Phoebe, between blustering neuroticism and almost aggressive laziness.

And I had been dropped right into the centre.

Chapter 5

The Battle for Roscree Library

Visitors Daily (average) December: 62
Enquiries Daily (average) December: 19
Printed Pages Daily (average) December: 61
Violent Incidents December: 0
Children's Event Attendance: 69%
Photocopies Daily (average) December: 31
Free Watch Batteries Supplied to Public (total) December: 18
Free Dog Waste Bags Supplied to Public (boxes, total) December: 2

Meeting Emily was like meeting an old friend.

I tended to arrive fairly early for my shifts. It had happened naturally, as I began to fit in with the rhythm of the place. I'd arrive an hour or so before opening time, grab a coffee en route, chase the night's shadows from the place and shake off the silence as I sipped coffee, opened curtains and dusted-off displays. The building had a habit of growing oppressively stuffy overnight and I liked to think of the steam from my coffee as something akin to the sage smoke used to ward off malingering spirits in cleansing rituals the world over.

This time, however, I had only begun my morning ritual when my colleague arrived. The loud *clunk* of the staff entrance door was accompanied by a blast of icy winter air. At the sound, my stomach dropped slightly.

I'd tried to get along with Phoebe. I'd tried to get past that maddening smirk and the blunt, hostile questions and even the temper tantrums, all for civility's sake. Ultimately, not only had I failed to salvage any kind of familiarity with her, I had begun to get stomach aches in her presence. Her rudeness repulsed me. A sort of cold would wash over me, a cold that I forced into my gut to quell the anger she provoked whenever she shoved a bony finger in my face and demanded to know what medication I was taking today and why, or when she hissed through her teeth as I tidied around her, as though by cleaning the place I was somehow offending her.

The thought that Phoebe's abhorrent presence had begun early, barging into my hallowed cleansing and preparation time, horrified me.

'Hello? Somebody in?'

Emily was, like me, a part-timer unknowingly thrust into the middle of a battle zone. Just a couple of years younger than me, she was well-spoken and an absolute breath of fresh air. She had the air of an old Hollywood starlet, big blue eyes framed with thick black lashes. Her black hair was stylishly parted and pinned in a style reminiscent of Audrey Hepburn. She moved gracefully, like a trained dancer.

She shook my hand gently and seemed utterly delighted to meet a new member of staff. I would soon learn that this was the way that Emily approached all things in life: wide-eyed, curious and with an optimism that quite frankly, terrifies me.

Before long we were exchanging the names of our pets (her, Flower, an old rescue dog whom she obviously loved deeply, and me, my pet snakes and my cats whom I often refer to as my supervisors). She was a great lover of animals, spending time between shifts in the library volunteering at local charities and animal shelters. A child of church ministers, this was her calling. I admired her zeal, even if it did rather tickle at my own insecurities.

She was also an artist. I had to pry that information from her. Not only did she paint, but she was a published poet. Again, I had to coax her to share the extent of her achievements and even though I might normally end up childishly resenting someone so bloody talented *and* humble to boot, I just couldn't dislike her. Within the first hour or two of meeting her, Emily's wicked (and truly filthy) sense of humour had me laughing until I cried.

Some people take a while to grow on you. Others crash into your life in a blaze of talent and dirty jokes and shared interests. Emily was most definitely the latter.

The shift went far more quickly than any other I've ever had. Despite the low visitor numbers, we kept each other busy and laughed riotously.

By the next morning, we already had nicknames for one another as we set up the library for the day. Opening was a breeze and then all we had to do was wait for the regulars to arrive. We sat and watched the revolving doors spin. I found myself smiling as the first visitor of the day approached the desk.

Cheeto was a regular IT user. He came to do his mandatory job search like so many of the others and, just like so many of the others, he should have been receiving benefits for his disability. He was a short, skinny man who could have been aged anywhere between his late thirties and early fifties. His thinning grey hair was always pulled back in a greasy ponytail and, up until recently, his face had been dominated by an equally greasy, shaggy beard.

Without the beard, the extent of Cheeto's malnourishment was clear. He had the pocked, angular face of someone who had known starvation and had known it for a long time. I'd come to know the look – the hollow cheeks, the loose skin around the jaw. He didn't appear to be a drug user (again, I'd come to know the looks) but he also clearly wasn't well.

When Cheeto arrived at the library, his smell often followed. It was a mixture of the roll-up cigarettes he would stamp out at the entrance and the sour tang of dirty clothes and old sweat.

His hands always shook as he handed over his library card, eyes averted, mouth trembling.

Cheeto was a mumbler. It wasn't just that he spoke quietly but that his every thought, action and inclination was quietly broadcast to the world via a never-ending string of whispered, involuntary commentary.

'—*got to buy some more and get the computer*. Computer please, miss,' he said, trembling fingers releasing the card. '*Do the fuckin' job search then the shops then the bus. Search first*—'

He was far from the only IT user with mental health difficulties but, despite his appearance, I had a soft spot for Cheeto. I always knew what he was thinking. Everything he deliberately projected at the outside world (that is, the speech he could control) was polite, hesitant and even slightly apologetic. Some found his constant muttering alarming or even threatening but I'd spent long enough around him to know that even the more vulgar murmurings were involuntary and quite clearly a reflection of his own anxieties. His goblins, it seemed, had found a way to speak out loud.

Once or twice, I'd had complaints from some of the Bookbug mums about Cheeto's presence. I know that Phoebe had generally 'resolved' these particular situations by shouting 'shut up!' in

Cheeto's direction. This had almost always resulted in an increased urgency (and vulgarity) to the commentary-stream, punctuated by apologies in his more deliberate voice.

I tended to hand-wave the mums' concerns with a reminder that the library was for everyone, including some of the more vulnerable members of the community. Cheeto was harmless.

I had no idea why everyone called him Cheeto. To this day, I have no idea.

Cheeto was an example of another of my rules for working in a library: **Just because someone communicates differently doesn't mean they're communicating incorrectly.**

It's a librarian's job to bridge gaps. We bridge the gaps between those who have access to information and those who don't. We bridge the gaps between the rich and poor by providing free access to essential services. Just as importantly, wherever there is a gap in communication, we must try to find a way to bridge it.

Bridging a gap in communication may be as simple as writing information down on a piece of paper in an accessible way. It might involve remembering that not everyone has the same level of literacy as we do. It might be learning a little bit of British Sign Language – as I and many of my colleagues have – just enough to be able to ask some yes or no questions.

Not all communication gaps arise from disability or even a difference in language, which leads me to an important point: swearing.

Some people swear casually. Some people swear without realising it. Many of our regulars pepper their speech with swears the way one might pepper a paragraph with punctuation. It's simply part of their communication pattern and that is why I believe that it's important to make a distinction between swearing used as part of everyday speech and swearing intended to insult.

Just because someone is swearing doesn't mean they are swearing at *you*. This is a point that I would write across the sky if I could.

When you work in a library, you must accept that your cultural standards are not the same as everyone else's. Your norms are not necessarily the norms of those you serve.

At Roscree, we have quite a few 'sweary' regulars. Some staff, especially those who may be used to working at branches with a more middle-class clientele, can find themselves shocked and offended when they overhear the odd f-bomb or, God forbid, a hard c-bomb. I've found myself in situations where a newer member of staff had come to me after refusing to serve a regular due to the language used in the request.

Frankly, I find a blanket, offence-taken approach to all forms of adult language rather naive and completely counter-productive. Nine times out of ten, the person doing the swearing isn't even aware that they have used foul language. Some even apologise as the word slips forth and the vast majority of the time, all that's required is a quiet reminder that the word or words used are not generally seen as appropriate for the setting. Either that or a reminder of the presence of children is enough to solicit an apology. Don't patronise but don't get up on your high horse either. Be reasonable and most will respond in kind.

I do not have time for pearl-clutching around language and neither do the people who need the library most.

Slurs, of course, and language intended to demean or intimidate are another matter entirely. For this, I would like to refer to the next rule of library work, which is derived from a phrase that

I've seen mostly banded around the pagan, Wiccan and otherwise witchcraft-adjacent realms of the internet for a good number of years: **Do no harm but take no shit.**

I believe that one speaks for itself.

*

As Cheeto shuffled off to the IT section, Emily picked at a corner of one of the posters that had been lopsidedly taped to the wall behind the desk. It read: *CHRISTMAS PANTO 2010 TICKETS: £5 EACH.*

'You know,' she said, 'I hate this. Look at how out of date it is!'

I reached over to pick at the tape on another corner of the poster.

'Phoebe will go off her head if she thinks we've been messing with her displays,' I said.

Emily laughed as she finally got purchase on the paper itself, tearing it down in one swift movement.

'I think this place could do with a makeover, don't you?' she said.

'Definitely.' I looked around. God, there were so many out-of-date posters! They'd been bothering me from day one but Phoebe was so *bloody precious* about what did and didn't go up in the place. She'd hiss at me if I even approached her crumbly old displays.

I became acutely aware that we were two grown, adult women living in fear of our batshit insane colleague. Sure, Phoebe had been in the public sector – what, forty years? – and yes, she was unpredictable and quite frankly terrifying, but so what? This wasn't the playground. We weren't children. Why were we kowtowing to the mad emperor just because she liked to stamp her feet?

I tugged at another poster, tearing it in half with a flourish.

'What's she going to do, complain to Heather?' I said.

'Exactly,' said Emily, scraping at the remaining tape with a plastic ruler.

'And anyway,' I continued, balling another sign and tossing it in the recycling bin, 'how would she know which of us to complain about if she's not here when it happens?'

'You know ...' Emily said, putting down the ruler. 'When I first got this job, I thought that this was the kind of thing I'd be doing. Putting out books for display, making up posters for banned book week, that sort of thing.'

'Why don't we?' I suggested. 'Why don't we just do it? I won't say anything if you don't. We can just shrug and say it was like this when we got here.'

My grandmother always said that it is easier to ask forgiveness than permission. My parents hated it when she told me that.

Emily grinned and offered me a tiny, dainty hand. I shook it. 'Deal!'

'The pact is sealed!' she announced. 'The library shall be transformed!'

''S'cuse me, missus!' Cheeto called across from the IT section. 'How come my emails look weird?'

*

That was how our guerrilla campaign began. While the adult section may have been the official setting of Heather and Phoebe's war, Emily and I quietly conducted our own little operations on the front line. I'd come in after her shift to find a brand-new display on Scottish authors, complete with banners, tartan ribbon trim and Burns quotes.

Meanwhile, I'd surreptitiously print off signs encouraging readers to ask for recommendations, or pointing out which lesser-known authors were similar to the more popular ones.

Phoebe went on the warpath.

'Who did this?' she'd demand, gesturing to the new displays, to which I'd shrug in response.

Later, I'd wait until Phoebe had gone for a 'fresh air break' and I'd rotate out the large print displays. I'd make a featured author section in the time it took her to finish a lap of the car park.

Heather's presence during some of my shifts with Phoebe made absolutely no difference to my guerrilla work. It became clear that Heather was more than content to sit in the tiny, smelly management office all day, emerging only for the odd toilet break. Even when she did grace us with our presence, she was so preoccupied with flustering over her own neuroses that a truck could have driven through the side of the building and she wouldn't have noticed.

I brought in my own tools and discovered that Emily had been quietly borrowing from – and restocking – the arts and crafts materials reserved for children's activities. I started doing the same.

Soon, we had beautifully mounted signs indicating upcoming authors of the month. We filled our favourite books with pre-made bookmarks that contained information about similar authors and brief reviews of their books.

All the while, Phoebe's expression soured, her cigarette breaks increased in frequency and – vitally – book loan rates (known in the library business as 'accessions') went up.

Whenever I was on a shift with Heather, I would hear her fielding calls from Phoebe or furiously chicken-peck-typing out ALL STAFF emails that would go along the lines of:

To: Roscree Staff
From: Roscree Team Leader Account
Subject: UNAUTHORISED SIGNAGE

IT HAS BEEN BROUGHT TO MY ATTENTION THAT NEW SIGNAGE HAS BEEN PUT UP WHICH HAS NOT BEEN PRINTED ON OFFICIAL COUN-CIL HEADED PAPER. I WOULD LIKE TO REMIND ALL STAFF THAT THE LOCAL AUTHORITY LOGO MUST BE PRESENT ON ALL OFFICIAL COM-MUNICATIONS FROM THE LIBRARY AND THIS INCLUDES SIGNAGE.

ADDITIONALLY, BOOK DISPLAYS MUST BE INOFFENSIVE AND IN LINE WITH THE BOOK DISPLAY STANDARDS SET OUT IN OFFICIAL COUNCIL LIBRARIES OPERATING PROCEDURE DOCUMENTATION, ALL OF WHICH IS AVAILA-BLE ON THE COUNCIL INTRANET.
HEATHER

Each screeching, all-capitals email would send a rush of child-like, rebellious excitement through me. Emily and I would spend our shifts together reading them aloud whenever the library was quiet. I particularly enjoyed putting on my very best Patrick-Stewart-recites-King-Lear voice for them.

We noticed, however, that those quiet moments were becoming few and far between.

Heather and Phoebe weren't the only ones who'd noticed the changes at the branch. Visitors had taken to commenting on the new displays, the hidden messages for readers and the signage. Soon, we had groups of teenagers traipsing in on their lunch break to read – a phenomenon virtually unheard of in modern libraries.

Susan, the children's assistant, had caught on. We set up a secret message group and would bat ideas back and forth. We discussed linking children's activities with adult events. We swapped tips and resources. We found ways around each of the rules passed down in Heather's emails. I printed off stickers with the council's logo so that all of our signage met her increasingly ridiculous standards.

There's nothing quite like being technically right.

Roscree's visitor rate continued to climb.

One day, Heather emerged from her office, flushed with anxiety, to inform us that a local crime author had requested to use the branch for a meet-and-greet.

Phoebe and I spoke simultaneously, her grunted 'why?' colliding with my 'wow!'

'Well, I'm not working overtime,' she grunted.

'We can't afford to pay overtime,' Heather began but I cut her off.

'I'll do it. I don't mind.'

Neither Heather nor Phoebe could summon an objection and I silently rejoiced as the meet-and-greet was scheduled into the branch diary.

*

I should have known that Emily would also volunteer to organise the author signing event. We spent much of our next shift brainstorming promotion ideas and producing posters. We were just getting into the logistics of leaking a notice to the local press about the event without going through official authority channels when Emily paused, frowning at her screen.

'Everything okay?' I asked.

'Have you seen this?'

She turned the monitor to face me. She gestured towards an email marked URGENT in the library's inbox.

To: Roscree Library
From: Roscree Cluster Management Account
Subject: Departmental Changes

ALL STAFF,

Please be aware that, following the recent departure of Iris Wilson from the position of Cluster Manager, I will be acting as Temporary Cluster Manager for Roscree area branches.

I appreciate that this change is sudden and will be visiting all of the branches and speaking with all affected staff over the course of the next few weeks.

Linda Chapman

'Huh,' I said noncommittally.

'Yeah,' Emily replied. I could tell she was judging my reaction before providing her own.

'Sudden departure,' I offered tentatively, 'seems a bit uh ... unexpected.'

Emily nodded and looked around. It was very early. Very few library users were within eavesdropping distance. She gestured me closer anyway.

'You were at Colmuir, right?' she whispered.

I could barely hear her, but I nodded. 'Yeah.'

'So, um … you know about the situation. With the violent incidents.'

I remembered the dent in the wall, just above my head-height, and the chair that had made it. I gave a small, bitter laugh. 'You mean that there are loads of them, all the time? Yeah, that's why I'm here.'

Emily nodded. 'So, you know the violent incident reports go to the cluster manager, right?'

'Er … do they?'

'Yeah. They go through Heather, then on to Iris. It's her job to implement changes or bans or whatever.'

'She didn't do a whole lot of that. Just left me to it.'

'Exactly.'

Emily straightened up as a woman approached the reception desk. After an exchange of books and an expert flurry of date-stamping, the woman left. I was only just starting to digest the information about Iris when Emily sat down again.

'So,' I said, 'Iris got the boot because she wasn't dealing with the violent incidents properly?'

Emily shrugged. 'Don't know for sure. I do know that word got round of just how bad it was out there. You must have been terrified! Did they really follow you home?'

I scratched my head and nodded sheepishly. 'I uh … yeah. We had some problems with that. The police were more interested in the gang stuff, I think.'

Emily was about to reply when Mr Lewis arrived at the desk, bushy brows furrowed as always. He plunked his books down on the desk with a grunt that, over time, I had come to recognise as meaning 'these are returning to the library.' He had a similar, longer grunt that he would often use in lieu of pointing out that the books being dropped on the desk were being borrowed.

'I wonder if that's why she got the sack,' Emily pondered once the old man had gone.

Serves the coward right, I almost said aloud. Instead, I pointed to the signature on the email.

'Do you know this Linda Chapman?'

She shook her head.

I shrugged and held up my magnificent A3 poster, glossy and colourful and guaranteed to cause another email-lecture from Heather on economical use of printing resources.

'I wonder if she likes crime.'

*

I'm not sure what I expected the local gritty crime author, Jack Murray, to look like. His books were, by and large, fictionalised accounts of the very real gang crime that existed in the Glasgow area. Rumour had it that his father had been involved in the real thing before moving to Roscree, where he apparently abandoned the life of crime for something more respectable while bringing up his sons.

The man who arrived for the signing was shorter than me by several inches, making him easily one of the shortest men I'd ever met. He had a wind-beaten, weathered face, as though he made a living between writing books either working at sea or out in the moors somewhere. He must have been in his late fifties and had a broad Glaswegian accent.

His bald head was crossed with two or three scars that stood out against his honeyed brown skin and suggested – though this was most likely my associative bias after reading one or two of his books – that his interest in violence may have been more than academic at one point. Still, he had the battle-scarred appearance of a man who'd done a lot of hard physical work and had grown a thick skin over the years.

He'd arrived to a respectable queue of readers waiting to meet him, clutching a plastic carrier bag full of copies of his novels and the day's newspaper in one hand and the groceries he'd picked up from the local corner shop in the other.

Something about his request to pop the skimmed milk he'd just purchased in our staffroom fridge really tickled me. I suppose I had expected an eccentric, artistic type. Instead, Jack Murray was as down to earth as any man who might visit Roscree for a quick spin on a computer to check their emails or a browse of the true-crime section.

It was just as well that the author was so humble and forgiving, as this was the day that our branch IT server had decided to give up the ghost. We'd discovered the problem that morning after a cursory inspection of the server room revealed that the air conditioning had failed and the system had massively overheated.

What this meant in practical terms was that not only had we lost access to the internet but that our entire cataloguing system was unavailable to us and that was the day that I learned yet another of library work: **Expect hardware and software to fail.**

Unfortunately, having never experienced a server outage before and being a tech-reliant millennial, I was about to have a crash course in manual library stock-keeping: namely, in the use of The Big Red Book.

The Big Red book is a ledger that – in times of emergency – can function as a record of stock movement. Its usage requires noting the title, author, ISBN and catalogue number of all stock returned to or taken out from the branch. Each entry is accompanied by the ten-digit card number of the user either borrowing or returning the book.

Veterans of library work will be rolling their eyes when I complain about the labour-intensive process of manual cataloguing. Many will remember the pre-digital systems of index cards and other similar filing processes and you have my utmost sympathy because quite frankly it is near impossible to do anything other than process returns and accessions when you're tethered to a great big bloody book without autofill or barcode scanning or any of the other luxuries us library workers have come to take as standard.

Still, the server could not have picked a worse day. Poor Jack Murray was left to set up his own signing booth as Emily and I juggled queues of irate and impatient members of the public and calls to and from our IT service – managed remotely by an external contractor and seemingly staffed exclusively with condescending older English men who spoke to us as though we were confused little girls on our first day at school.

'I'm sorry I just *can't* understand your accent. Can you pass me to someone more senior?' I was asked more than once.

'No, look, I'm trying to tell you that the server has overheated and we can't restart it. You can't do this remotely. I need someone here.'

'Come again?'

'Server's down. Send an engineer.'

'What? Sorry? Is that English? I can't understand you.'

'Pass. Me. To. Someone. Who. Can,' I snapped finally.

Emily almost choked as she passed by with a cup of tea to our wonderfully patient author, who seemed to be finding my struggle with IT 'support' just as, if not more, interesting than the group of readers who'd come to discuss various plot points and murders in his work.

'You girls have your work cut out for you!' he announced after the last of his fans had left, signed books in hand. 'In my day, we never had computers at the library. Closest thing you got was the photostat.'

Whenever a library user became aggressive or demanded that something was done about the lack of internet access, Murray would gently rebuke him for 'harassing the young ladies' and fire up a spiel about how we all managed just fine before the invention of the internet. Didn't you know that he still typed his books up on a manual typewriter? If it was good enough then, it was good enough now.

In the end, we muddled through and though no IT engineer showed up, a combination of Emily's relentless optimism and Jack Murray's cheerful commentary made the whole episode much easier to bear and by the end we were taking bets on the sort of reaction we'd get from each user who approached the desk with books, expecting them to be quickly scanned and instead spending five minutes as we pored over each one and painstakingly entered them into The Big Red Book.

*

Shifts with Emily passed far more quickly than those with Phoebe but all too soon I found myself in the presence of the smirking mantis once again.

I was scanning Cheeto's card (*'fuckin' job search journal fuckin'* Thanks, miss!') when an uncharacteristically quiet Phoebe spoke up for the first time that morning.

'Have you spoken to Heather yet?'

Returning Cheeto's card and waving him off, I returned to my chair and turned to face her.

'Heather? Not lately,' I replied.

The smirk deepened. 'She's all upset about her friend being fired.'

I glanced around. Phoebe had never developed the habit of lowering her tone when we had library users in. In all honesty, I'm not sure if it's something she even considered. She clearly loved the sound of her own voice and treated each grunted syllable like a blessing bestowed upon us unworthy mortals.

'You mean Iris?'

Phoebe nodded. Despite wanting to appear professional, I was curious. I'd been thinking about Iris's departure and what Emily had said a lot. Was I really in some way responsible? Should I feel guilty? Angry? She'd obviously neglected her duty to keep her staff safe but was that all that had been going on? I was hearing all of this second- and third-hand after all.

'She and Heather are close?' I prodded.

Phoebe sat back and laughed so abruptly that I flinched. It didn't even register as a laugh at first. For a brief, mad second I honestly believed that she'd started barking. It wouldn't have surprised me at all.

People were starting to stare. I pressed the lever on my office chair to lower myself out of sight behind the standing desk.

Phoebe caught her breath and gestured towards Heather's office. '*That one*,' she drawled, 'and Iris are *best pals*. They go way back. Two peas in a pod.'

She scooted closer to me and I instantly regretted lowering my chair. She towered over me, even sitting. 'She was crying *all day* yesterday.'

My discomfort peaked as that gloating smirk hovered above me and I instinctively stood up, backing away.

'That ... sucks,' I offered finally.

Phoebe waved my feeble attempt at empathy away with a bony hand and a snort.

I was distracted by the arrival of Mr Priestly.

Mr Ben Priestly (no, really) was the councillor for the Roscree and surrounding areas. He held a surgery every second Tuesday of the month in the library itself, or at least that was what the glossy posters featuring his hilariously airbrushed mug declared.

In truth, he showed up for around maybe half of the scheduled surgery sessions and of those that he did attend he was, without exception, an hour or so late. He would arrive in a cloud of tangy aftershave that seemed to assault the sense of taste, bypassing the nostrils entirely. His patent shoes glinted under the library lights and his female assistant (about my age) would follow, bent over a pile of paperwork in a manner reminiscent of Heather's perpetual fluttering.

Priestly didn't so much radiate an aura of smugness as taint nearby water supplies with it. From the pressed pinstripe suit to the crotch-first swagger of a man who has laid off more assistants than I've had hot dinners, he was a living embodiment of the hot-shot politician caricature.

I feel at this point I must emphasise that Priestly was a local councillor. Not an MSP. Not a member of Westminster Parliament. He was a local councillor (one of a cluster) for the Roscree area.

As always, he strode past the reception desk without so much as a word. I'd once managed to glean a nod from him by waving overenthusiastically as he passed by, much to Phoebe's ire.

Priestly liked to leave the little details to his assistant, who dumped the pile of paperwork on our desk and immediately began the semi-monthly ritual with Phoebe.

'Tea?'

'Coffee. Two. No milk. Biscuits if you've got them.'

'Water?'

'Please.'

Priestly had a power that none other seemed to wield and yet he was rarely present to see it in full action. He could reduce the praying mantis to a grovelling schoolgirl. It was quite the sight to see her running after him, fetching coffees and biscuits and offering sugars and pens and notepads in a strange, simpering voice I've never heard her use for anyone else.

Phoebe was not the only member of staff strangely afflicted by this man's power. He managed to achieve another impossible feat: coaxing Heather out of the management office to do some work. She, too, became a starry-eyed sycophant to him as though all women felt compelled to act the part of the young fifties secretary in his presence.

Watching these two women who, for all their flaws, had until that point seemed ostensibly modern and relatively feminist develop these submissive personae was nothing short of bewildering to me. Eventually, the whole excruciating charade became too much for me and I summoned the courage to ask Phoebe about it.

'So, um … what's the deal with the councillor?'

'Mr Priestly?' Phoebe asked.

'Yeah. Is he a celebrity around here? Nobody ever seems to attend his surgeries.'

Phoebe 'shushed' me so suddenly and sharply that I physically flinched. She beckoned me closer with a short, frantic gesture.

'Think of him as your boss's boss's boss's boss's boss,' Phoebe said, counting out each 'boss' on her fingers. 'The council control the budget, right? Well, he's in charge of the library budget. Pretty much, anyway. He's Oscar Coates' boss.'

Of course. No wonder he walked in like he owned the place. Theoretically, he did.

'I see.'

'So if he asks you for something, you do it, right?' Phoebe hissed. 'If we keep him onside, we might get some new computers by the end of the year.'

I glanced over at the IT section. The PCs were running on a version of Windows I hadn't seen in years. The server itself was prone to overheating and backup supply failures. Hell, even the keyboards and screens were in dire need of replacing, having been manhandled by God-knows-how-many members of the public in their time.

I was genuinely surprised that Phoebe cared about the state of the library equipment or the place's budget at all, given how little she seemed to care about the footfall numbers and retaining any sort of air of professional service in the face of the general public. It occurred to me that a computer upgrade would probably benefit us too, as the vast majority of our IT-related work tended to revolve around overcoming or working around the decrepit nature of the available systems.

'Gotcha,' I said. 'Man with the budget. Be nice.'

The surgery – if it could really be called that without any attendees – was supposed to last until late afternoon and would take place downstairs in the storage area, where a table and chairs had been set up. We were instructed to accompany any constituent who wished to attend downstairs and to phone ahead to announce their presence, the area having its own extension line left over from the days when a real meeting room had been set up down there.

As always, Priestly left two hours before the official end of the surgery, swanning past and leaving his secretary to announce their exit.

'Have a nice day!' Phoebe called to him as he left, though no response came.

As I popped the next scheduled surgery into the library's digital calendar, I noticed Mr Taylor approaching the front desk from where he'd been sitting in the IT section.

'All finished?' I asked him as I typed. Priestly's secretary continued to hover beside me.

Mr Taylor huffed, resting himself on the desk for a moment. I looked up from the computer.

'That ... man ... is that the councillor?' Mr Taylor asked between breaths.

'Mr Priestly? Yes.'

'Is he ... coming back?'

I already knew the answer but I looked at the secretary, who glanced at the front door, back at me and shuffled some papers.

'No, erm, he had to leave early today for ... family reasons,' she answered.

Mr Taylor made a non-committal noise, brow furrowed.

'Tell me, hen, does he have a phone number?'

'Mr Priestly would prefer if you contacted him via email or attended his next surgery, should you have any enquiri—' the secretary began but Mr Taylor cut in.

'It's about the Miners' Welfare.'

Back when the Roscree colliery had been in full production, many of the miners had chipped in to create the Roscree Miners' Welfare centre. It was a tiny hut of a thing that had functioned as a working man's club for decades. Many in the community, especially the elderly, had come to rely on the place just as dearly as they relied on the library for education and socialisation. A local befrienders group used the place to run informal meetings and a sort of friendship speed-dating service for the members of the community who couldn't leave home due to age or disability.

The Miners' Welfare was almost an extension of the library, remaining open after the library closed, as well as on Sundays. It was a two-minute walk from the library itself and those who volunteered there would often visit the branch with posters and leaflets advertising upcoming classes and clubs.

I'd read in the local paper that very week that the building that housed Roscree Miners' Welfare had been condemned, ironically due to subsidence caused by old mining work done beneath that part of town. Last I looked, the building was cordoned off, another boarded-up face on Roscree's high street. A relic of a time that may not have exactly been more prosperous but had definitely seen more populated streets.

While Mr Lewis was one of our more technologically literate library users, he certainly wasn't the kind of person who could simply rattle off an email to the local councillor. Even if he did manage to send the thing off, it would be a struggle for him to remember how to check his inbox for a reply.

Besides, having freshly encountered Priestly that day, I was feeling more than a little bit of resentment towards the man.

As his secretary spoke, I ran a quick search on the council website and scribbled down Mr Ben Priestly, Councillor for Roscree and Surrounding Areas' office number on a Post-it.

'Here,' I said, 'there's his number.'

*

I'm not sure how I'd pictured Linda, but it hadn't been like this. When she first walked into the library, I'd assumed she was a regular patron. She appeared sporty, her blonde hair pulled into a tight bun and a polo neck that wouldn't have looked out of place on a PE teacher. The only items giving away her corporate status were the immaculate pinstriped suit jacket and the corporate lanyard around her neck which, at first glance, I'd assumed was a sports whistle.

She was tall – not quite on a par with Phoebe's height but close – and wide. There was quite obviously a lot of muscular bulk beneath the suit jacket. The ways and angles in which the polo neck strained and stretched confirmed this. She must have been in her late forties, though she had the sort of skin that had seen a lot of sun. She wasn't *ugly*, far from it. She was the kind of woman the Victorians would have referred to as 'handsome'. She was ageless in a tanned, well-maintained way. I could well see her on a golf course, breaking records, or perhaps dwarfing her opponent on a tennis court.

She assessed the room like a police officer taking in a crime scene before setting her gaze on the two of us behind the reception desk, expression unreadable. Silently, she pointed a finger at Phoebe and told her to 'sit down' in a gruff voice. There was no 'please'.

I expected rebellion, or a huff, or *something* from Phoebe but perhaps she had finally met her match. She silently sank into her seat and crossed her spindly legs.

It was only then that I spotted Heather shuffling through the rotating doors behind her. The poor woman was dwarfed by

Linda's enormous outline and looked as though she'd been jog-
ging to keep up with the pace. As always, she was carrying more
paperwork than she could reasonably handle.

'Ah, Allie! Good!' she huffed as she stepped out of Linda's
wake, adjusting her grip on a stack of envelopes, 'Linda, this is
um … well, you know. It's Allie. Now you have a face for the
name, heh …'

Linda's dark eyes met mine and something sparkled in
them. Her mouth twitched – the barest hint of a smile – and
she nodded.

'I'll start with you, Allie,' she announced. Her voice had
softened somewhat, though she continued to speak so loudly
that several nearby library users turned their heads. I felt as
though I'd been picked for the school football team.

'Will you be using the store?' Heather ventured.

'The store' referred to the storage space in the basement.
Dank, dark and I'm pretty sure slightly damp, it housed various
items including Christmas displays of yesteryear and older reference books that couldn't be left on general display.

'No,' Linda replied, the gruffness back, 'we'll use your office.
You can wait out here.'

Heather opened her mouth to speak. Nothing came out.

In the time I'd been at Roscree, I could count the number of
times I'd been in Heather's office on one hand. Her room was
sacrosanct: always locked, except when Heather was present. One
bare light bulb gave the place a sickly yellow tint and the under-
desk heater emitted a smell that I can only describe as akin to
that of burnt cat hair. A potted plant had long ago withered to
nothing on the windowsill.

Now, Linda was plucking a brown envelope from Heather's
hands and directing me towards the door while Heather gawped

silently beside Phoebe, who was wearing that sour, boiled-piss expression once more.

I scratched my nose to keep myself from laughing. Linda had ruffled so many feathers with so few words that I felt a strange sort of respect for her. Imagine having the power to command a room like that!

She closed the office door behind us, which in itself was no mean feat. The room was a repurposed storage cupboard with barely enough room for one occupant, let alone two.

She squeezed her brawny frame past me and behind the pathetic little desk, gesturing for me to take a seat on the tiny stool opposite. As I perched, she continued the procedure of manoeuvring herself into Heather's office chair, which groaned and sank several inches further than I'd ever seen it go.

There was a tense moment of silence as both of us waited – but endeavoured not to acknowledge that we were waiting – to see if the chair would hold out.

It did.

'Allie Morgan,' she said finally, retrieving the paperwork from the envelope that I now saw bore my name on it.

Now that we were alone, her entire demeanour shifted. She tossed the paperwork on the table and relaxed, leaning back into the chair (which creaked only slightly) and raising a hand to rub at her broad jaw. She glanced around the place and puffed her cheeks.

'This place has seen better days, hasn't it?'

I'd been expecting some kind of interview. To be honest, I'd half-anticipated an interrogation regarding the circumstances of Iris's departure.

'The office?' I followed her gaze.

She sighed and sat up once more, straightening the papers on the desk almost idly.

'The branch. The whole library. Shame, really.'

She dropped the papers back onto the desk. They were violent incident reports. I recognised my own handwriting.

'It's ... a bit dated,' I offered.

She nodded. 'I'm sorry you've been put in this position. I've got to watch what I say.' She glanced at the door before continuing. 'The fact is that this place used to be a four-man branch. Sometimes five. We had more space, more books. Your store was a children's library. I don't know if you knew that.'

I shook my head. She leaned forward, lowering her voice further.

'Cards on the table, this place is in danger of closure, Allie. Colmuir too. A few other branches in the North. I think this is a great wee library, I really do, but ... the numbers aren't great.'

'The footfall numbers?'

'Exactly. The children's events are the only thing keeping this place open and even then ...' she paused. 'I didn't tell you any of this, okay? I shouldn't know myself, really. Thing is, Iris has been left too long with this place and nobody's bothered to check up. We need events. We need displays. We need stock rotation and colour and ... we just need to get people through that door.'

I thought about Emily and our pact. I thought about the silly, childish thrill of our illicit poster-making campaigns and guerrilla pop-up displays.

'I can do that,' I said.

Linda looked taken aback. 'Hmm?'

'I mean I can get people in. Me and Emily. We've been trying. We have ideas for events ...'

I was about to say more but Linda was smiling and it caught me off guard. Her eyes twinkled for a moment before her face fell back into its neutral, businesslike expression.

'That's exactly what I'd hoped you'd say,' she announced. 'So here's the deal: email me your ideas. You and Emily keep doing what you're doing. Don't think it hasn't gone unnoticed, by the way.' She grunted approvingly. 'I'll work on the red tape. We don't have a budget for funding events but if you can scrounge whatever you can for free, I'll help you with whatever you need.'

'Actually,' I paused, 'we've had some … uh … resistance.'

'From Heather.'

I nodded.

'And Phoebe.'

'Yeah.'

Linda sat back once more.

'You leave them to me.'

Chapter 6

Death and Rotas

Visitors Daily (average) January: 77

Enquiries Daily (average) January: 28

Printed Pages Daily (average) January: 82

Violent Incidents January: 2

Children's Event Attendance: 75%

Photocopies Daily (average) January: 49

Free Watch Batteries Supplied to Public (total) January: 34

Free Dog Waste Bags Supplied to Public (boxes, total) January: 4

Damaged/Lost Books (total) January: 13

Free Sanitary Products Supplied to Public (boxes, total) January: 32

Days Tracking Checklists Not Complete: 3 (staffing changes, lost sheets)

'Tell me about the crying at work,' Graham said. 'I thought you were enjoying the role.'

The standard NHS-blue plastic seat squeaked as I shuffled awkwardly. I could feel the sweat collecting beneath me. The tiny rooms in the psychological clinic were always stifling.

Must be the studio lights, I mused.

'No, I mean … I mean yes, I am. Enjoying it. More than I thought. I want the place to do well …' I trailed off.

Graham allowed me a moment before gently pressing. 'But …?'

A halogen light was buzzing. Had been buzzing the whole time I'd been sitting there, feeling louder and more insistent by the minute. I had the maddening urge to take off a shoe and throw it at the damn thing.

'It's the people,' I said. 'We've got more people coming to us than ever and they're really desperate. I've never seen anything like it.'

'Does it upset you?'

I nodded. 'Yeah, it does. Not that they're so poor, it's more … the system. It's shit. They get treated like shit. It makes me feel guilty.'

'Why?'

'I don't know … I mean … Can I give you an example?'

'Go ahead.'

The first time Emily and I arranged a tea morning, we hadn't expected such a turnout. We figured that lots of people came to the library to socialise, so why not try making it a formal thing? If it went well, we could grow it from there, maybe try some kind of community outreach thing. We'd already spoken to local care homes about bringing in some of the residents for knitting and crochet groups.

Linda had been on board, though she'd already warned us that we wouldn't be able to get any sort of funding through official channels. That's when the thought had occurred to me to run the day as a charity event. We'd stick out a collection tin for a local charity and ask nearby businesses to donate things like tea bags, coffee and maybe some biscuits.

The response had been overwhelming. I had arrived the next day to a frankly enormous delivery from a local grocer. They'd sent us an entire pallet of cakes, biscuits, sandwiches and tea bags. Other locals had joined in on the idea, bringing in jars of instant coffee and even pints of milk from their homes.

When we first started up the rotating doors that morning, Emily and I realised that we'd started something big.

In what we were later assured by local residents was the first time, we unlocked the front doors to find a queue outside. People had wrapped themselves up for the brisk spring morning and came bearing cakes, tea towels and mugs.

It seemed that all of Roscree had shown up for the morning and Emily and I had our work cut out, running back and forth to the staffroom to refill kettles and urns, dragging old chairs up from storage, counting and emptying the donation tin into the library safe.

All in all, the visitor count was in the hundreds. Not bad for a branch that currently averaged around 70 people a day.

In the midst of it all, several familiar faces grinned as they cut into home-made cakes and handed out napkins to each other. Sophie, the Colliesh mum I'd tried to comfort on that first day, was there with her baby. Margaret soon arrived with baby Cameron and a group of other elderly, unofficial childminders. Even our regulars joined in.

'Is-is it free?' asked Cheeto as I offered him a tray of biscuits.

'It's for charity but you don't have to give anything. It's all free.'

His eyes lit up. 'Thanks, miss! *Fuckin' hungry.*'

By the afternoon, the bustle had died down and Emily and I were able to take turns cleaning out mugs in the staffroom while the other held the fort at the reception desk.

It was Emily's turn to wash up when the boys arrived. I say 'boys' but the young men were probably in their early twenties. A couple of regular jobseekers. I recognised their faces.

Poor doesn't begin to cover it.

These young lads had been let down from day one. Tossed back and forth through the care system, they'd ended up left to look after their respective disabled mothers as soon as they'd been dropped out of the foster system. They'd had various jobs from time to time but always seemed to end up back at the library, back on the punishing Universal Credit grind.

Skinny as rakes, they hovered in the entranceway, whispering to each other.

Finally, one of them approached me at the desk.

'How much is the tea, miss?' he asked.

'It's all free,' I said. 'It's a charity thing but we're packing up. Take whatever you like.'

The boys just about fell over themselves. They thanked me, over and over. They kept asking if I was sure that nobody would miss the cake.

I told them that it would go to waste if they left it, so they may as well take it.

'Thanks, missus. Thank you, miss. Can I take a slice for my mum? She likes Madeira. Can't get out the house.'

'Tell you what,' I said, lifting an unopened cake from the stash we had behind the desk. 'Here's a whole one. It'll last longer. It's just going to go to waste back here.'

I handed him the Madeira cake and when I looked up, I realised that he was crying. Tears streaked his hollow cheeks.

He looked a lot like my younger brother, I thought, if my brother hadn't eaten properly in years.

This poor kid was starving, I realised. They'd probably been starving their whole shitty life. Both of them. Their wee disabled mums were probably sitting in a cold flat, also starving.

I glanced around. There were very few people left in the library. We didn't have CCTV.

Fuck it.

'We've got to-go cups here. Grab some tea and coffee.' I wasn't offering any more, I was instructing. 'Then pick another cake. Does your mum like shortbread?'

I bundled a box of biscuits up with the Madeira, along with an unopened pack of cupcakes.

'Oh, missus, I can't take all that ...'

'You're doing me a favour,' I said. 'I'll just have to clear all this up otherwise.'

I got a hug from the pair as they left. It was like hugging a couple of warm skeletons in ill-fitting tracksuits.

That's when Emily returned. I excused myself to the staff toilets and I cried.

There I had been, not six months ago, ready to end it all over ... what? Losing my job? Being unwell? Dropping out of university? And here were these boys without proper homes, proper jobs, without food. Here were two starving boys who'd been offered cake and the first thing they'd thought of was getting a slice for their housebound mums.

Nobody opts into depression but, my God, I thought, nobody opts into a life like *that* either. Two young men, reduced to tears over a few slices of cake.

*

'So you feel guilty because your life doesn't seem as bad?' Graham suggested.

'Yeah, a bit.' I scratched my nose, a nervous habit. 'I mean ... no. I was unwell. I'm still unwell. I'm still recovering so being suicidal doesn't compare.'

I looked up at him. 'Honestly, I'm fucking angry.'

He blinked. I don't often swear at our sessions.

'I'm angry that there are so many people in that position and I'm angry that there's nothing I can do for them.'

'Sounds like you did do something.'

I paused. 'For now. I helped them once. We should be doing that all the time! That's what the place is for! People come to get help with things. Libraries are the one place where you don't have to spend money. They're where people come to get help with their benefits and get information and if people like Phoebe and Heather had their way it would all go to shit! Then there are the councillors, like Priestly ...'

'What about him?'

After Mr Taylor's enquiry, more library users had started bringing up the fate of the Miners' Welfare Club. Until that point, I'd assumed that the place had only been used by a handful of locals and the odd charity or two. It soon became clear that I'd vastly underestimated the building's significance to the people of Roscree.

We began getting visitors from a group calling themselves 'Friends of Roscree Miners' Welfare'. They'd heard from Mr Taylor that I'd been the one to pass on the councillor's contact details (even though they were readily accessible to any member of the public who visited the council website) and would arrive in twos and threes to probe me about the councilman.

'What does he look like? Is he the one we should be speaking to about this?'

I'd pointed out the posters with Priestly's face on them, highlighting the surgery hours.

'And it's here, is it? Where he holds the surgeries?'

I'd nodded.

After the fifth or sixth visit by the campaigners, I was pulled aside by Heather. She had me squeeze into the management office to look at an email.

To: Roscree Team Leader Account
From: Roscree Cluster Management Account
Subject: FW: Contacting Councillor Ben Priestly

TO WHOM IT MAY CONCERN,

Please note that due to the large increase in enquiries, Mr Priestly will no longer be able to discuss constituency matters over the phone.

It has come to our attention that one or more members of staff at Roscree Library have been advising constituents to contact Mr Priestly in this manner and we would like to reiterate that the correct channels for all enquiries relating to constituency matters are via email or by visiting Mr Priestly's constituent surgeries in person. Details of the dates and times of these surgeries have been outlined in the attached poster.

Please make your staff aware that Mr Priestly is often out of the office and therefore telephone enquiries are unlikely to reach him in a timely manner and have them convey this to any constituent seeking advice on council matters.

Yours fully,
Pamela Boyd, on behalf of Councillor Ben Priestly

'Was this you?' Heather asked bluntly. 'Have you been giving out Mr Priestly's office number?'

I blinked.

'It's on the council website,' I replied diplomatically.

Heather's brow furrowed and she stared at me for a moment. I could feel the panicky anger just bubbling beneath the surface of her gaze. Finally, she said, 'I'll print this out for all of the girls to sign. That includes you.'

Frankly, I was more than a bit irritated by this dressing-down for doing my own job but I knew that Priestly held the library to ransom, whether Heather admitted it or not.

'Okay,' I said curtly. 'Do you need a hand with anything else?'

Heather shook her head, still scowling.

I turned to leave when she called my name.

'Allie,' she said sharply and then, more quietly, 'be careful with him, okay? Just ... be careful around Mr Priestly.'

A look passed between us that I'd known in a previous life. Back in my engineering days, I'd come to know this look and the quiet comments that often accompanied it as the 'whisper network'. In a male-dominated industry, the whisper network is what keeps the few women afloat amid a sea of testosterone. The whisper network was a safety device, a warning system against those men who'd earned a silent reputation for cruelty, wandering hands or a particular kind of attitude towards women.

'I will,' I said.

I meant it.

*

'He's been in the job for years, absolute sleazebag, soaking up the money while people struggle and suffer. He's got the power to change things, he just doesn't care. That's what makes me angry.'

Graham nodded. 'So, what are you going to do with this anger?'

'I'm going to … I'm going to help people. I'm going to do what I can, and, if I can, I'll keep the library open. I'll make people see how important it is.'

*

There is a knack to spotting illiterate people. Before I started working in libraries, I had assumed that very few people in modern society had never learned to read or write. I'd assumed that they would stand out like sore thumbs. After all, how much of our communication is text-based nowadays, especially now that we rely on digital communication more than ever?

The truth is that illiterate people are everywhere. They are our friends, family members and colleagues. The vast majority of them have developed a number of tricks and techniques to work around their inability to read and write. The more aware I become of these methods, the greater the respect I have for those who've lived their secret inability their whole lives.

The stigma against illiterate people is enormous. It's no wonder that they usually do everything within their power to hide it, sometimes even from their own parents, children and partners.

A common technique is to claim poor eyesight when confronted with text. This goes hand in hand with the excuse that 'I've forgotten my reading glasses'.

There are an awful lot of non-existent reading glasses out there.

People who can only read to a certain degree often become agitated when confronted with complex written word or large amounts of text. Another common refrain is that of 'I'm too busy to read all that'.

Whenever I talk about the illiterate people who come to the library, I'm often greeted with scepticism. Why would someone who cannot read come to a library? How do they function in society?

The answer to the first question is quite simple: they come for the same reasons that people who can read and write come to the library, with one exception – they're not here for the books.

Over the years, the Jobcentre has sent increasingly large numbers of illiterate people to our branch with the promise that we will help them claim benefits, especially Universal Credit. Sadly, the fact is that I am legally not supposed to even see a library user's Universal Credit account. I certainly am not supposed to ask for or enter any of their personal information.

Just last week, a couple arrived at the library having been sent here by the Jobcentre. They must have been in their thirties, relatively nondescript, obviously poor and with telltale signs of having experienced starvation throughout their lives.

In a quiet voice, the woman, Claire, pulled me aside for some help. They were both library members and while she came semi-regularly to use the computers, her partner had been told that he must start filling in his job search journal online. The only problem was, he had never learned to read or write.

His story was typical of most illiterate library users: he'd come from an unstable home and had experienced trauma throughout his early life. That, combined with a suspected learning disorder, had led to him struggling at school and eventually choosing to forgo it altogether. Between foster homes and the instability of the care system, nobody had ever really picked up on the fact that he'd stopped attending school. He'd fallen through the cracks.

Still, he'd found work whenever it was going. He'd met Claire young and eventually confessed his secret. Now, she did any reading and writing required to keep him in work.

Sadly, there are only so many jobs out there for someone who can't fill out paperwork and once again he found himself back on the job search.

Claire's reading and writing abilities weren't great either, I discovered. She spelled phonetically and tended to use emojis in lieu of words wherever possible. Of course, when it comes to job applications, few employers tend to accept a CV riddled with emojis and misspellings.

According to what little training I've had and privacy regulations, I should have helped them get to the Universal Credit website and left them to it. Quite obviously, this was all the help they'd received previously because their benefits had been stopped and they'd been sanctioned for failing to respond to letters and emails.

The two were desperate, hence why they'd revealed all to a library worker they'd never met before. I'd like to think they chose me because I seemed approachable but, in all likelihood, it was a case of almost literal beggars being unable to be choosers.

Whenever I have a situation like this, my first action is to take stock of who's in the library. Who am I on a shift with? Are they sympathetic to desperation? Are they willing to turn a blind eye to me bending the rules to help someone? Second, I'll try to find a computer in a quiet spot, away from nosy Joe Public or anyone else who might be inclined to ask a few too many questions about why a library assistant might be getting so heavily involved with a stranger's DWP details.

In this case, the library was quiet and we had the IT section to ourselves. I gave Emily the signal that we both knew meant 'keep an eye out for management' and escorted them over.

The man, who I'll call Darren, clutched a grubby Post-it in his hands. I recognised it as the kind handed out by the local Jobcentre, usually with a list of passwords and important information that would help him access his Universal Credit account. (The miserable bastards wouldn't even splurge on an actual sheet of paper or a printout. The damn things were always grubby, torn and hand-written.)

I talked them through the login procedures. It took Claire four attempts to spell her partner's name correctly. She began to get flustered, so I pulled up a chair beside her.

'It's okay. I always struggle when someone's watching me type too,' I said. 'Want me to read out the password?'

There's a fine line between being supportive and being patronising and it varies from person to person. Claire seemed to appreciate the offer once I was sat beside her. I suspect she'd have found me hovering over her somewhat off-putting.

'You'll get a few questions,' I explained to the pair. They should have had this explained at the Jobcentre but I never assume anything about that place any more. 'Your place of birth, that kind of thing. Then I'll show you how to get your journal.'

I spent a good twenty minutes with the pair. Thankfully the place was quiet enough to leave Emily to man the desk for that amount of time. I rarely get to do that.

We had a good chat about remembering where things were on the screen. I grabbed a sheet of paper and drew the Universal Credit interface. I highlighted the important menus. I circled the login section.

Every time a website (especially a government one) has its layout changed, our branch is flooded with people requesting a one-to-one session like this. It's not part of our job and I've been reprimanded more than once by various managers for doing it but until a better system is in place I honestly don't see what choice I have. It would be far too easy for some to turn people like Darren and Claire away, who'd probably then end up unwell, homeless or worse. I just don't think I'd have the stomach for it.

Finally, I borrowed the Post-it note and typed up all of the information on it. I printed off a copy in as large and clear a font as I could manage. Emily and I refer to these as 'cheat-sheet' prints. We don't charge for them. We've been reprimanded for that, too.

When Claire began to get teary I had to step away. I couldn't help but think of those boys again, crying over a free cake. She hugged me.

*

This is where an important rule for your own mental health in library work comes in: **You will get angry. Use it.**

Priestly failed to show for his surgery.

This wasn't a surprise, of course. He had a track record for no-shows. The problem for him, this time, was that the library was bustling with Friends of Roscree Miners' Welfare (FORMW) members. They'd come in coordinated t-shirts. They had leaflets. They even had a petition.

A short, middle-aged woman with a quite frankly incredible head of curly, silver-tinted copper hair identified herself as Moira, head of the FORMW group and architect of the petition that was now being handed out around the library to Bookbug parents and somewhat bewildered IT users.

I knew immediately that I liked Moira when she slapped a leaflet down on the desk and said, in the kind of voice that can only be cultivated from years of chain-smoking, 'So, where's Mister Councillor? Hiding from us, is he?'

Despite her coarse voice and gruff exterior, there was a motherly warmth to Moira. After I explained that Mr Priestly had been due to arrive almost an hour ago and that I, unfortunately, could not get through to his office number (emails be damned), we got chatting.

Moira's father had helped found the Miners' Welfare in Roscree. She'd been volunteering in it since she was a teenager, cleaning, serving drinks, arranging educational activities for the miners and anyone else in the community who chose to visit. She helped establish the kitchen and before long, coordinated a team of volunteers to run it most weekdays.

Anyone who wished could pop in, pay a small fee and have a drink, a meal and a chat.

Somehow, Moira also had time to volunteer with the Men's Shed Association and used the Miners' Welfare as an informal 'shed', where men would meet, carry out crafting, building and gardening activities and, more importantly, get some judgement-free socialisation. I was impressed to hear just how busy and vital the little building had become.

'You could tell it was needing work,' Moira admitted, 'but subsidence? That's a killer. We'd just had the kitchen renovated too. Cheeto used to pop in every day for lunch.'

I had a look at the petition, which already had gained several pages of signatures.

'So what's the plan now?' I asked.

She pushed the clipboard towards me.

'There's plenty of empty buildings in Roscree. We just need somewhere to start. We can raise cash once we've got somewhere. It's down to the council. They just need to give us a base.'

I thought about Priestly. How utterly arrogant must a man be to take his constituents for granted like that? It was beginning to look like he wouldn't show at all.

'Give it here. I'll sign it. I'll take a couple of copies and we can keep it here, too.'

'Good for you, hen. Thanks.'

Priestly never did show up that day, though his contact details made the rounds once more. I made no effort to stop them, either. I made a token effort at pointing out that we'd been told to contact him via email or in person but, given the fact that the latter seemed pointless, I wasn't at all motivated to belabour the point.

I rattled off an email of my own to Priestly's office, pointing out that we had a number of concerned constituents waiting to see him and could he please call us at his earliest convenience to let us know whether or not he would be attending this month's surgery.

Later in the day, we received a phone call from a man claiming to work for the *Roscree Post*, the local paper.

'Is it true that Mr Priestly failed to show for his constituency surgery today?'

I opened my mouth to reply but Heather's warning rang suddenly in my ears. *Just be careful with Mr Priestly.*

'I ... can't really comment,' I replied.

'I understand. Do you have the contact details of someone who might be able to discuss it?'

'Er ...' I paused. *Oh, sod it.* 'If you have a look on the council website, every councillor's office number is listed there. I have been told to give out his email address too if you'd like it.'

'Yes, please. Oh, and while I'm here, do you know anything about the Friends of Roscree Miners' Welfare?'

I hesitated again. *Careful, Allie.*

'I can't really comment but um ... if someone were to pop into the branch, there are a few leaflets and a petition here with some contact details on them, as far as I know. That's all I can say, really.'

'Will you be there if we pop in today?'

'Er ... yes.'

'Thank you for your time.'

As I read Ben Priestly's email address aloud, I began to wonder if I was getting drawn into a conflict that was way over my head. Still, I remembered the reverent way Moira had spoken about the Miners' Welfare. She and her FORMW group weren't the only ones who'd brought up the closure. Plenty of our regulars had expressed sorrow at the loss of the facility. Some had even stopped showing up at the library as much since its closure.

Like it or not, the Miners' Welfare and the library were two parts of the beating heart of Roscree. There was no doubt in my mind that with one gone, the other would suffer and the community would be all the worse for it.

I don't know if the reporter showed up later that day. If they did, they certainly didn't mention it to me in person. Plenty of people inspected and even signed the FORMW petition. Several more took leaflets, some vowing to share them with friends and family who also relied on the place.

Later that week, a story appeared in the *Roscree Post* entitled 'Save Our Miners' Welfare'. It was only a small piece, the front page being dedicated to an ongoing expenses investigation within the council, but it featured a picture of a stern-faced

Moira standing in front of the boarded-up welfare centre and included a link to the online version of the petition.

*

I had always scoffed at depictions of recovery from suicidality in the media. How could a person go from the belief that the only way to end their suffering was by ending their life to simply … not believing that any more?

The 'suicidal urge' is a strange beast borne of many goblins but the most striking thing about finding yourself in the position of actively planning your own death is the silence that accompanies it. In my experience, it was as though someone had pressed 'mute' on the fever-pitched roar of responsibilities, failures, shame and fear that had been pressing down on me, threatening to crush me into a fine powder. The knowledge that I simply did not need to *be,* to experience any of this, was like coming up for air after being held underwater.

Of course, that feeling is also a lie.

It is entirely possible for one person to flip back and forth, suicidal and then not-suicidal, kicking and fighting, letting go, then fighting again.

What I realise now is that most suicide attempts are not an active choice to die but simply a reach for silence, a (rather permanent) leap away from the turbulence and trauma that so many of us carry with us. Our own goblins.

When you have survived a suicide attempt, as I have, or even simply come out of that headspace where dying seems like the right thing to do, everything changes. It will always be with you and, crucially, once that door has been opened, it can be very difficult not to see it as an option whenever the turbulence threatens to overwhelm again.

I will fully admit that even now, whenever life begins to pile up on me – the trauma flashbacks return, the experience of loss, stress or difficulty – I do find myself glancing over my shoulder to that doorway. I used to experience a great deal of shame in that glance. I'd chide myself for being selfish, irrational, ridiculous ...

If you've ever felt that way, you, too will know that there's no shaming someone out of that doorway. Instead, I treat it as an old friend, a dark comfort. I know now that I am indescribably glad to have never stepped through the threshold and so I know that tomorrow or the next day I will most likely experience that gladness, no matter how dire things may seem. I nod to my goblins and my demons and doorways and I acknowledge them. I thank them for warning me of where my mental state is headed and I take the necessary steps to avoid falling back into old habits.

After living with it for a long time, I know that I'll never stop making that backwards glance and, in some small part, I'm glad for it.

I've learned to see that look in others.

One afternoon in January, a young woman approached me at the counter. Initially, she seemed to simply want access to a computer. Then she seemed to want to talk about housing and other council services.

Her tone was robotic, slow and quiet. Her shivering fingers grasped at each other.

I asked her if she wanted me to accompany her to a computer, just to get her set up. That was the first time she met my eyes. It felt like making eye contact with someone falling from the sky. She was miles away and falling fast and yet also, somehow, right here.

She nodded.

We hadn't even finished sitting down together when she said it. She didn't want to live any more.

Most library staff aren't trained in mental health first aid. Some local authorities have begun rolling it out but the training tends to be expensive and more geared towards corporate clients. Look after your colleagues, check on Dave in the staffroom, etc. All well and good but not exactly helpful for those of us on the front lines.

There is very little official help out there for those of us who work with the public like this, not unless we become mental health workers or charity volunteers in our spare time. There's certainly very little official training available for free.

I will admit that the first time a library user admitted their suicidal ideation to me, I too felt as though I were falling without a parachute.

Still, I sat with the young woman. I chose my words carefully. Most of all, I listened. I know that when I was in that position, what I needed more than anyone else was to know that I was being heard, seen and noticed. I needed to know that I was still a person, still a real human being, worthy of some kind of existence.

She was, like so many of our users, in the midst of real financial difficulty, having been tossed out by her parents the moment she turned seventeen: alcoholic, abusive parents. She had applied for hundreds upon hundreds of jobs. She'd printed CVs, attended every course the Jobcentre offered (which, nowadays, wasn't a whole lot), she'd tried to follow the demands that the DWP had placed on her but she'd missed a couple of appointments due to clerical errors. The letters had been sent to her parents' address. She'd been sanctioned. She could barely afford to eat.

The pattern was so familiar to me that I could probably have predicted many of the pitfalls. She had started off determined to work for a living but after two years of failing to get a single interview, of being messed around by cash-in-hand, exploitative employers and con-men, she was at her wits' end. Who wouldn't be?

I didn't have the answers. I still don't. Instead, I waited for her to finish and told her, candidly, that I had been in her position, at least mentally. I told her that the only reason I was alive today was that I'd been lucky enough to get help at just the point I needed it and the only reason I'd had a hope of *that* had been because I'd reached out, just as she'd done.

She was making the first step without realising it.

I did what I could. I helped her call to apply for a crisis loan. I helped her register with her local GP and arrange an emergency appointment. I printed out a guide of what she could ask from her doctor. I gave her the number for Samaritans and pointed out that what she really needed was crisis care but I could help her get some other help in the meantime.

Importantly, I tried not to patronise her. I didn't promise that things would get better right away. I told her that what I was giving her was what would have helped me.

I honestly don't know if it helped. She seemed less upset by the time we were finished talking. She seemed to have a plan, one that involved a future with her in it.

This is the problem with being the last port-of-call in a crisis: we library workers may be the safety net, or, at the very least, the last Hail Mary for those in the worst of states, but once we've done what we can, we may well never know if it was the right thing. People might revisit their doctors and psychologists to review their progress but who thinks to revisit a library once you're out of the pit?

That young woman was the first of several people who came to me in their darkest moments. It never gets easier, even after I've researched and self-educated as best I can.

Another unexpected by-product of having experienced suicidality is a strange affinity with death. Having come close to the precipice, I no longer flinch away from the thought of mortality. That's not to say that I want to die (because I absolutely do *not* want to die) but instead I feel a sort of closeness with those who are dying or may die soon.

Many scientists say that trauma is inherited and, if that is the case, then my family – lines of Jews fleeing pogroms and genocides on one hand, Irish Celts and Catholics surviving famine and persecution on the other – has gifted me with more intergenerational trauma than I dare calculate.

The first time I knowingly encountered a terminally ill person at work, my own reaction surprised me. An elderly man, who – to all the outside world – appeared in good health, popped into the library to have some documents photocopied.

As I ran the documents through the machine, he explained that he was getting his affairs in order. These were the legal documents required to ensure that his wife received as much as possible in his will.

He had been told by his doctor that he had three months to live. Terminal lung cancer, he said. He said it all in the same tone one might expect another to use when commenting on the weather, just a passing thought.

I laughed. It was a strange sort of laugh that I had to choke back. Not a laugh of mirth but something borne of a dark, nervous little place that I hadn't known existed within me until that point.

I managed to cover it with a cough.

There was nothing funny about the man's predicament. I didn't *feel* amused. I felt nothing but bone-deep sorrow for him and his loved ones, and yet . . . there was this little part of me that wanted to laugh at the cruel absurdity of the situation.

Man finds out he's dying. Man walks into a library, asks to use the photocopier. Man spends 15p a sheet copying his own medical and legal records, all of which state that he's going to die. Man shrugs as he explains the situation to the library worker. *C'est la vie.*

Or in this case, *c'est la mort.*

Before that point, I suspect I'd have felt more than a little bit awkward, given the situation. After all, what do you say to someone who has so little time left? How do you respond to a statement like that?

Now, though, my own times on the precipice filled me with a feeling of a kind of kinship for this man. Suicide attempt aside, I've had a few near-death experiences in my life – one involving an open lift shaft that should have been locked, another a sudden onset of anaphylactic shock – and they've left me with an occasional sense that I have outstayed my time on this earth.

I still wonder whether or not I'd prefer to have a few months' warning when my time comes.

Transaction complete, the man tipped his cap to me and told me to keep the change.

'I won't be needing it.'

Out of nowhere, that laugh threatened to burst forth again.

Man pays for photocopies. Man leaves without change. Can't take it to the grave.

Out of habit, I waved to him and said, 'See you later.'

'Probably not,' he replied.

As soon as he was out of sight, I laughed until there were tears in my eyes. Then I cried until the tears were gone.

I have this same bizarre, momentary reaction whenever I'm confronted with death and mortality now. I've gotten good at pushing it down. I suppose it's just another item of proof of my particular kind of madness.

I often wonder if that first terminal man really did get his three months. I hope they were comfortable.

*

As the visitor numbers continued to climb, so did the frequency of emails from Heather and the dourness in Phoebe's demeanour.

Both Heather and Phoebe had outright refused, more than once, to participate in any extra activities that Emily and me arranged. This suited us to a degree but it meant that we were restricted to organising things around those rare shifts that we shared. As time went on, this limitation impeded our ability to plan ahead as we tended to work around the schedules of the full-timers.

Linda's visits became increasingly frequent. More than once, I would return from a break to hear raised voices coming from the office. Phoebe was not taking well to the new style of management and she needed everyone, including the general public, to know it.

If anything, I'd hoped that the shared animosity towards Linda would have helped ease the tension between Heather and Phoebe but it only seemed to escalate matters. Clearly feeling disenfranchised by Linda's more hands-on approach with the staff, Heather had taken to enforcing ever more obscure and draconian rules. Her justification was always a reference to some sub-section of a sub-paragraph of a council operating procedure guide but the intent was clear: she needed us to know that she was still in charge.

Things began to change in the branch itself. Displays would be 'mysteriously' vandalised or go missing entirely. Posters would be torn down and replaced by bizarre, ALL CAPITALS warnings about tolerated behaviour. These were always printed on standard council headed paper.

The signed Miners' Welfare petitions mysteriously went 'missing' before Moira had a chance to collect them.

The in-fighting came to a head when Heather demanded that Phoebe work back her smoking breaks, at which point Linda arrived. The demand became a dispute, which was moved into the office.

Five minutes later, Phoebe stormed from the office, and then the building itself.

We were informed that Phoebe had gone on long-term sickness leave.

A week later, Heather followed suit.

Linda arranged for Emily and me to cover as many shifts as possible. We were no longer confined to the odd shift every few weeks together.

Until Linda could arrange further cover, we had free rein of the library. She would manage us wherever possible and we were to report to her either in person or by phone each week. Other than that, she thanked us for taking on the responsibility and left us to it.

*

It's the dream of many a bookworm to have the run of a library and I'd be lying if I said that I wasn't excited about the prospect. Emily and I spent just as much time off-shift discussing the running of the place as we did during our working hours.

Between us, we set up groups, activities and events for every day that the place was open. We drew inspiration from other libraries all over the world, sending each other links to pieces about food bank initiatives in a library in Ontario, a 'blind date with a book' event in a library in England, simple crafting events, displays and activities that we could adapt to Roscree Library.

It was hard work, especially when coupled with the seemingly endless avalanche of paperwork that had now fallen our way. We updated operating procedure documentation, arranged deliveries, took stock inventory and processed all of the cash coming into the branch.

Over time, it became clear that many of the Team-Leader-specific duties were either being performed incorrectly or not at all. While we didn't have access to Heather's inbox, I was certain that it must have been bursting at the seams with demands for backdated paperwork that had never been filled out: invoices that hadn't been processed, orders for stationery never fulfilled, reports never filed and spreadsheets never collated.

Any respect I had for Heather began to dwindle until all that remained was a vague sense of sympathy. While digging through and reorganising the back-end of the library, I began to realise just how out of her depth she really was. It was little wonder that she always seemed breathless and flighty when she was so far behind on so many tasks.

None of this is to say that we performed all of her role for her. The fact was that we didn't have the training nor the access to be able to do everything required to run the place. Instead, we'd do what we could and forward everything else to Linda, who promised to handle the rest.

I had a growing sense of embarrassment as time went on. Not for myself, but for the branch. It was clear that Roscree was being held back by its regular staff and it angered me to see just how badly the library users and the community itself was being let down. Heather and Phoebe had become a bottleneck through which very little work or progress could pass. With both of them out of the way, I spent more time correcting historic errors and attempting to undo the damage that had been left unchecked for many years now.

I began to get the urge to apologise to members of the public when they approached the front desk and especially when they commented on the apparent change in staffing. That they had stuck with a branch that had so many (in my eyes) obviously wasteful practices and such poor customer service said far more about the resilient and at times forgiving nature of the community.

Still, I couldn't help but wonder just how many users Roscree had lost over the years through the sheer incompetence (and, make no mistake, I had given up trying to empathise and excuse away what was, I was now convinced, pure incompetence) of the permanent staff.

The visitor numbers began to soar.

That's when the new challenges began.

Being at the bottom of a funding bracket meant that we had a long way to go to bring in the kinds of numbers that would allow us more funding and – crucially – more staffing.

Queues began to form at the reception desk. The computers were always busy. This led to us having to enforce a one-hour time limit on their usage.

The printer, furniture and other facilities were requiring more regular maintenance and since we were on the same measly budget as before, things often went un-maintained until they became dangerously broken.

On top of all this, Emily and I were working the maximum number of hours allowed for our branch. Too many extra hours would qualify us as full-timers and would have all kinds of implications for our contracts. (Namely increased rights, job security and holiday allowance, the horror! Of course, this would have eaten into our budget and left us worse off overall.) This led to some bizarre shift-patterns as Linda juggled us around to ensure that at least one of us was present whenever we had staff covering in from other branches.

We received assurances that more cover would come, but, in all honesty, I relished the work. I had no time to ruminate, no time to allow myself to worry about symptoms, goblins and night terrors because I was *needed*.

I hadn't felt needed for a long time.

If I had any regrets, it was that we had increased usage to the point where we could no longer afford to give the one-to-one attention to our more vulnerable users.

I no longer had time to comfort anyone who came to request advice on accessing food banks. We had two or three of those a day. I found myself becoming impatient with the sheepish way that these people would approach the counter, barely whispering the request. I could feel myself hardening to their clear discomfort as the queue began to form behind them.

I didn't want to end up like Phoebe.

One Tuesday evening, when the flow at the desk had slowed to a mere trickle (Tuesday nights being the quietest time for the library), I called an informal 'crisis meeting' with Emily.

'I snapped at a food bank user today,' I confessed.

'The one we were holding a parcel for?'

I nodded. 'I was helping her to the car and she snatched the box from me. I twisted my back ... but still. Wasn't really her fault.'

Emily sighed and rubbed her face. She glanced over at the still-busy IT section.

'It's stress,' she said. 'I shouted at a child. I *never* shout.'

Stifling a yawn, I nodded.

'One of the lights in the public toilet is broken again,' I said. 'That's three.'

The council had decided that we were only to receive repairs under 'emergency circumstances'. Having asked for clarification, I was helpfully informed that an emergency consisted of three or more broken lights in a single area.

I had taken to fixing things myself. Linda bought a toolbox. I'd re-assembled desks and glued signs together. Susan had even helped re-stitch some of the fabric on the chairs.

I spent one particularly memorable afternoon screwing the legs back onto one of the children's reading tables and gluing a chunk of wood that had somehow been ripped from the back of one of the bookshelves. (It looked as though a large animal had taken a bite out of the thing. To this day I have no idea how it happened.)

There just weren't enough hours, never enough hands and no resources left to speak of.

We were dragged from our reverie by the arrival of Cheeto, who slapped his card down on the counter with shaking hands.

'Are you okay?' I asked him.

His muttering was louder and more nonsensical than ever. He couldn't meet my eyes and his limbs twitched agitatedly. If I didn't know him better I'd have guessed he was having some kind of seizure.

'C'n I get more time? An hour?' he managed to stutter, mid-stream.

'Of course,' I replied, scanning his card.

He kept glancing over his shoulder, back at the entrance. The street was deserted.

'Cold out there tonight,' I said and offered him as warm a smile as I could muster.

'Yeah. Yeah. Thanks, miss.'

Emily had answered the branch telephone as I'd been serving Cheeto, and as soon as he shuffled away, she tapped my shoulder.

'It's Linda. She sounds serious.'

Chapter 7

The Battle for Me

Visitors Daily (average) February: 86
Enquiries Daily (average) February: 38
Printed Pages Daily (average) February: 90
Violent Incidents February: 1
Children's Event Attendance: 77%
Photocopies Daily (average) February: 56
Free Watch Batteries Supplied to Public (packs, total)
February: 40
Free Dog Waste Bags Supplied to Public (crates, total)
February: 5
Damaged/Lost Books (total) February: 17
Free Sanitary Products Supplied to Public (boxes, total)
February: 28
Days Tracking Checklists Not Complete: 2 (no reason given)
Book Requests Fulfilled February: 107
Free Food Waste Bags Supplied to Public (crates, total)
February: 3

'Sorry, can you repeat that?'

'It's coming from higher up, Allie. There's nothing I can do. Two members of staff have submitted grievance procedures and the contracts are being reviewed. You're technically still contracted to Colmuir. Iris never changed that, plus there were the complaints from Lisa—'

'Hold on. Lisa, the children's assistant at Colmuir? What's her deal?'

I could hear Linda shuffling through papers. 'Well, it seems a number of complaints were made by her. All to my manager. Something about … something about police harassing her. Oh, that'll be the incident with the assault—'

The way she spoke was so businesslike, I could almost picture her hand-waving the term *assault* away. A little while after she'd taken over Iris' role, Linda had asked me about the ongoing case. I'd informed her that it was no longer ongoing, explained that Lisa had given a conflicting statement and that was that.

Now, though. Now I was wondering just what *else* Lisa had said and why. What did she have against me? Why was she *still* complaining about me?

'Yeah,' I replied slowly.

'There's also the complaints she made about the computer incident.'

'The *what?*'

'About the files. You didn't know about this? She claimed you deleted all of her files right after the recent IT upgrade. As retaliation.'

My eyes glazed over as I stared out into the cold, dark street. Linda continued listing off complaints that had been placed against me by Lisa – mad, spurious things, some of which would have been physically impossible for me to pull off.

'Why wasn't I told about any of this?' I asked finally.

Silence.

'Linda, what the fuck is going on?'

Emily spun to stare at me and I glanced around. No nearby eavesdroppers. I mouthed an apology to her, even though my blood was boiling.

'I don't have all of the notes here,' Linda confessed finally. 'I'm as in the dark about this as you. She went further up.'

'When does she claim I magically wiped her hard drive? What about the thing with her car?'

Linda reeled off some dates.

'Right,' I said, fury building in my chest, 'I'm going to email you the rotas for Roscree. You'll see my name on the shifts on most of those dates. I don't want to discuss this any further without a union representative present.'

This wasn't my voice. This was someone else's voice. I hadn't heard speech like this since long before my breakdown, before all of the antidepressants and sedatives and hospitals and psychologists.

This was old me, head of archiving, onsite product engineer, and old me was *furious.*

'I understand ...' Linda began.

'Then understand this: I am working, I am very busy and I am in public. I will call you back if I get a spare moment. If not, I will speak to you tomorrow. *Goodbye, Linda.*'

The phone clattered in its cradle.

Emily hesitated.

'Are you ... okay?'

'*I need,*' I began, but I was almost shouting. I cleared my throat and tried again. 'I need to call her back. From the office. In a minute.'

Emily nodded and handed me the office key.

I had this almost cartoonish mental image of launching a fire extinguisher across the room, Hulk style. Instead, I let myself into the back room and screamed every expletive in my vocabulary into the back of my arm until I ended up laughing at the absurdity of it all.

Semi-satisfied, I picked up the phone just as a wave of cool detachment washed over me, right on cue.

*

All human beings will experience a form of dissociation at one point or another. The problem comes when the experience becomes episodic, lasts for extended periods of time or comes on at inappropriate times and interferes with everyday life.

I was, and still am, no stranger to dissociation. It is the hallmark of my disorder. It is also a survival technique.

The typical depiction of PTSD is that of the wounded soldier, returned from combat only to have the battle rage on in his mind, and while there are plenty of veterans and ex-soldiers out there who do experience PTSD, it is far from the most common version of this insidious beast.

To put it simply, human beings detach from reality when reality becomes too much. The problem with that is that it's not as simple as flicking a switch. Memories are still formed during trauma; they're just stored haphazardly. A smell goes here, a sound goes there, everything gets scattered.

Then, later, when the survivor of the trauma is least expecting it, he or she may experience one of the aspects of the traumatic memory – say, the smell of stale cigarette smoke, an unexpected car horn, or the specific blue of a certain wallpaper – and suddenly another aspect of the trauma comes to the fore. Usually emotion.

Likewise, once the body has used dissociation to avoid the immediate impact of trauma, dissociation becomes a habit.

Too stressed? Dissociation. Angry? Dissociation. Sudden noise? Dissociation.

The memories are broken, you go into survival mode. You lose time.

I don't remember exactly what I said on the phone to Linda that day. I do remember the smell of the office and the exact faded pink of the curled Post-its around the office monitor. I remember the way the orange street light created a shaft across the desk and the way the motes of dust in the air seemed to appear and disappear as they passed through that shaft.

I have a record of the email I sent, purely because it remains in my 'Sent' folder to this day. I remember attaching the rotas and all of the other evidence required to clear my name with regards to Lisa's accusations.

I remember coldly informing Linda that the email was sent and her replying that there would be an investigation.

I also remember her stopping me before I hung up.

'Look, I'm sorry but there's something else. As I said, Lisa wasn't the only one who complained. Remember when I said you were still contracted to Colmuir?'

'Yes?' I intoned robotically, though I could feel my *self* – my own consciousness – sliding back into place, overcompensating and then sliding back out the other side.

'I've been informed that you need to return to your original post.'

'Why?'

'Because things have changed.'

That was it. *Things have changed*.

I remembered the feeling of being followed back to the bus station in the evening, of wondering which of the hooded figures just happened to be going my way and which of them were Stephanie's 'friends'. I remembered a young man with a white face and blood on his shirt. Call after call to and from the police.

'I'm not going to do that,' I replied.

'Then I'm afraid I'll have to terminate your contract.'

'I suppose you will.'

Heather's warning drifted to the forefront of my thoughts once again. *Just be careful with Mr Priestly.*

Could this be his revenge? No. The man might have had influence with regards to budgets but he wouldn't be petty enough to have me fired in such an oblique way, would he?

Would he?

I don't remember the rest of the shift. I can only imagine that I was of very little use to Emily. I was probably downright rude.

From what I can tell, she took most of it with grace. I didn't tell her what the phone conversation had entailed but I suppose when I didn't arrive at work the next day, she'd have figured it out.

Thus ended my library career for the second time.

*

The goblins were back and louder than ever.

Laughter rang in my head as I scrolled through the old, familiar job search sites. Here I was again, back to square one. Back to being unneeded.

Stupid of me to think I could make a difference. Stupid of me to expect a career. Stupid of me to forget that I had this thing in me, this *abnormality* that seemed to bring out a violent revulsion in people. Lisa had sensed it. Maybe those teen boys who'd attacked me had sensed it.

Stupid, stupid, stupid.

My vision began to blur. How many times had I passed by the IT section on my rounds of the library and watched so many unfortunate others going through this same routine?

Selection, application, rejection.

I thought of Cheeto and the way he'd started to seem a bit more confident for a while, right up until my last week. I thought of those skinny boys, weeping over tea and cake.

No. Not stupid.

The thing about rock bottom is that once you've been there, you'll do anything in your power not to go back. You also learn to recognise the fall and, often, the recognition in and of itself is enough to keep you afloat. We tread water by instinct after we've learned how to swim.

I closed the laptop.

I wasn't going to let myself fall into this pit again. Not after everything I'd seen. If the struggling single mums and the starving boys and the disabled jobseekers could get up, day after day, and push themselves through the unemployment meat-grinder then so could I.

My phone buzzed.

Linda's number.

I'd answered before I'd made the conscious choice to do it.

'Allie?'

I gave a raspy croak, cleared my throat and tried again. 'Speaking.'

'Allie, I wanted to let you know how sorry I am for the way everything went down.'

Was that it? An apology? I rubbed my tired eyes.

Linda seemed to take my silence as an invitation to continue.

'You should know that Lisa has been placed on immediate suspension and, between you and me, once the investigation is concluded, she'll probably lose her job.'

'Oh ...'

Not stupid. Not abnormal. Wronged. Screwed-over.

I realised that I hadn't been all that far off the mark with Priestly, nor had I been overly paranoid in my feeling that someone had been out to get me.

'While I can't fix the contractual issues,' Linda continued, 'I can offer you a zero-hour contract. Rolling. I tried to reinstate your hours, I really did ...'

'So ... like a casual role?'

'Yes. Not just at this branch, either. If you accept, I mean, which I'd personally love. You could also be asked to work at other branches but on your terms. You'd have complete say over where you work. You'd be doing cover work, mostly.'

I thought about Emily and our pact.

'If you're not interested, I'll completely understand,' Linda continued. 'Truth is, even if Heather returns there are going to be big changes at Roscree. There will be more positions becoming available, now that we've found a replacement for Phoebe.'

'Phoebe's gone?'

'She has been ... relocated to another position. Adam will be taking her hours. He's great, Allie. You'll love him. He *cares*. I really feel like the three of you could turn this place around. You've already done so much ...'

I glanced at the laptop and tried to picture myself adding my brief time at the library to my already patchy CV. I thought about never arranging another author visit, or tea morning, or charity event. I thought about never talking about colon health with Mrs Collins or singing along with another Bookbug.

'It's a rolling contract,' Linda added. 'Monthly. So you can leave at any time. You can say no to any shift you want.'

'All right,' I said. 'Put my name down.'

There was an enormous sigh of relief over the phone.

'Thank you, Allie. I mean it. We need you here.'

Not stupid. Needed.

'When do you need me in?' I asked.

'Tomorrow morning. In fact, if you could take up your old shifts that would be great and then if you've got a pen and paper, I've got a list here the length of your arm.'

For the first time in a good week, I laughed.

'Go on, then.'

*

Adam was a library veteran. Now in his fifties, he'd worked just about every position in the entire system. He'd done archiving, delivery, stock management, front desk, reference ... If there was a position that needed covering, he'd done it.

More importantly, he was funny, bright and enthusiastic about the service.

'There she is!' he announced as I arrived for that first shift with him. 'Linda told me all about you.'

I'd arrived just under an hour early, expecting an empty building. Instead, all the lights were on, shutters up and shelves tidied. He'd replaced the old newspapers and magazines and even set up the tills.

'Adam, right?' I asked, shaking his hand. 'You're here early.'

'Got to get my tea in or else I'm no use to anybody,' he replied cheerily and hoisted a truly enormous travel mug in the air. 'Anyway, a little bird tells me that there's a pact on the go in here. Something about saving a library. I hear you're the one to thank for that.'

I could feel my face burning as I put my own, far smaller coffee cup on the counter.

'Well,' I replied, 'not *just* me.'

He tapped at his monitor with a biro. He'd pulled up the visitor figures spreadsheet.

'Looks good, but I reckon we can do much better. What do you think?'

I shrugged my coat off with a grin. 'My thoughts exactly.'

*

'So I hear you transferred over from Colmuir,' Adam said after we'd seen off the first computer users of the day and had settled into a morning routine of paperwork and stock rotation.

I winced. 'Yeah. Do you know it?'

He laughed. 'Aye, I've done my time there, for my sins. Back in the eighties. Place used to be a right shithole.'

I snorted and ducked behind my computer monitor. There were no visitors within earshot but my ears burned nonetheless. I turned to look at him. He seemed to be waiting for my response.

'Yeah, it's … it's not the nicest,' I said awkwardly, my best attempt at being diplomatic.

'I could tell you some stories about that place,' he said with a wink. 'Had a few encounters there myself.'

The barcode scanner in my hands beeped and I dropped the book I'd been processing into the box for outgoing deliveries.

'Was it always a one-man branch?' I asked.

He cleared his throat. 'Not in the beginning. Used to be a gorgeous big place. You know, before the gym and the pool were put in. Waste of time that was, by the way. That must've been … what, the early nineties? *Leisure facilities* were all the rage, then.'

I scribbled down the details of the next book in the pile onto a stock transfer form. The romance books were rotated regularly as they were small, easy to transport and quickly devoured by readers who would often take out as many as sixteen at a time. This way, we kept relatively fresh stock without having to buy in new titles every month.

'There were two floors, so you'd have your reference library upstairs, with its own reference librarian. Meanwhile, I'd watch the desk downstairs, the fiction and children's stock. Me and Ruth.'

'Ruth Black? Little old lady?' I asked, recalling deaf-as-a-post Ruth writing me out lists of regular Capital-R Readers and their preferences so I could order reading material in advance for them.

He chuckled. 'Not so old then, but yes, tiny wee woman. Lovely. She got transferred not long after the first hold-up.'

I paused, scanner in hand and turned to look at him. He laughed at my reaction.

'Aye, it's always been a bit of a hotspot, Colmuir Library.' He chuckled. 'In my time it was the McLean family. Bunch of nutters. The older brother Jamie decided to rob the library in the middle of the day, on a weekday! Idiot. He walks in, demands the money from the till from poor Ruth and walks out with a few quid extra in his pocket. I was on a delivery run at the time, came back to find the poor wee woman shaking like a leaf.'

'Oh my God,' I whispered. 'What happened? Was she okay?'

Adam sipped his tea. 'Ruth? Aye, she's a tough cookie. Took a week off and it was decided that she wouldn't be left on her own around there.'

'What about the robber ... uh ... Jamie?'

'Jail,' Adam replied. 'That and some other things. Everyone knew the McLeans; bunch of thugs. He admitted it, got a few months in the jail and that was that. The funny thing is, while Ruth was away, his younger brother Ryan tried the same thing again!'

'No way!'

Adam dropped a book from his work pile into the delivery box with a chuckle.

'Yeah,' he continued, 'not the brightest bunch, the McLeans. I came into my shift and found him chipping away at the front door – you know, the big wooden doors inside the centre? Those were the front doors to the library. He was chipping away with a knife. Just putting big scratches in the paintwork, not even like he was writing something. Stupid boy probably couldn't spell his own name ...'

If I hadn't had my own baptism of fire at Colmuir I might have suspected that Adam was having me on. Honestly, I have no idea if he was telling me the truth that day. I have heard from others since then that the hold-ups really did happen with alarming regularity in the eighties. Another branch manager once let slip that in the nineties there was almost always a police car sitting outside Colmuir Library, the crime was so bad. They'd spend the day ferrying people to the local station until it was closed down.

'So what did you do?' I asked.

'I asked him what he was up to. Don't think he expected the place to be closed, because he told me he wanted the money from the till. I told him he'd have to at least wait for me to unlock the bloody door.'

'Did he?' I asked.

'Wait? Aye. Stood there like a lemon while I unlocked the door and set the place up. I took my time, too. By the time I got round to switching all the lights on, he seemed to have figured out that there wouldn't be any money for him to take, but by that point, he was so dug in that he just followed me about the place.'

I laughed, picturing Adam casually strolling around the library, trailed by a morose would-be robber.

'Did you call the police?'

'Nah. Not right away. Sat the lad down, gave him a cup of tea. He just seemed confused at that point. I would've felt sorry for him if it wasn't for the shock his brother had given poor Ruth. We sat, had a chat. I asked him why he was scratching at the door. He seemed to have forgotten all about the money at that point.

'He just shrugged, said he didn't know. Said he was angry about his brother. The thing is, I don't think the lad was bright enough to connect the dots. The way he saw it, jail was just something that happened to his family. His mum, his dad, they'd all been in jail at some point or another.'

'So he wanted to punish you for calling the police?'

Adam shrugged, dropping another book in the box. 'Don't think he even thought that far ahead, if I'm honest. Some folk just figure that they'll end up dead or in jail anyway, so why not just do what they want? The folk that work in the library, we're just part of the system to them. We're not like them. We don't react the same way they do.

'Say that boy – Ryan – was to threaten somebody from Colmuir, from the high-rises. You know, the really rough parts. Say he pulled a knife on them. Well, they'd just pull a knife right back. That's what you did in those days around there. You didn't wait for the police to come. You hit me, I hit you, kind of thing.'

You hit me, I hit you. The words brought to mind the image of Vicky, face swollen and broken, crying blood. I remembered Stephanie's lingering, threatening presence, the way she seemed to always be on the verge of violence towards me and the way she seemed to think better of it every time I delayed our interactions.

It seemed that some in Colmuir still lived in the old eye-for-an-eye ways. No wonder I'd felt so utterly out of place.

'There was one woman,' I began, 'I tried to help her. She came in all beat up, I offered to call the police for her.'

'Bet she didn't take that well.'

I shook my head. 'No, and her friend took it even worse. The one who beat her up in the first place.'

Adam nodded. 'It's mental, I know. Some folk just live like animals.'

I paused, thinking about the way Vicky's broken fingers had curled around the note I'd handed her with the victim support number on it.

'I don't know about that,' I said and I turned away from my work to look at him. 'I think some people just get stuck in a rut. They're trapped in a cycle. Maybe if they'd had some help—'

Adam interrupted me, though his tone was still soft. 'Some folk can't be helped. Allie, you're a nice girl but you'll learn that the hard way. Some folk could have every opportunity to make things better and they'd bite the hand that offered it to them. The McLeans had had help in the past, and look at them. The two lads in jail. Now they've got weans of their own and *those* boys are forever in trouble with the police. Some folk are just rotten.'

I pursed my lips. Was I naive? Probably but I just couldn't bring myself to believe that entire family lines were somehow inherently tainted.

'Maybe … but maybe it wasn't the right kind of help. Like you said, they just see us as an extension of the system. Maybe if they'd grown up knowing council workers, or they had friends who worked in libraries or whatever, maybe they'd realise that it's not us versus them. Maybe they look at people like us trying to help them and think it's some kind of trick.'

Adam sighed. 'Could be,' he conceded.

'Maybe what they need is to see other people from the high-rises or the community or whatever succeeding to see that it's possible. I don't know … maybe not the ones who would hold a knife up to a wee old lady working in a library but maybe their kids … or something.'

I had so much more I wanted to say but I was painfully aware that I was sounding childishly naive. I've never been great at expressing myself verbally but ever since the breakdown I've struggled even more with putting complex thoughts into words out loud.

The truth is that I had felt a twinge of revulsion when Adam referred to people and families as 'stupid' and 'animals' because it sounded all too much like the same sort of arguments made by fascists and eugenicists the world over. The idea that anyone was tainted by way of their genetics or family line was and is unconscionable to me.

In the years since our first discussion of this, Adam and I have had many more discussions (some more heated than others) on this subject. He's not a bad person, just a jaded one who's seen a lot of violence, but what he has come to realise is that I, too, have seen a lot of violence in my life.

I've been in and out of the UK psychiatric system since I was a child. I've experienced traumas that to this day only I and my psychologist discuss. I've seen deprivation on levels akin to what I'd experienced in Colmuir, and while at the time of working there I had been in a bit of a post-breakdown fog, I wasn't the sheltered little girl I may have seemed back then.

Library work has taught me many things and one of those is that, yes, some people cannot be helped. Not by me. Maybe not by anyone. Those people usually don't want to be helped.

Still, I would much rather be a naive fool than a person whose experiences of violence had led them to become numb to human suffering. I'd rather be childish than someone who could have helped and didn't.

This is where quite possibly the hardest to follow rule comes in: **Never lose your empathy, but learn to leave the anger at home.**

This is definitely the rule I've broken most.

When just doing your day job can be the difference between someone starving and not starving, between being employed and unemployed or simply between understanding something or struggling on without that knowledge, it is very easy to become complacent. Most days you won't make all that big a difference. Most days you're just a face at a desk, or you're a pair of hands putting books on a shelf and so it can be easy to miss that moment when your words and actions become pivotal to someone else's existence.

I have no illusions about my job. The vast majority of what I do means very little to the library visitors. Still, some rare days I might suddenly find myself playing the role of a therapist, or a counsellor, or teacher. I would never pretend that I am qualified for that role but when those little pivotal moments come up, I'll always err on the side of trying, even if someone else might see the person reaching out to me as a lost cause.

It's terrifying but it's also, if I'm being perfectly honest, a little bit exhilarating. It can also be infuriating and downright depressing.

So if you ever find yourself working in a library, remember that. Remember to leave that fury at the door before you head home and never let the opportunity to make a difference pass you by.

*

Adam offered me a lift home that night. My husband ended up working late and so I accepted.

As we pulled out of the car park, I spotted a crow with a crooked wing hopping across the grass. As though sensing my gaze, the creature hopped once, twice and then took off on a glide across the tarmac.

It wasn't quite flight, but it wasn't a fall, either.

'So you've been working with Heather a wee while, eh?' Adam asked.

I turned from the window to look at him. His expression was unreadable, though the corner of his mouth twitched.

'Yeah, I've been working with her here and at Colmuir,' I said.

'I take it that she still hides from everyone,' he said, eyes still on the road. He was smirking.

'In the office? Hardly ever see her out of there. Have you worked with her before?' I asked.

'Once or twice,' he replied. 'Over the years, I think I've worked with everyone. She's always been afraid of her own shadow. I met her when she first got the team leader post at Colmuir. Before that, she'd only worked one-man branches. To be honest, I'm surprised she's running Roscree.'

'Why's that?' I asked.

He glanced at me and then turned back to the road.

'She's afraid of people,' he said. 'Haven't you noticed? If Roscree gets any busier, she'll barricade herself into that office and never come out.'

I pictured her as I'd seen her on my very first day: flustered, overburdened, breathless.

'That's too bad for her,' I said.

'What is?'

'The branch will get busier,' I replied. 'Once we get those visitor numbers up, I mean.'

Adam laughed.

*

I collapsed on my couch. The shift had gone at breakneck speed. Between Adam's chatter, a record number of visitors and a flurry of emails between Adam, Emily and myself, I'd been kept on my toes all day. Still, I'd loved it.

We'd planned more tea mornings, a knitting club, a crochet club, adult colouring groups, children's art sessions, a Lego club, author visits, lectures from local experts on subjects ranging from gardening and foraging to local history, activities with the local care homes and a frankly genius baking competition charity event.

Better still, Adam had enough experience in local libraries to hook us up with various contacts and grants that not even Linda had known were available to us. He sent me the details of all of the charity coordinators at our local supermarkets, all of whom – he assured me – were given a budget each month to donate supplies for local charity events.

I couldn't shake that day's shift from my mind when I got home. I found myself scrolling through my work emails on my phone that evening, though I normally only check them during my working hours or days off.

'Are you still looking at work things?' my husband commented from behind his own phone.

'Yes, but so are you,' I replied indignantly.

He shrugged. 'I get paid for that.'

I pulled a face and glanced at my phone again.

'The front door broke again today,' I said.

'At the library?'

'Yeah. The revolving one. People kept walking into it, even after I put a sign up.'

'Should've recorded it.'

I chuckled. Looked back to my emails once before closing the app. Still, I couldn't stop thinking about the library. My mind raced with all of our planned activities and events. I thought about the regulars and how they'd react to the planned baking competition.

I smiled. I couldn't remember the last time I'd felt this optimistic. I wanted to hold on to that feeling, or somehow document it.

I opened my Twitter app and logged in to my anonymous account. I'd had the thing for ten years. Some of my friends knew me on it, but for the most part, it was a place to vent, especially on matters like mental health. More than once, I'd found the support I'd needed in difficult times on that little blue-bird app.

I began typing.

Things I have learned about the general public while working at the library

It began as a bit of a rant. Having been a product designer in my previous life before the goblins had made their Big Debut, I'd never really shaken the habit of people-watching.

If people are interacting with a product in a way the designer hadn't intended, that becomes the standard interaction with the product, I remembered my lecturer saying. Library work was like one long observation exercise across a varied cross-section of society:

1. *A huge number of people under 20 can't read face clocks, having grown up with a digital one.*
2. *Most people don't know how to spell 'library'. It's in our email address. This causes problems.*

I smiled to myself.

3. *A disturbing number of young people don't actually know how book-lending at the library works. They assume it costs money! Teach your children about libraries!*

I remembered Olivia and every other surly teen who'd been dragged into the branch by a well-meaning parent. There was always that moment of incredulity when they were informed that it cost nothing to borrow books.

The millennial generation (myself included), it seemed, had grown up expecting to pay for things.

4. *Crime and thriller are basically the same thing in many cases. In fact, we have doubles of books because of that.*
5. *People use hidden codes like asterisks to mark which books they've read. Please don't do that! The system will let you know if you've already borrowed something! Just ask.*

I've since learned that libraries in America are legally bound to erase every reader's borrowing history for privacy purposes. As much as I sympathise with the reasoning, I also know that I'd be utterly lost without a record of what I've taken out before.

The most commonly coded books are the large print. When I have the time, I like to flick through some of our older copies and note the various kinds of iconography used to mark a book as 'read' by a particular patron.

I like to imagine that in some distant future, historical archivists will write papers attempting to decipher the meaning behind an underlined page number, or a set of initials on a back cover, or even a minuscule rating out of five left on the thirteenth page of a Nora Roberts novel.

6. *If an automatic door breaks, people will walk into it instead of reading a sign at face height.*
7. *Libraries are a godsend for blind and deaf people and not just for audiobooks. They can come for help with filling out forms and getting directions.*

One of our regulars was a lovely little blind lady called Mrs Bennie. She had a guide dog named Rosie. To this day, Adam is convinced that the dog can recognise which audiobooks Mrs Bennie has taken out before. Personally, I'm fairly sure the dog just barks at random when she lifts the CD case from the shelf but I'm loath to burst Adam's bubble there.

Sometimes she'll arrive with a parcel of the mail she's received over the past few weeks. When we have a quiet moment, one of us will take her aside and help her sort the important mail from the junk. She'll then take the important stuff to her granddaughter, who will send off bills to be paid and so on. Her granddaughter doesn't know that the library staff help to sort the mail first and neither does our management. Technically, we're not supposed to, but it's one of those gaps in community services that, increasingly, people reach out to library staff to fill.

Whenever I put on my uniform I remember Mrs Bennie and the hundreds like her who recognise us council workers and trust us completely to do what's best for them. I try not to take that responsibility lightly, even if I do feel like a bit of a pompous git for wording it that way.

8. *Some elderly people go through books at a TERRIFYING rate. They are to be feared and respected.*

Some of our Readers-with-a-capital-R will quite easily read two to three books in *a day*. I can only assume that they have some kind of Eidetic memory. When I first encountered such superheroes, I assumed that they'd browsed each book and decided against it. That is, until they started discussing the plot twists towards the end of the books and the way that some of them deviated from the plot of the television series.

I have nothing but admiration for those people. I hope that one day I can read at even one-third of that pace.

9. *Some people are so afraid of computers that they will come to you with a query and then become upset if you offer to look it up on a computer instead of in a book.*

Once upon a time, the library was a place for answering questions. We had desks specifically for that purpose. They were called Reference Desks and it would work like this:

The library user would either phone or come to the desk in person with their query. They would provide contact details. The query and the details would be noted on a card and placed in the query pile. Later, the user could return to check on the status of their query. In the meantime, the reference librarian would use their extensive knowledge of the Dewey Decimal system, coupled with an enormous archive of non-fiction reference books, to find an answer, or something similar to the query. They would then contact the enquirer and provide the answer.

Alternately, the librarian could assist the enquirer by locating the relevant reference books for them and passing those books over so that the library user could conduct their own search.

Entire careers were built upon being the fastest and most effective at answering enquiries.

Now, we library assistants have one primary point of research and its name is Google. This often perplexes and, very occasionally, infuriates some of our more elderly enquirers.

Still, Google is not the only source we can tap into. When it comes to more specific enquiries, we have access to local historical documents, educational databases, ancestry records ... I still couldn't list all of the information sources at our disposal because I regularly discover new ones.

10. *Some people have never, ever used a telephone. Especially older women. Their husband did it for them.*
11. *The DWP fuck everyone over but especially the most vulnerable and I haven't met a single library worker who hasn't helped struggling library users with food or phone calls or even a cup of tea when it's cold and they can't afford heating.*
12. *The Jobcentre regularly lie to people and like to tell them they can get services in the library that simply do not exist. We will try our very best to get you the help you should have been given in the Jobcentre.*

I think of people like Claire, who could barely read and write, having to try to help her friend Darren apply for jobs and even just read his Universal Credit statements. It shouldn't be this way. There should be provisions made for people like them. It wouldn't be hard and it would save them a world of indignity and frustration.

13. *Most banks assume that everyone has an email [address] now. In fact, some people have trouble proving that they exist at all without one.*

Homelessness very rarely looks the way it's depicted in films, especially American ones. While there is indeed a great number of people sleeping rough in the streets, there are far greater numbers of the 'hidden homeless': people without a steady address or access to contact details.

To put it simply: most companies and organisations assume that you have a way of being contacted. Things that you or I might take for granted, like bank accounts, an address for receiving mail, email, internet shopping, etc. become inaccessible to the poor and homeless.

Two-factor authentication is another major issue that makes certain aspects of society inaccessible for the very poorest. Most email providers will ask for a second form of contact in order to make an account secure. Those who are more tech-savvy might be able to find a way around this but for the average library user who just wants to check the status of their Universal Credit application, the quicker, less secure methods are easiest.

In order to get around the demand for a mobile number, the poor and homeless will usually 'share' a number around. Perhaps they have a friend or family member who owns a mobile phone. They'll borrow the number for the purposes of signing up for an account, unaware that they will be required to have access to the phone itself in order to access the account later.

Then there are the people who change numbers frequently, due to theft or simply being unable to keep up with a phone contract. They, too, lose access to their accounts once they are no longer able to receive a confirmation text or call from the bank or email provider.

14. *Library folk are good folk. We do this because we are passionate about it. We have to be.*

The pivot away from specialist librarians to library assistants has meant that the average library worker earns far less than they used to. Frankly, unless you're looking to go into management or are very lucky indeed, the role is not a steady career. This is why only the most motivated of the staff survive and, even then, every available role posting becomes a scrum of rolling-contract, zero-hour workers looking for a little bit of job security.

Needless to say, job turnover is extremely high.

15. *Libraries aren't quiet any more. They're community hubs now. They may have quiet study areas but most libraries are bustling with activity. Between kids' classes, singing and memory groups for those with dementia, craft sessions and noisy office equipment, don't expect silence.*

Sally visits the library at the same time every week. She comes with a group of her peers from the local care home for the elderly. Now in the advanced stages of dementia, Sally sits in the same chair every week. She becomes agitated if the chair is unavailable, so I've taken to leaving a 'reserved' sign on it every Tuesday morning.

Sally doesn't speak. She used to grunt and sometimes cry but now she barely makes a sound. I have no idea what's going through her mind but she seems to enjoy her library visits. When our managers are off at other branches, Adam, Emily and I will make the Roscree Care Home group cups of tea and coffee.

Sally likes to pocket the sugar cubes when she thinks nobody's looking.

Last year, Emily and I decided to set up a knitting club. Neither of us could knit but we'd hoped that by providing the materials and a space to work, the group would naturally form itself. Unfortunately we were denied our request for materials and so I put up a small sign requesting donations of needles and wool. By the first week, we had everything we needed, which was just as well because Heather took down the sign, citing some council regulation about risk assessment and donated materials.

In the beginning, few people attended. It's hard to get a group going without a few core, regular attendees. That's when Emily had the idea to email the Roscree Care Home, who were more than happy to bring along a few residents to the sessions.

The first time Sally attended, I'd expected her to sit in her usual silence. To everyone's amazement, she spotted the materials and immediately reached for a pair of needles.

'Mammy's teaching me how to make socks.'

The announcement was so unexpected that even the nurses who accompanied the care home residents stared.

Sally's voice was a muffled croak, as though it had gone stale through lack of use. It was little and light, like a child's.

'Mammy bought me nice green wool.'

We watched as Sally expertly prepared the wool and got to work, her wrinkled hands deftly working the needles.

'Mammy said I can keep the socks when I'm done.'

Those are the only words I've ever heard Sally utter. She still attends the knitting group and she still works on her green socks (thankfully, we have a good supply of green wool) but she does so in silence. She still slips sugar cubes into her pockets when she thinks I'm not watching.

16. *Libraries remain the only place where you can spend hours in a publicly accessible building without being expected to spend money. Parents come to entertain their children for free on wet days. People in poverty come for a warm place to sit. Libraries are a haven.*

When it snows, Roscree is always the first place to be hit. The place seems to have a microclimate of its own. No matter what the weatherman says, Roscree experiences something different.

The first time I was snowed into the library I was thankful that I'd prepared in advance. I'd built a little store of pot noodles and tins of soup in my locker as the rotating doors ground to a halt and the shutters refused to sink into the ever-climbing drifts.

In all honesty, having a library to myself was a dream I'd harboured since I was a child.

I spent an hour or so picking up books at random, reading the first few pages and popping them back. There was so much to read, how could I possibly decide? I had a 'to read' list that had to be categorised by genre, length and priority.

Someone tapped the window.

I looked up to see a young woman shivering. She was a regular IT user, someone I'd helped apply to food banks and for crisis funds. She wore a thin, summer jacket and tracksuit bottoms and was so pale she seemed grey in the evening light.

We'd been warned not to let anybody into the library after closing time.

I had to fight to open the side door, shoving snow aside.

'S-sorry . . . the buses are off . . .'

I gestured her inside.

'I know about the buses,' I explained as I filled the kettle. 'My husband gets off work in a few hours. His car can get through snow. It's got winter tyres. Have you got heating at home?'

The girl nodded. 'Got a wee electric heater. Don't like to run it, but . . .'

'It's expensive, I know.'

I handed her a cup of tea. The steam seemed to restore some of the pink to her skin.

'Need a lift?'

This wouldn't be the last time I made a cup of tea for a library user who was ill-equipped for the cold.

In the end, the snow stopped and the buses returned but I still think about that girl, white with cold. I hope she really did have a heater.

17. *Some people will go their entire lives only reading two to three authors but still have enough material to read a book every month. (See also: Danielle Steel, James Patterson, Clive Cussler, etc.)*

18. *A library lives and dies by the staff on the counter. You can have the best funding, all of the books and tech in the world, but you'll only get footfall if your staff go above and beyond. Sometimes even that doesn't work, though, and it's frustrating.*

19. *We're funded based on footfall. I've seen staff cry because we lost a youth group to a private hall that has fancier facilities like a café. We need all the footfall we can get.*

20. *Staff are hitting their heads against walls volunteering to create events, classes and groups only to have them shot down because local councils don't understand social media or want to charge for it. I can't overemphasise just how much unpaid work staff do.*

Just that day I'd purchased a couple of packs of whiteboard markers. My idea was to use an old, disused meeting board to direct people into the library. We could tie it to a post outside and make a note of the day's events. Unfortunately we'd later find that board in pieces after it was left outside overnight. We're still saving for another, more sturdy whiteboard.

21. *Most of the facilities are only working because staff pay out of pocket to get things working. My manager bought a new laminator when we couldn't afford one. She buys in colouring materials for kids. We sometimes bring in our own stationery. We even buy lightbulbs in.*
22. *Authors don't like to visit little libraries because they don't get paid. Bookstores often pay.*
23. *The 'sexy librarian' trope has actually done a LOT of harm and has caused countless incidences of sexual assault by men who can't tell the difference between porn and reality.*
24. *Old ladies keep libraries in business. Old ladies who read are the best. Old ladies who can tell you exactly which page features the most gruesome murder scene are the very best.*
25. *Library staff ALWAYS want to know what you thought of the book. We want to know what to recommend to others!*
26. *I'm not supposed to have favourite library users but I do: I love library couples who bicker over each other's reading*

tastes or share books and then argue about the themes. I also love the autistic kids with special interests. I will crawl over hot coals to get you a book about the specific type of train you are interested in, tiny child. I will listen to you tell me about it in great detail. I will try to remember for the next time you come in.

27. *The single best moment, for me, is when a library user graduates from Young Adult to Adult and suddenly the entire library is open to them! They can read anything! No more tiny teen section! All of the classics! Sci fi! Horror! They often get overwhelmed.*

28. *And finally, because I've spammed you long enough and because my typos are mounting up, remember this: Library staff can overcome many challenges but Book Gods help you if you deprive us of caffeine. You don't want to see what happens then.*

That evening, we watched a film together. It was good to relax after the uncertainty and stress of previous weeks. Meanwhile, my phone began to buzz with unnoticed notifications.

Chapter 8

Going Viral

Visitors Daily (average) March: 94

Enquiries Daily (average) March: 40

Printed Pages Daily (average) March: 99

Violent Incidents March: 3

Children's Event Attendance: 77%

Photocopies Daily (average) March: 66

Free Watch Batteries Supplied to Public (packs, total) March: 38

Free Dog Waste Bags Supplied to Public (crates, total) March: 6

Damaged/Lost Books (total) March: 24

Free Sanitary Products Supplied to Public (boxes, total) March: 31

Days Tracking Checklists Not Complete: 7 (no reason given – **this isn't good enough. We must complete these tracking stats EVERY DAY** *– Linda)*

Book Requests Fulfilled March: 145

Free Food Waste Bags Supplied to Public (crates, total) March: 5

Book Donations (crates, total) March: 1

Adult Event Attendance: 60%

1,000+ notifications.

I stared at my phone. The little bird icon was unmistakable but there must have been something wrong with the notification count.

It was 6am and I had two texts from friends, a flurry of Facebook messages and a whole cluster of Telegram messages from my Twitter mental health support group.

'Omg look at those numbers!'

'Stephen Fry is following you!'

'YOU WERE IN THE NEWS.'

'NEIL GAIMAN RETWEETED YOU!'

I opened the Twitter app and stared.

Overnight, the first tweet I'd rattled out had hit over seven thousand likes. The last one in the list had gained over *fifteen thousand*.

Fifteen thousand people had seen my thread about the library, had read through it and had hit the little red 'heart' button to voice their approval.

Fifteen. Thousand.

'Are you okay?' my husband asked as I stared at my phone in disbelief. 'You made a weird sort of squeaking noise.'

I turned my phone to him wordlessly. He squinted.

'Don't have my glasses on ...' he muttered.

'I think ... I think my Twitter thread went viral.'

'What do you mean?'

'I mean ... fifteen thousand people have liked it.'

My husband is not, as he puts it, a 'Twitter person'. He has an account. I believe it may have three followers.

Before I had posted my thread, I had just under one thousand followers. That morning, I had over eleven thousand. As I watched, the number kept on climbing.

'Look at the numbers,' I commented. 'They keep going up.'

'Is that happening right now? Are those all people following you right now?' he asked.

'Yeah.'

'Holy shit!'

'Yeah!'

*

I'm not all that good at keeping secrets. I'd been very good at keeping my work and private life separate until the breakdown.

The breakdown had brought my private life crashing down to obliterate my work–life balance, my career, my dignity and any hope of 'passing' as a sane person in public ever again.

It wasn't a gradual thing. At least, not towards the end. I'd started getting headaches at work. These had progressed to migraines, which had progressed to insomnia.

I had handled all of that with a combination of strong pain-killers and espresso shots.

And then the hallucinations had started.

When you hallucinate as a child, especially to the degree that I had, you are described as having an 'active imagination'. If the hallucinations keep you awake at night, they're described as 'night terrors'. Then, if you treat them as such, they start to disappear. You think that this is because you're growing out of such childish experiences. In actual fact, you are repressing them, just like you've repressed the trauma you've experienced to the extent that you are no longer aware that it exists.

Occasionally, the odd thing will slip through. You'll start crying when you catch a whiff of a certain brand of cigarette. You'll put that one down to hormones. Maybe you'll see a cluster of dead rabbits at the side of the road and you'll put that one down to tiredness, too.

When, decades later, a colleague's face began to melt and morph into a face that I neither fully recognised nor acknowledged as a stranger, I knew that painkillers and espresso were no longer the answer.

There had been warning signs at university. The day I'd had to leave a lecture because I'd developed a belief that the lecturer was talking directly to me (only me, in a hall of over one hundred students), and was about to leap across the desks and strangle me, should have been, in hindsight, something of a clue.

Strange, too, had been the time I'd burst into tears during a cosy evening in with my husband because for a terrifying moment I'd been sure that there was a man standing in our living room doorway with a dentist's drill.

My complex trauma, it would later transpire, had involved abuse at the hands of an orthodontist who was later struck off. The cigarettes were the favourite brand of another childhood abuser.

This day, though, what I was trying to keep from bubbling over into my public persona was not a symptom. At least, it wasn't a symptom of my complex PTSD.

It was a compulsion.

Stupidly, I'd kept the phone in my pocket. The damn thing had been buzzing all day, even though I'd switched off Twitter's push notifications.

By the time my lunch break came round, I had just over thirteen thousand followers. Several newspapers had picked up on the thread, which had led to another flurry of retweets and, from there, the whole thing had ballooned far beyond anything I could have imagined.

'Good news?' Adam asked as I put my phone away.

'Hmm?'

'You're grinning. Did you get some good news?'

'Oh!' I hesitated. 'Yeah. Just … family stuff.'

'Nishe,' he replied through a mouthful of sausage roll. 'Always nishe to hear shomething good on a workday.'

He went back to reading his paper – the latest issue of the *Roscree Post*. Today's front-page headline: *Friends of Miners' Welfare Stage Protest Outside Council Building.*

*

There are very few careers that will force you to keep your feet firmly on the ground the way that library work will.

Moments after returning from my lunch break, I served a stressed and rain-drenched mother who was returning the enormous stack of nursery books she'd stowed in her toddler's pram. As I was scanning each book back into the system, she began to pull yet more books from various bags and pouches located within the pram.

Frankly, I am always impressed by the sheer volume of *things* that parents find a way to stow in their baby-carriers.

As she handed one particular hardback to me (*Cooking for Toddlers,* I believe), I noticed a little smear of mud on it.

Her eyes followed my gaze.

'Oops, sorry.'

I shook my head. 'No worries.' Life happens. Mud happens. It was a horrible, blustery day and she had probably had to navigate several muddy puddles on the way here.

I grabbed a tissue to give the book a wipe when the smell hit me. It was just a whiff at first but potent: something akin to what I imagine week-old, curried sprouts might smell like.

I was already wiping with a tissue when I made the connection and froze.

It wasn't mud.

'Is that, uh … dirt?' I asked her, mentally begging for it to be so.

'It came like that when I got it,' she snapped, hastily zipping various pouches and compartments, including, it seemed, a nappy carrier.

I found myself staring at the very obvious toddler shit on my fingers as she all but fled the scene.

This rule may be obvious but if you want to survive library work, it's best to remember: **Wash your hands. Wash them regularly.** Books and children are the perfect plague vectors. Don't overthink it. Just keep washing your hands.

'Everything all right?' Adam asked over my shoulder.

'We need … antibacterial spray.' I stared at the shit-smeared desk. 'Wipes. Bleach. I'll go get them.'

As I cleaned the human faeces from my workstation, I wondered whether my newfound Twitter popularity was a one-off thing. How many of my new followers would still be here in a week or two? Would my celebrity endorsements continue in the days to come or was my thread a 48-hour flash-in-the-pan?

Then there was the logistics of my new contractual situation. I was now, essentially, on a zero-hour contract. Sure, I had enough shifts to keep me going for the next couple of months but what about after that? Would I have to ring around the branches and beg for work? Would I get it?

The turbulent mix of uncertainty was punctuated with occasional jolts back into awareness that I had a thirteen-thousand strong (and growing) audience to whatever brief messages I decided to share with the phone in my pocket. What a strange irony, to be worrying about my continued employment in one moment, only to be rewarded for my frank discussion of it in another.

I couldn't keep myself from sneaking, periodically, to the staff toilets to have a quick glance at my phone. I had dozens upon dozens of private messages. Librarians from all over the world had sent me notes of solidarity. I came to realise that the battle for Roscree Library was a microcosm of something that was happening in libraries all over the world: namely, those who cared deeply about the service and its users were in constant conflict with an increasingly capitalist and consumerist culture in management.

Even once I was home, I could barely keep up with the direct messages. It was the same scenario, over and over: a library worker would get in touch to say that they, too, worried for the future of their service. They worried about the users, who tended to be members of the most vulnerable groups of society. They worried that those people were relatively voiceless and that increasing pressure to create something from smaller and smaller budgets was already having a devastating effect on the service, with smaller branches being cut back or closed entirely, staff being laid off or unable to provide the help that these people needed.

There was a comfort in knowing that there were hundreds, maybe even thousands of others like Emily, Adam and me, people who cared not just about the job itself but the very concept of the library: a place of safety, of shared knowledge and, most importantly, a great equaliser for society.

In my diary, I had taken to alternating between brief bullet points and rambling paragraphs. I knew there was something to all this. We strangers all had a shared cause, and, by the looks of the replies to my silly little thread, we had support.

People truly love libraries, I've learned; those who use them and those who have known them as children really do see the magic for what it is. Just as I did. Just as I do now.

We had to save them.

That evening, I scribbled down what felt like the beginnings of a manifesto or, at the very least, a statement of belief.

I get the feeling that in this hyper-capitalist society, spending your time helping someone, be it a stranger or a friend, is seen as foolish and wasteful.

Lately, I've been feeling more and more like many people confuse kindness for weakness or stupidity. It means that others are afraid to ask for help. There's no time for a human face to our interactions when everyone is on the clock. If your transaction doesn't go by the script, it's seen as a waste of production time.

I don't blame staff who are paid by the hour. Hell, I don't even blame library staff who work this way. We're all held to targets and there's no incentive to spend time with just one person at a time.

It's all about numbers – but think of the difference in life quality a slightly longer interaction can have with someone who's struggling! No wonder so many of us have mental health issues. No wonder we struggle.

With increased financial pressure on everyone, we need to have a serious look at how we disincentivise human interaction at the cost of health and well-being. We are all time-poor.

We should incentivise caring more! It's the most important job! It's literally keeping others alive! Pay carers and nurses more. Hell, pay them better than politicians and

CEOs and footballers. Start from the ground up. Use the hierarchy of needs.

Who is keeping us alive? Who feeds us? Who keeps us sheltered and safe? Value that first. Profit should be far, far down that list.

Libraries aren't free. You have already paid for them in your taxes. We shouldn't have to be profitable because you have already paid us!

At the time, it all seemed patently obvious to me and perhaps that is a sign of the radical shift in my thinking. I had spent a long time blaming myself for the goblins in my head but the reality was that we are not floating brains existing free of context in our own bubbles.

Looking back, my breakdown had been inevitable. I had ignored my hierarchy of needs. I had fallen into the same trap of valuing productivity over humanity. The attitude that had crushed me was now threatening to crush a service vital to society's well-being.

Without libraries and community spaces, societies become sick.

This is what I expressed to Graham the next evening before we got started on the EMDR processing session.

To his credit, Graham seemed (or at least made a very good job of pretending) to be almost as excited as I was. He stopped me now and then to remark on my passion, on my elevated mood and even the lack of severe symptoms that I'd experienced lately.

We prepared to start the EMDR session properly.

When most people think of talking therapies, they often picture some sort of Freudian psychoanalytical conversation, one participant (the patient) reclining in a chair or couch and waffling on at length about their relationship with their mother in an almost narcissistic manner.

There certainly are forms of talking therapy that involve a lot of conversation and introspection for the duration but those tend to take the form of counselling or are a prelude to the harder stuff.

Anyone who has had EMDR therapy will tell you the same: it is hard bloody work.

Short for Eye Movement Desensitisation and Reprogramming, the technique might seem strange or new-agey to anyone unfamiliar with psychological therapies but the truth is that the technique has been around for decades in one form or another. It involves the introduction of a stimulus that moves left to right and back again, which the eyes of the patient must follow as they go over their trauma or traumas in a controlled setting.

When I first had it described to me, I imagined the swinging pendulum of the hypnotist, the commanding voice: 'You are feeling very sleepy'.

Graham doesn't use a pendulum. He uses a lightbox. The simple device contains a row of LEDs which, each session, I try to follow with my gaze without blinking. Sometimes he also introduces a pair of buzzers, one for each hand. These emit a sharp vibration each time the LED light reaches the corresponding side of the lightbox.

Yes, it feels strange. Yes, it looks even stranger and, no, I don't know exactly how it works.

What I do know is that every week or two, I would sit for up to two hours following that little light with my eyes. We would begin with a stimulus: did something trigger flashbacks this week? What was it? Now go into that headspace. Feel the panic but don't let it take over ...

After a few minutes, Graham will stop the lights and I will, in theory, 'return to the room', so long as I haven't gone into a full flashback. Treading the line is extremely difficult, which is why we would often spend several sessions practising grounding techniques to make that easier.

We then analyse the memory. How intense are the feelings? Was that a full flashback, or more like watching a film?

Let's say you walk the same way to work every day. There's a billboard on your route and you notice the sign on it. The more often you walk that way and the more often you pass that sign, the more accustomed to it you become until it's simply part of the background noise of your commute.

That's the basic theory behind the repetition and re-experiencing of the traumatic memory (or memories, in the case of complex PTSD like mine). The eye-movement theoretically keeps you from going too deep into a flashback, at least that's what I've been told. As I've said, the mechanics of the thing are far beyond me.

There are two things you should know about EMDR. The first is that it works. It works incredibly well. Before I began working with Graham I honestly believed that I would never leave the house without a panic attack again. Flashbacks plagued my waking hours and, when I did eventually sleep, I experienced sleep paralysis and night terrors. Lack of rest made me hallucinate. I jumped at every noise. I existed in a world with one foot in the past and only a tenuous grasp on the present.

Now? I work. I write. I campaign and I speak on the radio about Twitter threads I've made that have gone viral.

The second thing you should know about EMDR is that it is *exhausting*. Each session, whether half an hour or a two-hour marathon, may appear to flow quickly but that's because you're slipping between different states of consciousness. Make no mistake: the patient is doing a *hell* of a lot of work in those sessions. You and only you are the one who can get yourself into that headspace and safely out again. You – and only you – are the one who can put words and number-ratings to your emotional and mental state, over and over.

When I finish a session, I am often ready to collapse and utterly ravenous. My husband and I often scheduled our evenings out around my therapy sessions. We'd visit anywhere with a buffet and he'd watch me consume the kind of meals an active man twice my size would call 'a bit much'.

At the end of this session in particular, I was ready to eat a horse and it took me a minute or two to process what Graham was saying as we wrapped things up.

'Just a question,' he repeated. 'When we first began these sessions, we talked a little bit about identity and how yours had been damaged by your inability to work.'

I nodded slowly, eyes still slightly unfocused.

'Would you say that helping people, especially in the context of the library, has become part of your identity?'

I thought of the messages in my inbox, the way I'd already been referred to as 'anonymous library worker' by a few of the media sites that had picked up on my thread's popularity. It gave me a little thrill at the thought.

'Yeah, I think it has.'

*

'A competition,' Adam said with a grin. 'A big one.'

Adam, Susan and I were clustered in the staff kitchen. Susan lifted a sheet of paper to reveal a wonderful, glossy poster.

'A baking competition!' she announced. 'Kids and adults! Right here!'

The poster called it *The Great Roscree Bake-Off,* with a provisional date in two months' time. Just in time for the summer holidays.

'Three categories,' Adam explained, gesturing to the poster. 'Young kids, teens and adults. Entry is free. Everyone's a judge! You pay for a badge, then you anonymously vote for your favourite cakes. I can get prizes. All for charity! We'll pick something local. What do you reckon?'

'I reckon we have a lot of promotion to do,' I replied, grinning. 'What does Emily think?'

'It was her idea,' Susan said, rolling up the poster. 'I really think we can make this big if we push it hard. Linda's on board.'

'Count me in,' I said.

'Perfect.'

As Susan was putting away the poster and Adam tucked into his lunchtime soup, I began my lunch break ritual of replying to as many direct messages on Twitter as my overstimulated brain would allow.

One of them caught my eye.

Hi @grumpwitch. I work for BBC Radio 4's Today Programme. We'd love to have you on to chat about your thread and libraries generally. Send me a message with your phone number and we'll arrange something!

I almost choked on my sandwich. I coughed and cleared my throat.

Navigating to the sender's personal Twitter page, I double-checked the bio. She had a blue-tick, which meant that she was a relatively public figure and had officially verified her identity on the site.

This was no joke.

We exchanged numbers and email addresses and I promised to call her as soon as my shift was over. I then frantically texted my mum and my husband to fill them in.

All of this communication, in silence, while my colleague sat directly across from me, slurping his chicken broth. My phone vibrated furiously.

Buzz. Buzz.

'*OMG!!! When do they want you on?*' my mum asked.

'*Tomorrow, I think,*' I replied. '*It's my day off so I can head into the studio.*'

'*OMG!*' This was followed by the usual string of emojis that my mum is fond of punctuating her texts with. In this case, it was a party popper, a balloon and, curiously, a smiling cat.

Buzz. Buzz.

'*Get an autograph from Evan Davis,*' my husband replied a minute later.

'*He's in London.*'

'*Well … ask them to send you one.*'

'*I'll try.*'

'Can you pass me a paper towel?' Adam called across the table.

'Hmm? Oh. Yeah. Sure.'

Buzz. Buzz.

'You're popular today,' Adam remarked.

I grinned. 'No kidding. Sorry.'

*

I arrived at the BBC Pacific Quay building – a great, perpetually wind-whipped, glass block on the side of the River Clyde – a full two hours early.

I'd intended to grab a coffee at a nearby café, but my stomach was too restless to allow the consumption of much more than a few timid sips from a bottle of water. Instead, I perched myself on a bench overlooking the river (frigid despite the bright sunlight, thanks to the funnelled sea gusts blasting off the water) and fidgeted with my phone.

My contact, a lovely, eloquent woman in London with whom I'd had a couple of phone conversations, had sent me a list of instructions regarding security in the building via text but I still couldn't shake the feeling that this whole thing was some kind of elaborate set-up for a prank.

I'd spent most of my life listening to Radio 4 in some form or another. I'd always imagined it being produced in a magical, far-off place where everyone spoke with the Queen's elocution and every guest speaker was either a high-flying politician, a celebrity or a crumbly old professor, preserved by academia and harking from a bygone era, clad in tweed and pipe smoke.

By comparison, the Scottish arm of the BBC had always struck me as a younger, unruly sibling. The building itself seemed less 'British institution' and more 'trendy industrial start-up space' especially once I stepped inside.

After picking up my ID tag (misspelled in three separate ways), I snapped a surreptitious picture and sent it to my mum. She'd been gushing by text all day, as had I. When I confirmed to her that I'd be speaking with Evan Davis, she replied with a smiling, heart-eyed emoji and a waving hand, which I chose to interpret as positive.

If you've never been in a recording booth (which, until then, I don't think I had), it's essentially a very well sound-proofed broom closet with a microphone. The air is so well contained that it feels like sitting in a box full of cotton wool. You don't

213

realise how disconcerting pure silence can be until you experience it.

I realised that even my brain goblins, usually chattering incessantly, were quiet.

Once in a previous corporate life, I was tasked with giving a presentation via conference call to justify a budget increase in my department. I'd spent weeks preparing, rehearsing and refining until I was relatively confident I had my speech perfected. About a minute into my call I felt my mouth go dry. By the five-minute mark, my voice had disappeared entirely. I ended up having to make my excuses and run to the nearest water cooler mid-call. The memory still makes my stomach gurgle and my face tingle uncomfortably.

Now, in the recording booth, I felt that familiar dryness. I licked my lips, made sure my security escort had left and then snuck a water bottle from my bag. I'm sure the tech who was testing levels heard every part of my guzzling gulp, but, to his credit, he didn't mention it. Instead, he continued to talk me through using the equipment (press the button to hear my own voice, leave it unlit to mute it, keep the headphones on, don't leave until the 'live' light is off).

When Evan Davis first addressed me, I had a bizarre, out-of-body moment where all I could think was *I must be mad, the man on the radio is talking to me.* I can only thank whatever deity was on duty that day that the interview was pre-recorded because I do not doubt that my anxiety could be heard over the miles all the way to London.

Davis, by the way, is a consummate professional and a fantastic reassurer. The interview itself felt more like a friendly chat, and, within what felt like minutes, we were done.

Of all of the wonderful things that have come from my work in the library, I must admit that hearing Evan Davis enunciate my Twitter handle ('grump, as in grumpy, witch as in ... witch. Grump. Witch.') has to be in my top five. I'll take that memory to my grave.

Of course, in the wake of that broadcast, my Twitter account experienced another surge of followers but it was a call from my grandmother that meant more to me than all the retweets and followers in the world:

'I wish your grandpa was alive to see this, Allie. He'd be *verklempt*. He'd be so proud of you.'

My grandfather was a witty, dry-humoured, mischievous man who was sparing with praise and high in expectation for his grandchildren. I adored him. He used to cut out articles from science, literature and technology magazines for me and would collect them in a plastic pocket for when I visited. He bought me my very first Terry Pratchett books. We would take turns reading them, then the Harry Potter books and so many other novels featuring magic and monsters. He and my parents helped stoke my love of library magic from a young age.

When he died, he left me his collection of beautiful Parker fountain pens, knowing that I loved to write my own fantasy stories.

I hope that wherever he is, he gets reception for Radio 4.

Chapter 9

A Cathedral of Knowledge

Visitors Daily (average) April: 103
Enquiries Daily (average) April: 38
Printed Pages Daily (average) April: 95
Violent Incidents April: 1
Children's Event Attendance: 85%
Photocopies Daily (average) April: 70
Free Watch Batteries Supplied to Public (packs, total) April: 29
Free Dog Waste Bags Supplied to Public (crates, total) April: 7
Damaged/Lost Books (total) April: 19
Free Sanitary Products Supplied to Public (boxes, total) April: 33
Days Tracking Checklists Not Complete: 0 (**much better, please continue to train cover staff on tracking procedures – Linda**)
Book Requests Fulfilled April: 202
Free Food Waste Bags Supplied to Public (crates, total) April: 4
Book Donations (crates, total) April: 3
Adult Event Attendance: 75%
Reports to Building Maintenance (total): 7
Repairs Completed: 1
Outstanding Maintenance Requests: 6

'Excuse me. My son has shit himself.'

Library work is a dream job in that it is extremely surreal, unpredictable and does not take place on any recognised plane of reality. You can be selling raffle tickets in one moment, comforting a starving single mother the next, and, still, the public will find ways in which to surprise and baffle you.

After pointing out that not only does the library provide free nappies for parents in a pinch (donated by library staff out of necessity) but that the bookshelves are not an appropriate place to change your quite frankly *violently* feculent toddler, I sighed and fetched the body fluid kit.

Every library has a procedure for body fluids. You'd be amazed how often it has to be implemented.

Or perhaps not.

Remember the rule, **'do no harm but take no shit'**? I should have mentioned that sometimes the shit is literal and sometimes you have no choice but to take it. Sorry.

*

Since my Radio 4 PM interview, my thread had been picked up by more news outlets and several Twitter-scraping clickbait sites that seemed to only exist to farm content from social media and reproduce it, unaltered and often uncredited. The *Sun*, amongst others, had referred to me as a 'man' then 'boy' then finally 'person' in their version, though I've been informed that they've corrected my pronouns since then.

Credit where credit's due, several sites contacted me before running a story about my thread and libraries more generally. Some even allowed me to add further comments and clarifications including – both humiliatingly and wonderfully – a correction by Val McDermid regarding one of my tweets about author visits in bookshops and libraries, which I had immediately tacked on to my original thread.

I spent much of my free time answering messages and requests for more information. I took part in another interview for Radio 4 and was interviewed via phone for Radio Scotland, which was a far less formal experience, marred only slightly by my little rescue cat (who firmly believes she is my actual child) following me from room to room and meowing for attention.

Meanwhile, preparations for The Great Roscree Bake-Off were well underway. Adam had gotten in touch with local bakers again and the head of the chain had agreed to join the festivities as an 'expert adjudicator' in the case of a tie. He'd also gotten in touch with local supermarkets, who'd agreed to provide various baking-themed prize items, from baking tins to icing kits to a set of wooden spoons.

I created a set of 'invitations', small enough to slip inside a book as it was scanned out for borrowing. I even slipped them inside books being returned to other libraries in the area.

There was an unspoken but generally understood consensus that the Bake-Off would be our big chance not only to promote the library itself but to show management that, without the twin shackles of Phoebe and Heather, the branch could thrive. If our proactive approach paid off, it might well lead to further freedoms for frontline staff.

According to Linda, the attendance and accession figures at Roscree no longer put it in direct danger of being declassed and therefore stripped of funding and staff. However, if we wanted to do more than tread water there was still a fair way to go.

The main problem, Adam, Emily and I agreed, was that people (especially young working or studying people and those without children) simply weren't aware of the library's existence. When we'd trialled putting a simple sandwich board outside announcing that the library was open, we'd more than doubled the number of visitors, many of whom had expressed surprise that there was still a functioning library in Roscree. The board had later been ruined by weather and finally vandalised but the point remained: the community appeared to have some sort of collective amnesia around libraries.

We needed to remind them of what they were missing.

I had toyed with the idea of lifting my anonymity on the Twitter account. At that point, I had around fifteen thousand followers, many of whom were famous writers and other public figures. Imagine the reach we could have if I simply named the time, date and location of the Bake-Off ...

It was sorely tempting but ultimately impossible. The only reason I'd been able to make and publish my observations in the first place had been the security of anonymity. All local authorities have extremely strict social media and public relation guidelines. We'd already fallen foul of our council's PR team by hounding the one employee who managed the council's Facebook account to post about the Bake-Off. Even if the poor fellow had given in to our constant requests for exposure, any post made would have been immediately swallowed by the non-stop stream of information rendered useless by its corporate jargon and the sheer volume of things posted to the account.

The fact is that those in library management tend not to understand social media. To them, there's no reason to split a single Facebook or Twitter account for an enormous council area into smaller, more local feeds. The information is going online! Who cares that nobody follows the account because it makes 30 posts a day about the inanities of libraries, leisure and community centres 20+ miles from the user?

If I'd thought that Heather liked her operating procedures and guidelines, it was nothing compared to the PR department at the top of libraries. Every tweet, every post or quote or line in a paper had to be vetted by a team of lawyers and bureaucrats whose only role was to suck the joy and humanity from every sentence, rendering it vague, meaningless and as corporate as an auditor's committee meeting. By the time your promotion, advert or simple notification had been passed through this process, your event had already passed.

Like most things at the library, the only way to get anything done was to quietly go rogue.

It's easier to ask forgiveness than permission, after all.

*

Bad news comes in threes. My father always swears by the phrase and nowadays I have to admit that I do, too.

I found out about Cheeto's murder on a rare day off. I'd spotted his picture on the front page of the local paper and had immediately scooped up a copy.

He'd been slightly later home that evening, having stopped for a chat with another library regular and a visit to a nearby chip shop. The group of youths who'd been tormenting him for a while were clustered at the entrance to his block of flats. He'd kept his head down, but his unfortunate muttering-stream had been his undoing.

I don't know exactly what happened. I know that he would never have deliberately confronted the young men, who were all drunk and still drinking. He was a gentle, anxious soul.

They beat him. One of them used a glass bottle. He died.

The loss of a regular is always difficult but the violent nature of Cheeto's death and the resultant aftershocks manifested themselves in unexpected ways.

Each of us was hesitant to take bookings on Cheeto's computer – and it really was thought of as *his* computer – for a while, especially around the times that he'd usually visit.

The paper said that, before he'd become unwell (a euphemism, I suspect, for his having some kind of illness or injury that affected his mind), he'd been an IT specialist, had been renting a flat with his girlfriend and building a life and career.

Other regulars began to speak of him in hushed tones. I never asked for details but over time I began to form a picture of Cheeto's life.

I often wonder about the event that caused him to go from John, IT specialist, to the mumbling Cheeto we all knew. What I know is that after the event he fell into alcoholism. He drank to combat the anxiety that plagued him day in, day out. He lost the flat. His girlfriend left.

After his father died from alcohol-related illness, he resolved to get sober. As he did, his mental state began to improve. He was no longer chattering constantly. Instead there began the quiet stream of muttering that I'd come to grow almost fond of.

He wanted out of his little council flat. The estate was full of triggers for his alcoholism, drugs and, of course, violence.

He was on the waiting list for a new home when he died. The help we'd given him at the library had given him the confidence to get in contact with the local social worker, to seek changes to an existence he'd previously become resigned to. While the job search had never led to much more than a single interview, the friends he'd made at the library had supported and encouraged his sobriety, sharing tips and contacts.

The rules of library work can also apply to its users. **The people within the library are as important a resource as the books.** This is a rule which crops up time and time again.

Cheeto's story is not all that unusual, I would come to learn. Many of our regular long-term jobseekers are disabled, some recovering addicts, others with mental illnesses severe enough to impede their ability to work but not deemed severe enough by the DWP to entitle them to financial support. Many of them are actively working to remove themselves from harmful situations. Almost all are on waiting lists for better housing, training, support, therapy, healthcare specialists. Almost all have experienced trauma, just like me.

They're not wasting time. They've spent their whole lives having their time wasted by faceless bureaucrats and red tape. Most of them could work if they'd been given the support years ago, or had been shown how to apply for help that they, by all rights, are entitled to. They've been through more than many of us can even imagine and have been let down by the very system that was supposed to help them.

These are the people who need libraries and they're the ones least likely to have their voices heard when it comes to allocation of library and council resources. They deserve better.

*

We were informed that Heather's return to work would be phased: she would work two days, then four per week, before returning to full-time work, starting that very week.

Adam, Emily and I held a hurried meeting that afternoon in the storeroom. We knew that Heather most likely wouldn't leave the management office much (as had been the case before her absence) but it would still be prudent to keep our promotional activities on the down-low. The phrase 'plausible deniability' was used. Still, she would have to find out about the Bake-Off sometime, and, if her track record was anything to go by, she would most likely attempt some form of murder via regulation.

Nobody had heard from Phoebe and for that we were grateful. It would be much easier to keep Heather sufficiently distracted without the praying mantis picking apart our plan. Word through the grapevine was that Phoebe had taken out a formal grievance against both Heather and Linda, ironically, for creating a 'hostile work environment'. We could only imagine how she'd react to Heather being coaxed back into her role like this.

The next morning, I was surprised to receive a text from Linda at around 6am.

Bit of vandalism been reported at the library this morning. I can't get out but please be careful and call the police as soon as you get there. No alarm triggered so no intruders. Stay safe.

The morning was dark and cold. A vicious wind had picked up overnight and continued into the morning. The rain lashed against my glasses and so I had to fumble for the alarm panel when I finally got into the library.

The air was ice-cold. Something crunched under my foot.

The floor glittered with tiny glass shards. Every inch of carpet, every surface was covered. Combined with the icy wind, it felt like the place had grown a lair of frost overnight.

Several ground-floor windows had been smashed.

I tiptoed to the counter, brushed off the phone and rang the police. When I was done with mechanically reporting the crime, I contacted Linda, who instructed me, simply to 'do what you can to get the place safe and opened ASAP'.

I shivered as the cold wind whipped up the glass shards once again, sending them into little flurries like snowflakes.

I picked my way towards the staffroom, glass now embedded in my shoes.

A repairman was on his way, I'd been told, to board up the windows. I just needed to deal with the broken glass.

I closed the door to the tiny staff canteen and put the kettle on.

This is what I do when faced with a seemingly insurmountable task or setback: I make tea. I make one for me and one for the task. I invite it in. It may seem mad and were you to tell me as much I'd probably agree with you, but it keeps me from ruminating and provides an outlet for my frustrations. I can tell you with confidence that my little tea ceremony is 100% psychologist approved. At least with my psychologist, anyway.

You invite the difficulties in. Sit down with them. Drink tea. Stare them down. Tell them exactly what you plan to do and how you plan to do it. In that way, you are forced to come up with a plan, even if it's a very vague sort of plan. Productivity by spite.

I told the second cup that I would get the vacuum for the glass powder, then I would clear the surfaces and vacuum again. I would not let this get to me. If I had to, I'd pick the damn stuff up with my bare hands. I would *not* let this get to me.

The mug steamed at me, almost tauntingly.

'You think this is bad?' I said. 'You think this is enough to make me despair? I'm a madwoman. You'll have to do better to break me. I'm talking to a bloody teacup! I can do anything!'

I finished my tea, picked up the opposing cup and poured it down the sink. My own personal cleansing ritual. (At home, I'd have waited until it cooled down and then fed it to my plants.)

*

It is at this point, I suppose, that I should address the 'witch' in my Twitter handle, 'grumpwitch'.

When I was around twelve, a well-meaning friend or relative (I can't remember which), upon hearing that I was going through a 'goth phase' (a phase I have subsequently never come out of, apparently) bought me a book called *Spells for Teenage Witches* by Marina Baker. The book had an eye-catching orange cover and appealed to the 'alt-girl' preteen market that was all the rage in the late 1990s and early 2000s, with quirky illustrations and curly fonts.

Sadly, after many house moves and family upheavals, I have since misplaced my copy of the book, but I still recall the sense of mild bewilderment as I flicked through the pages for the first time. Then the sense of curiosity as I flicked through it again and then, slowly, a sense of revelation.

Looking back, the book was probably my introduction to the concept of feminism and, of course, witchcraft.

The book contained 'spells', which were essentially a series of instructions laid out in a recipe-style format for things that teenage girls might want or need: a spell to help with exam stress, a 'rainy spell' (to, you guessed it, make it rain) and spells for peace and so on. It was all very wholesome, empowering and kind and ultimately rather harmless.

It just so happened that the book came to me when I was first dealing with a lot of trauma and stress and I found deep comfort in those little rituals, even if they rarely resulted in the outcome promised. (And really, who needs a spell for rain in Scotland?)

What I took from the book was not that I, or any other teenage girl, was capable of influencing the weather or bringing about peace in the world. It taught me, a child raised without religion, that sometimes ritual brings comfort. Sometimes putting a little bit of faith or a simple intention (*I will have a good night's rest*) out into the world can, if nothing else, make a girl feel a little bit more in control.

God knows I had very little control over anything at that point in my life.

As I got older, the cynicism of teenagehood crept in and the book ended up stuffed in the back of a drawer somewhere. No self-respecting teenager would be caught *dead* lighting a red candle and standing at the appropriate angle to invoke some kind of mystical energy. I was all about science, and cynicism, and hard, cold reality. Facts, not feelings!

For many years I dared not admit, even to myself, that there was something immensely comforting in holding a shiny rock and making a wish, or seeking out a magic wand in the forest, or giving in to the freeing experience of just believing for a little while that I could change the world with the right amount of concentration and a bit of incense.

I fooled myself into believing that my new coping mechanisms – various forms of self-harm, self-isolation, burying myself in my schoolwork to the detriment of my physical health – were rational and even 'correct'.

I distinctly remember sitting in the CAMHS (Child and Adolescent Mental Health Services) waiting room after meeting with my assigned mental health nurse and realising, all at once, as though the thought came from outside myself, that the grounding techniques, the visualisation, the CBT thought exercises and (as it would later be called) the mindfulness activities we'd been performing were almost identical to many of the 'spells' I had performed as a pre-teen 'witch'.

I believe that we're all capable of magic, much like the magic that flows through the best libraries. We might not be able to summon rain or summon vast riches with a thought, but we *are* capable of changing ourselves. We are simple, primal things, fooled by placebos and simple illusions.

So when I sit with a second cup of tea, and I visualise another being in the steam, a personification of a problem, I'm performing magic of my own. I'm forcing my simple, primal brain to get into problem-solving mode. I'm summoning my own power. I'm making a goblin to vanquish or work alongside.

To me, trauma therapy is magic. It's literally reprogramming the brain! It's a shamanistic journey into your past with a wise guide at your side. It's a re-piecing of shattered memories and a sit down with some old goblins. It's setting a table for the beast that's plagued you and looking it square in the eye until you no longer blink first.

I call myself a witch not because I am religious but because I am spiritual. I call myself a witch because I believe in my own power. I call myself a witch because I believe that we are all more mighty than we give ourselves credit for. We just have to start giving ourselves that credit. I call myself a witch because there's magic in overfilled bookshelves and in seeds becoming trees and in sugar pills tricking our brain into curing our ills.

If that makes me mad, well . . . too late. I was mad long before I started using magic and I'm pretty sure I'd be even madder without it.

*

When I was around five or six, my father took me to The Mitchell Library in Glasgow. My dad was never much of a fiction reader. He still isn't. While my mum has always been a frequent user of our local library, he was more interested in documentation and more physical or mechanical pursuits. Ever the engineer. At that point, he was researching his (*our*, I suppose) family tree and his search had brought him to The Mitchell Library, where the local authority archives (birth, death and marriage certificates) were stored.

It was a dreich, windy day and we had run all the way from the train station. I remember my hair dripping on my shoulders as I tiptoed around the stacks. In those days, all activities were performed in silence. I was fascinated by the students with their towers of books, lost in their own research.

I have a particularly strong memory of a man whom I now suspect was in his twenties, with thick-rimmed glasses and a set of headphones so big they'd have covered both sides of my head at that age. He sat with his head resting on one hand, the other hand turning each page with a gentleness that bordered on reverence, while his enormously magnified eyes darted across the text with frightening speed.

The air was muffled with dust and a sense of heaviness. It reminded me of the hush that had fallen upon my classmates the first time we'd been taken to our little local church – a veneration we didn't fully understand, something linked to the height of the ceilings or the high polish of the uniform pews. The church was, like many of the buildings of my hometown, a geometric, brutalist affair that seemed to have been designed to be as uncomfortable and uninhabitable as possible.

By this point, my dad had realised that I was no longer following him. He returned to where I was staring at the poor student, my sodding clothes creating a small puddle around me.

'C'mon, Allie. We won't be long.'

I think I recall the appearance of the student so clearly because of what he represented to me, of what the library itself represented to me. Until that point, I had only ever visited my local branch. Our school didn't even have a library and so my entire image of what a library could *be* consisted purely of that one little branch.

Never in my wildest bookworm dreams had I considered the possibility of a library so enormous, so full of documentation and tales, that it might require *signposts* to navigate! The previously labyrinthine stacks of General Fiction in my hometown were utterly dwarfed by comparison *and this was only the archive section*. The building had floors! Floors of books! Stacks of stacks and sections of sections!

The Mitchell Library is a cathedral and its religion is *knowledge*. Even now, when I step inside, I can feel the magic in the stone walls. Even after modernisations and renovations, the air is thick with compressed knowledge.

Decades after that first visit, I would have the honour of watching two of my closest friends exchange vows within those hallowed halls, as the local authority briefly allowed office politics, salary, shifts, rotas, conflict and poverty. touch of what had made me apply for the role back in those desperate days in the first place: the *magic*.

The contrast in myself between those early desperate days of my application – and they truly were desperate – and later was most emphasised when I summoned the courage to peek at my journals from that time. I had taken to bullet-journaling: giving myself brief bullet-point lists of tasks for the day, which I'd tick off or cross out depending on whether or not I deemed them completed.

My task for the weeks leading up to my interview and for a while after remained the same, day after day:

Get on the train, not on the tracks.

I had diligently ticked it off – task done! – like the good little student I have always been.

Even in those dire straits, something in me had acknowledged and reached out to the power of the library. I had pinned my last hope on the one place I had always truly felt safe.

Now, with the uncertainty of my employment, the still-raw memories of drug gangs and stabbings and chair-shaped dents in walls, not to mention the more subtle stresses from colleague betrayals and this mindless vandalism, I had almost lost touch with that spark entirely.

This would not do. I had to rekindle the magic.

*

By the time the repairman arrived to board up the windows, an unfortunate fellow casual staff member, Claire, had been drafted in to give me a helping hand. To her credit, she took to the job, such as it was, even laughing along with me when the head of the wonky old sweeping brush fell off and the vacuum threatened to give out.

The shoddiness of the cleaning equipment and the lack of proper tools became a running joke. Every time something broke, or we found ourselves picking glass out from behind bookshelves with plastic rulers and wads of Blu-Tack, we'd roll our eyes and mutter something like 'budget cuts, eh?' or 'well, that's show business!'

We were called incessantly throughout the work. First from irate library users, then irate managers who hadn't gotten the memo, then by Linda herself, who seemed to be under the impression that we were simply larking about and what was a tiny little bit of broken glass, anyway?

In response, I snapped off several photos of the glass that had gotten *inside* the pages of the books nearest the worst affected windows and wordlessly forwarded the images to her. She stopped calling after that.

Later, we began to get calls from the regulars and the same users who'd been irate about the library being closed.

'Oh, I've had a look and I hadn't realised it was so bad. Are you alright in there?' one of our crime-loving ladies had said.

'We're getting there!' I'd replied. 'The worst of it is done. We just want to be sure the place is safe.'

'Do you need a hand?' another had offered. 'I can bring round a brush and shovel if you need it!'

'Are you sure?' I'd asked. 'It might get full of broken glass.'

'Don't worry, it's old!'

Soon, people were hovering by the broken windows. Others knocked on the staff entrance to offer bin bags, another shovel, even an old vacuum cleaner and gloves.

By the time the repairman arrived, we'd had a dozen or so offers of help, though I'd had to turn away the volunteers who'd offered to help with the clean-up. The last thing I wanted was a member of the public to end up injured. I'd already had to pick glass from my shoes and fingers more than once. Nevertheless, the offers were always appreciated.

Still, the phone calls came. People offering teas and coffees. Requests to renew books over the phone. Offers of donations for replacement windows. Even Mr Lewis, who normally communicated purely in the form of grunts, called to ask if there was anything he could do to help get the place up and running.

In the end, we managed to get the library somewhat open that same day. By cordoning off the worst parts and with the boarded windows keeping the winds out, we'd cleared an area that we were sure was free of glass. We may have only managed a few hours of opening time but those were some of the busiest I'd ever experienced. Local regulars brought us biscuits just to express their sympathy for the place.

It was almost as though a dear friend of the community had been violated and now the community was rallying to support that friend. There was a true sense of sympathetic anger amongst the users that day.

Word also seemed to get around that I, specifically, was the one managing the clean-up. Before the end of the day, Linda called to let me know that she'd had several complaints from members of the public that Claire and I had been 'left to it'. She asked if I'd put them up to it. I laughed and told her I didn't have time to put anyone up to anything. We were too busy hoovering glass particles out of the photocopier.

I realised that the magic had never been in the stacks, nor the books themselves. The true magic of the library came from what it stood for and from the community that kept it alive. Without the people – without the hard work and the genuine love that stems from them – a library would just be a hollow building with some books inside, a warehouse for the written word, solemn and soulless.

Chapter 10

The Community Strikes Back

Visitors Daily (average) May: 157

Enquiries Daily (average) May: 44

Printed Pages Daily (average) May: 129

*Violent Incidents May: 0 (**does the incident with the child urinating on the large print count? – Emily**)*

*Children's Event Attendance: 125% (**additional events to cope with demand planned – Susan**)*

*Photocopies Daily (average) May: 100 (**we need toner! – Allie**)*

Free Watch Batteries Supplied to Public (packs, total) May: 51

Free Dog Waste Bags Supplied to Public (crates, total) May: 10

Damaged/Lost Books (total) May: 22

Free Sanitary Products Supplied to Public (boxes, total) May: 36

*Days Tracking Checklists Not Complete: 8 (**I understand your complaints and we're looking to streamline and automate the process. For now, please keep filling out ALL tracking forms EVERY DAY – Linda**)*

Book Requests Fulfilled May: 233

*Free Food Waste Bags Supplied to Public (crates, total) May: 6 (**that's us out! more ordered – Adam**)*

Book Donations (crates, total) May: 7

Adult Event Attendance: 90%

Reports to Building Maintenance (total): 14
Repairs Completed: 4
*Outstanding Maintenance Requests: 16 (**the basement is still leaking! – Allie**)*

'And this glue, is this the standard non-toxic stuff? I don't recognise the label.'

I stared at the auditor incredulously as he tapped the glue stick in my hand with the tip of his ballpoint pen. My initial response had been to laugh but now he was looking at me over the top of his half-moon glasses (where would someone even *get* half-moon glasses these days?) with a completely stony expression.

'Nah, this stuff's rubbish,' my mouth ran off before I had the chance to catch it. 'The good sniffing stuff's in the bins out back.'

Heather was making frantic slashing gestures towards her neck from behind the auditor. Linda was standing further off, pinching the bridge of her nose.

Ask a stupid question …

The auditor huffed, scribbled something in his notebook and continued to poke and prod at the workspace around me. He'd been inspecting the library for just over two hours now, 'hmm'-ing and 'huh'-ing and asking increasingly ridiculous questions. I was just trying to get on with my job.

I leaned around him and spoke to the library user dutifully waiting in the queue behind him.

'Hi there. How can I help?'

Mr Lewisham had a reputation for being one of the strictest health and safety auditors in the company. He inspired a form of terror in upper management that would have been impressive were it not for the fact that – and I cannot emphasise this enough – I did not get paid enough to give a single shit about him or his clipboard.

We'd had the honour(?) of a visit from Mr Lewisham when I'd been working at Colmuir. I, foolishly, had hoped that he might have picked up on the myriad of ways in which the lone worker on each shift was put in danger by violent members of the public. Silly, optimistic me had even hoped that he might suggest giving us some first aid training, or a panic button that actually functioned.

He'd spent several hours poking at fire extinguishers, asked me about the last test of water quality and left me to it.

To say I had contempt for the man would imply that I regarded him worthy of such emotion.

When a local authority overspends and thus intends to make cuts to services, several tell-tale signs precede the falling of the axe. One of these is a sharp uptick in the number of audits – particularly those of an opaque, bureaucratic manner such as health and safety inspections. Let's be clear: in all my years working in archiving and libraries, I have never known a health and safety audit to flag up any actual danger to staff, even after staff members have pointed out the glaring disparities.

This is not to say that I don't believe that health and safety generally has its place. I have also worked in plenty of other environments where audits have most likely saved lives. It's just an unfortunate fact that councils and large organisations the world over have learned that H&S makes a wonderful scapegoat when times are tough and budgets are tight.

I was, of course, still waist-deep in the trenches of the battle to keep Roscree Library open and was already well aware of the dangers to the branch, even as visitor numbers continued to creep up with our efforts. I just didn't feel that fawning over this pedantic little man or his clipboard would achieve much.

The main concern of the Roscree Defenders (as Emily, Adam and I had come to call ourselves – who said library workers were nerds?) was the impending Bake-Off. It was the last big event we'd managed to schedule before Heather's return and, as such, it was the last thing we had relatively set in stone. Heather had been doing her damnedest to ensure that every other idea or suggestion was shot down via a combination of staffing changes and more and more bizarre and specific rule enforcement.

Heather would never admit it aloud but it was becoming increasingly clear that Adam had been right on the day we first met: she was terrified of Roscree's increasing foot traffic and was doing a terrible job of disguising the fact.

I secretly suspected that there was more to her anxiety than a mere fear of people, though. Heather was at an age where retirement was really only two or three years away. It made sense that she would prefer to spend those few years in a quiet, even dwindling, branch. Sitting safely below the funding bracket for more staff (and more administrative work) meant that she could spend most of her shifts in that back office, counting down the days until her pension kicked in.

To her, our constant attempts to increase foot traffic and accessions and bump us up a funding bracket could well have felt like an attack on her peaceful, slow approach to retired life. Little wonder, then, that she seemed to take our every effort as a personal attack.

When Mr Lewisham eventually decided that he'd poked at a sufficient number of inanimate objects, he tore a sheet from his notepad and handed it to Linda.

'You can expect a call with the results in three working days,' he announced gruffly, like a doctor discussing a blood test.

And with that, he left.

Heather was already approaching the reception desk, where I was stealthily wiping the fines of a user who'd spent the last couple of months in hospital. I waved off the elderly gentleman, who winked at me.

Heather's face was like thunder. She tapped her fingers on the desk in front of me. I could tell from her nervous energy that she wanted to pull me up for the way I'd spoken to Mr Lewisham as elsewhere but didn't dare get into it in front of Linda, who was still within earshot. Instead, she cleared her throat in a forced, girlish manner and picked up a slip, which had fallen out of one of the recently returned books.

'What's this?' she asked.

It was one of the 'invitations' I'd created to promote the Bake-Off. I'd taken to not only slipping them into books as they were being sent out but placing them in returned books that I knew would be borrowed again soon.

Big mistake.

'It's uh ... a promotion. For the baking event.'

Heather's eyes narrowed. 'Did Linda authorise this use of resources?'

Linda perked up at the sound of her name and approached the desk.

'Uh ...' I glanced at Linda, hoping for a little bit of backup. It seemed as though she was still miffed by my attitude to the auditor because none came, so I replied. 'No. It was my idea.'

'Huh.'

I knew that *huh*. As predicted, she turned away from the desk without another word and headed for the management office.

Linda opened her mouth as though to speak, seemed to think better of it, and left.

I didn't like the silence that followed. I knew exactly what was going on in that little office. It was there that Heather would be furiously typing (well, as furious as one can be while typing with a single finger). Communications between her and upper management would be flying. 'Clarifications' of operating procedures were doubtless being sought before the announcements began.

There wasn't much use in worrying about it, so (as I had been trying to do all morning) I simply got on with the job. I gestured for the next person in line to come over to the desk.

'Hello, I'm looking for a book.'

'You've come to the right place. Is there something particular you're looking for?'

'Yes. I saw it here last week. Something like … Summer Oranges or Lemons … It had a woman on the cover. I think it's about lesbians.'

At Roscree, we've taken to calling overly vague requests 'blue-book questions' – as in, 'I don't know the title or the author but it had a blue cover.' I don't know a single library worker who isn't familiar with the phenomenon. Given that one of my particular tasks was the processing of new books, my ability to answer a surprising number of these requests has become a point of both pride and amazement for me. We call the process of drawing clues from the reader and narrowing possibilities down 'blue-book divination'.

Twenty minutes and a lot of gentle questioning later, the library user left clutching a copy of *Oranges Are Not the Only Fruit* by Jeanette Winterson and I basked in the warm glow of another mystery solved while resolving to take a holiday at some point. Clearly, I'd become far too familiar with the branch stock.

Unusually, Heather's email-chain process took several hours and when the first of the emails hit my inbox, I'd almost forgotten about the audit, the glue stick, the invitation and Heather's sour expression.

To: ALL LIBRARY STAFF
From: Oscar Coates
CC: Team Leaders, Community Librarians, Childrens' Assistants (all)
Subject: PROMOTIONAL COMMUNICATIONS

Dear All,
It has come to my attention that unofficial printed promotional materials have been used. These have been designed locally at branch level and do not match our official corporate standards. As such, I must remind you that no such materials should be distributed. All such materials should be designed and distributed by the council's graphic design department and/or be rendered in plain, Arial text on the corporate shell paper, in the corporate standard colours as referenced in SOP 207 (A).

Please contact myself or any member of my team should you require further clarification on this matter. Repeated failure to adhere to corporate standards may result in disciplinary action.

Please print this email and post it on your branch's staff notice board.
Regards
Oscar Coates
Head Librarian

Emily had joined me on the afternoon shift, and, in one of our rare quiet moments, we took the opportunity to dissect the email.

'I mean,' she said, as I handed her the hard copy of the email, 'it really depends on what we class as *promotional*.'

'I guess that these count,' I said, holding up one of the invitation slips.

She sighed. 'Probably. What about posters? Are we talking displays too?'

'What, every poster? Plain Arial on headed paper? That'll look terrible. Surely not,' I scoffed.

She gave me a look that immediately cut my scoff short.

'This is going to every branch, right?' I said softly.

'Every staff member at every branch.'

'Seems unenforceable to me.'

'We'll see.'

*

The next day, Heather arrived early. I'd never known Heather to be in early for a shift. It threw off my rhythm and had me questioning my own timekeeping.

Something about the library was off, too. It wasn't just the gloom caused by the boarded windows – I'd gotten used to those, as had most of the regulars – it was the walls . . .

'Good morning, Allie! Looks like the weather's finally improving!' Heather practically bounced past me on her way to the office, a stack of papers precariously balanced in her arms.

Every sign, poster and printed item had been stripped, removed, taken down. Some had been replaced by the blank, corporate-approved, black-on-white-headed-paper signage. Everything else was simply gone, even in the children's section.

Roscree Library was grey, empty and barren.

Once Heather had disappeared into the management office, I tiptoed over to the paper recycling bin and had a peek inside. As suspected, everything with a dash of colour had been thrown inside. How anyone could have taken a look at what had become of the branch and considered it an improvement was as baffling to me as the motivations of a junior book villain. (*Evil Mrs Corporate and the De-Colouring Ray of Doom*.)

I glanced at the staff notice board and homed in on the phrase 'printed promotional materials'.

My gaze fell on the children's colouring station, to the sets of glorious pens and crayons, which stood out so starkly against the new, joyless surroundings.

Sod your retirement, I thought, *I won't let you kill this library.*

*

As I've said, Emily is an artist. When she's not working at the library, she paints and draws and writes poetry. I've always been a little bit in awe of her creative ability, though I used to worry that I'd come across as a little bit creepy if I were to mention that out loud.

The hours we spent drawing and colouring, both in our free time and during the quieter parts of our shifts, were immense fun. There was a sense of revolution in our actions. Never at any point did either of us consider that we might be doing the wrong thing. We *had* to save the library from death-by-a-thousand-corporate-cuts. The community needed us and, besides, we needed to save our own jobs! Even Adam got in on the fun, tracing letters in purple pen and orange crayon, underlining them with a red felt-tip.

We replaced the posters in batches of one or two at a time. Sometimes they'd be torn down the next day. We'd replace them again. The three of us made sure that the others had alibis. We knew that the CCTV failed to cover the vast majority of the library.

Emily and I created secret Facebook accounts (Adam being less sure of technology and how to cover his tracks). We told no one the names on the profiles, not even each other. We used them to join various local groups like *Mums of Roscree; Colmuir and Surrounding Areas Neighbourhood Watch* and *Roscree News Discussion*.

The changes at the library had not gone unnoticed.

'What's with the weird signs at the library?' one commenter had asked.

'You mean the black and white ones?' another had replied.

'No, that's the same as every libary (sic) now. I mean the pictures.'

'I never saw them. Will have a look when I go shopping later.'

'My sister works at Cummore Library and she said it's management. They don't want staff making signs.'

'I heard it was because it's easier for blind people.'

'Blind people can't see, idiot.'

I must admit that I spent about as much, if not more, time reading through local people's commentary on the state of the libraries than I did reading through the replies to my viral thread. I wished I had thought of doing this before. I'd always been too afraid to join local newsgroups under my real name but now I had a window directly into the thoughts and opinions of the community.

With my sock puppet accounts, I had something else.

Using online tools to cover our digital tracks, Emily and I began posting digital copies of our original Bake-Off invitations to the Facebook groups. As agreed, we didn't reply to any of the comments, nor did we add any text-based information. We simply joined up, posted the jpeg which contained the details of the event and left.

We did the same on Twitter, though it's harder to gain traction with new accounts and even harder to link an image with users in an area without paying for promotions or spamming hashtags.

The Facebook trick seemed to work. Within a few days, comments on the original posts had had to be locked down by many of the groups' moderators, such was the level of discussion and debate on them. People demanded clarification on whether these were official communications from library staff. Some branded the images a conspiracy. Some groups blocked our sock puppet accounts, others welcomed the posts and the increased digital traffic that they brought with them.

Whenever a member of the public asked about the posts in person, I would do my best harassed politician impression, fight the urge to smile, and say, 'I'm afraid I can't comment on it. Council rules.' What I *could* confirm was that the details on the now semi-viral image were correct. We did have a baking competition coming up. Yes, it was open to anyone who wished to register. No, only those who wished to partake in the judging process would need to pay an entrance fee. Yes, registration for bakers was still open.

Within a week, we were fielding calls from the local newspaper. We'd already received two separate emails reminding us that under no circumstance were we to make a statement on behalf of the branch, service or local authority. All press communications were to be referred through the council's PR department, which I was more than happy to do.

Just over a week after The Great Poster Cleansing, the local Roscree paper had run two separate articles on the battle of the library, though they didn't explicitly name it as such. The Bake-Off invitation image was reproduced in all its technicolor glory in one of the articles.

Heather refused to leave the office, even when the queue stretched into the street, which it was starting to do with alarming regularity. She appeared to have given up on concealing her fear of interacting with people, instead only scurrying out to the printer to collect her paperwork whenever we were too busy to ask for help, or while the branch was closed to the public.

We had thought that our footfall numbers had been improving before. Now they skyrocketed.

The previously boarded windows were replaced ahead of schedule. I suspected that the increased visitor count had brought with it an increased number of complaints about the state of the building. My nightly visits to the community Facebook groups confirmed this. It seemed that the library had become a point of pride for the community, having visibly defied the council directive to strip all colour from its walls and displays.

Linda stopped visiting the library.

There were meetings, of course. Given the way our shift patterns worked (and the unpredictable nature of my zero-hour contract), it was difficult to get all of the library staff in one place at one time. Instead, sporadic half-meetings were held, wherein the minutes of the *other* meetings were read to the participants and we were then asked to agree, disagree or comment on the discussion.

Each of us refused to point a finger at the others. Heather started taking sick days again. The corporate directives began to come in at fever pitch.

To: ALL LIBRARY STAFF
From: Corp HR
CC: Library Management, Corporate Staff
Subject: Library Staff Annual Leave

To Whom It May Concern,
As of next year, all annual leave (Jan–Dec) MUST be booked by the 31st of January. Failure to do so may result in annual leave dates being denied. This applies to all Library Assistants and Team Leaders.
Laura
HR

Very few of them seemed particularly relevant to anything. All were nonsensical at best. Each new directive was punitive, petty and pointless. The aim was clear: if the council couldn't cut staffing directly, they'd create such a hostile environment that the staff would leave for them.

Perhaps it was a coincidence that the aggression from upper management ramped up in the wake of so much media attention to the libraries. Perhaps the cuts had been scheduled long in advance and this was simply a way of accelerating them. It seemed strange that, between irrelevant proclamations, certain procedural overhauls related directly to events at Roscree.

Coincidence or not, the directives made life much harder at Roscree. I would be lying if I said I hadn't considered applying for a role elsewhere. As the weeks went on, I ended up sending out a few CVs and even attended an interview for a paid position at a charity where I felt I could do more good for the community without continually having my wings clipped by corporate pettiness.

To: ALL LIBRARY STAFF
From: Oscar Coates
CC: Team Leaders, Community Librarians
Subject: Book Displays

Dear All,
In line with service streamlining, please see the attached list of approved displays for the upcoming six months. Please note that these displays have been agreed with our corporate charities and official partners and will take precedence over existing displays. As agreed, Team Leaders will choose display themes from the list which are most relevant to your local branch.
Regards,
Oscar Coates
Head Librarian

*

All this doom, gloom and pessimism melted away whenever I looked at the Bake-Off sign-up sheet. We'd had to stop taking on baker applications after we hit the 50-mark. I had serious doubts as to whether 50 cakes would even fit in the branch, never mind all of the accompanying people.

Still, the document made me smile. It reminded me of the outraged comments on the community Facebook groups. It reminded me of the locals rallying together to help us clear the broken glass. It made me think of the now thousands of comments in praise of local libraries in response to my tweets.

Something else was making the rounds on the local social media groups, too. The ongoing expenses investigation at the council was picking up steam. At first, rumours began to circulate about Ben Priestly's sudden departure from the council.

Soon, the *Roscree Post* picked up the story and it was confirmed: Councillor Ben Priestly had coincidentally decided to take early retirement from his role as councillor for the area right about the time his expenses for the previous few years had come under intense scrutiny. The implication was obvious but there was another aspect that had cropped up in the online conversations: with Priestly gone, who within the council would be responsible for the situation involving the Miners' Welfare? Would there even *be* an ongoing situation?

It would be easy for the council to dismiss the matter after all this time. The building was condemned. The man responsible for the decision not to provide a new home for the centre was gone. Case closed.

Moira had visited several times in the weeks building up to Priestly's departure and had explained that council intervention was vital for the continued survival of the Miners' Welfare. Though she and her various friends and associates had raised as much money as they could, the fact remained that buying or renting a new facility privately was just not on the cards. The ground on which the old centre sat was now useless due to the subsidence.

While Priestly had repeatedly ignored calls for help in this matter, the pressure on him had been mounting. Having a figurehead – albeit in the form of a scapegoat – for the campaign had been a great way to keep the community motivated. Nothing unites people like a common villain.

Now, with Priestly gone, the matter could be swept under the carpet. The FORMW would have to start anew with their activism – new protests, new petitions, a new councillor on whom to put the pressure.

'Unless,' I suggested one day, 'whoever replaces him is a bit more sympathetic? You never know.'

Moira laughed bitterly.

'You don't know the council like I do,' she said.

She sighed and glanced out at the car park and across the street. Her eyes narrowed and she turned back to me.

'How long has that care home been lying empty?' she asked.

I shrugged. 'It's been that way since I started here.'

'Interesting . . .'

Before I had a chance to ask what she was thinking, she popped some new petitions down on the desk and said, 'I'll be in later. Can you do the usual with these?'

I nodded and she left. I looked out at the abandoned care home. Could she be considering it as a potential new miners' welfare centre? It was certainly convenient for the library and everything else in the middle of town.

I left copies of the petition in strategic positions around the library and, once again, vowed to deny all knowledge of how they got there should any member of library management ask.

*

People have an image of what a library should be. The image might be a little bit outdated or old-fashioned but, by and large, we all know what a library should do and what it is.

A library is incompatible with unregulated capitalism. Its core function is incompatible with a drive for profit and efficiency which is measured in cash flow. Ultimately, libraries require money from those who need them least, to help those who need them most.

The day when local libraries are no longer needed is the same day that every person can access every story, every reference and every form of education for free. Until that far-off day, libraries exist to even the playing field. They are the repository and dispensary of a community's knowledge. They are the brain and beating heart of the community, as necessary as air.

The vast majority of people know this on some level. They may have forgotten about the individual services that the library provides but every single person I have encountered who has grown up around a library knows just how important they are.

As the day of the big Bake-Off approached, I think that most people began to realise that this was about more than just a silly baking event. We began to receive more donations, in book form and other ways. A local historian offered to provide a series of lectures on the history of Roscree, for free. Others provided old maps and photographs for the event. We had authors calling to ask if we ran signing sessions.

Just as it had on the day of the broken windows, Roscree rallied around its heart and made a stand against austerity's axe.

We use this service, was the message. *We use it and we need it. We won't let you take it from us.*

Chapter 11

Cake and Community

Visitors Daily (average) June: 190

Enquiries Daily (average) June: 52

Printed Pages Daily (average) June: 145

Violent Incidents June: 0

Children's Event Attendance: 100% **(deposit scheme seems to be working – Susan)**

Photocopies Daily (average) June: 90 **(photocopier broken again! Waiting on engineer – Allie)**

Free Watch Batteries Supplied to Public (packs, total) June: 42

Free Dog Waste Bags Supplied to Public (crates, total) June: 9

Damaged/Lost Books (total) June: 21

Free Sanitary Products Supplied to Public (boxes, total) June: 33

Days Tracking Checklists Not Complete: 3 **(Please keep an eye on branch emails for updates to the tracking targets – Linda)**

Book Requests Fulfilled June: 280

Free Food Waste Bags Supplied to Public (crates, total) June: 8 **(ordered more – Adam)**

Book Donations (crates, total) June: 5

Adult Event Attendance: 85%

Reports to Building Maintenance (total): 15

Repairs Completed: 10

*Outstanding Maintenance Requests: 21 (**basement leak fixed, but floor still wet! – Allie**)*
*Event cancellations: 2 (**timetable conflict: events rearranged and deposits refunded – Allie**)*

I adjusted my name tag and ran my hand over the stubborn cowlick that had seemingly sprouted overnight. The rain, which had pelted down for most of the night, had slowed to a grey drizzle the morning of the Big Bake-Off.

My outfit was a delicate balance. I wasn't technically on shift for the Bake-Off and so I couldn't wear my uniform, yet I didn't want to be mistaken for another member of the public when I moved behind the desk to assist those who *were* officially working that day. I also needed to smooth the damn cowlick, fix my name tag, which did not want to sit straight, and was I wearing too much make-up? What if there were press? Should I have gone without the eyeliner?

My stomach gurgled unpleasantly as I forced down the last of my tea, saluted the cats and headed out for my commute.

I squinted through the rain-streaked windows of the bus and wondered if the sombre weather would be enough to put people off the event. We hadn't charged any sort of deposit, had we?

My grim reflection and worries were cut short and immediately replaced by a new kind of anxiety when the bus rounded the corner at the library. Even forty minutes before opening time, there was no mistaking the library as the source of the truly enormous queue that snaked down the street.

People holding cake tins and umbrellas, pushing prams with plastic covers, smiling faces beneath waterproof hoods. I spotted a few familiar faces in the crowd as I disembarked from the bus. Many of our regulars dotted the queue, waving and gesturing to their own covered cakes as I approached the staff entrance to the library.

I could hear Emily's voice as I stepped inside. As I had suspected, our shifts had been mysteriously changed the week before so that no members of the Roscree Defence Squad were due to be working for the Bake-Off. Instead, inexperienced call-off staff had been drafted in. A cynical person might have noticed a pattern here but it hadn't mattered. We'd all put too much work in to be deterred by a little thing like not being paid for our time.

'Morning!' Adam announced cheerfully from atop a step ladder. He gestured towards the bunting in his hand and pointed down at a box of tacks. 'Give me a hand, will you?'

The recent de-colouring of the library only served to highlight the dramatic transformation the branch had undergone for the day. All of the stacks that could move had been pushed back and covered in plastic sheeting provided by Susan. She'd been encouraging the children at her classes to make cake-themed paintings and crafts. These were now stuck to the shelf-coverings. They'd made posters and bunting, too, which now festooned the walls and windows.

Adam had brought in an industrial-sized bag of balloons which we spent a good twenty minutes inflating and pinning to the walls and pillars.

Emily, with characteristic artistic flair, had created signs and little toothpick flags to insert in the cakes, each with a hand-painted number so that the submissions could be anonymous.

We'd previously managed to source some paper tablecloths. These were scattered with glitter (again, a gift from Susan's art cupboard). Alongside the library's tables, we'd managed to borrow some fold-out craft tables from local schools and other branches. I had no idea where we'd managed to find all of the chairs. It seemed we had enough to seat half of Roscree.

With five minutes until opening time, we (Susan, Adam, Emily and I) stood back to admire our handiwork.

'Not bad, eh?' Adam chuckled.

I was surprised to find that a lump had formed in my throat when I opened my mouth to speak. Emily seemed equally lost for words. Instead, she pulled us into a hug with an excited squeak.

'All right, team,' she said finally. 'Let's do this!'

I had never experienced noise like it. The moment we lifted the first set of shutters, muffled cheers came from the crowd outside. By the time the rotating doors started up and the queue began to spill inside, the muffled roar became a buzz of excited chatter.

Despite our best efforts and my finest spreadsheets, the organisation of participants soon descended into chaos. We quickly discovered that far more people had brought home baking than had actually registered to participate and so the tables were soon groaning under the weight of so much delicious confectionary. Pastries and cakes and pies sat on the windowsills, on the tops of the bookshelves, in and around the IT desks until the place began to smell more like a bakery than a library.

'Hey, Allie!' a voice called. It was Sophie, the Colliesh mum. She brandished a tray of cupcakes triumphantly. 'I made loads!'

The turnout was far beyond anything we had hoped for. A host of unfamiliar faces bearing baked goods far outnumbered our regulars, though I was grateful to see so many that I recognised. Those who didn't bring sweet treats were happy to pay to judge and all were keen to stress the importance of the cause we had chosen (a cancer charity).

Throughout the day, we received additional donations until our collection tin was packed full and had to be emptied into the safe in the basement for safekeeping. Even once the queue outside had filed into the building, yet more people came in couples and groups until we had to impose a limit for the sake of safety.

Somehow, despite the chaos, we managed to get the submissions separated by age category. Cakes were dropped, sprinkles were lost and biscuits fell behind bookshelves but, with all who attended pitching in, the Great Roscree Bake-Off was a resounding success.

What struck me most that day was the electric sense that we were on the threshold of something new and exciting. There was a shared sense of almost purposeful anarchy that went beyond the Defence Squad's rebellion. The sight of cakes all over the library, of so many people packed into what had quite recently been a dreary, business-like space and the buzz of chatter and chaos felt like a reclaiming of the branch by the community at large.

At one point I found myself watching a group of elderly library users who were looking over the promotional materials we'd set out for our chosen charity. In a rare moment of relative quiet, their conversation had carried to where I was collecting paper plates and plastic cutlery.

The four of them were discussing the charity and all that it had done for them and their loved ones who had been diagnosed with cancer. As more people came to join the conversation, the tone became somewhat reverent. Those that I could see had a tear or two in their eyes as they spoke at great length of their gratitude for all that had been done for them.

As I scraped sponge crumbs and icing into the bin, Mr Lewis approached me, clearly looking to speak. I straightened, expecting the usual grunt from him and was surprised to see that his eyes, too, were glistening with the first pinpricks of tears. He grasped my free hand, suddenly, and firmly pressed a £20 note into it.

I met his eyes and was about to speak when he said, more softly than I had ever heard him speak, 'This is for the charity. My wife had it. Cancer. Hell of a thing.'

I dropped the paper plates into our bin and clasped the note. I was surprised to find a lump in my throat as I spoke.

'Thank you,' I said.

He tipped his hat – the hat I'd never seen him without – and nodded.

'You take care of yourself, Allie,' he said.

We must have signed up at least thirty or forty new members, between tastings and the tallying of scores. People were taking selfies, tagging the local council in their Instagram posts and sharing calls with friends who couldn't be there.

It was beyond our control and it was glorious.

*

Sometimes, when I speak to friends about the harder times at the library or the more outlandish experiences I have had in my time here, they ask me why I don't look for something else. Don't I ever want a job with better security, where I know that, in six months, I will still be employed and safe and nobody can walk through the door, and, say, throw a chair at my head?

The truth is that by the afternoon of our big Bake-Off day, with prizes handed out, sponge trampled into the carpet and dripped icing decorating the edges of tables and chairs, I knew that the little niggling feeling I'd had about libraries was true. I belonged here, amongst the Colliesh mums and the Cheetos and the special interest kids and the nurses and the teachers and every other person who had gravitated towards their town's little hub.

I had laughed until I cried that day. I had tasted cake and helped elderly library users navigate enormous trays of biscuits and walkways narrowed into gauntlets by towering confection. I had handed out voting forms and paper plates and fixed bunting knocked loose by shuffling chairs.

Once the revolving doors had come to a halt and the last shutter had been lowered, I looked around our little branch. Adam was chatting with Emily as he collected chairs. Emily was sweeping, face flushed and grinning. Their laughter filled the air which otherwise would have been curiously silent after all of the din of the day.

Susan was pulling protective sheeting from the stacks, while some of the community volunteers wiped down tables. All were laughing, even though we had a long clean-up operation ahead of us.

'Oi, slacker!' Adam called.

I turned as he threw a handful of balled-up dirty napkins at me and flinched.

'Your phone's ringing!' he said, gesturing towards the desk.

I pulled a face at him and binned the napkins as I unlocked the desk drawer and retrieved my phone.

Linda's name popped up on the caller ID. I wondered why she hadn't called the branch phone as I picked up.

'How did it go?' she asked before I had a chance to speak.

'Great. Really great.'

'Big numbers?'

'BIG numbers,' I confirmed with a grin. We'd lost count at around two hundred or so but I was fairly convinced we'd come close to three hundred. We had probably exceeded the safe capacity of the library at some points during the day.

'I'm glad. I really am. We'll talk more tomorrow but listen, I know you're busy. I wanted to let you know now because I've got some news. Can you talk for a minute?'

I had moved away from the chaos of the clean-up committee and stepped into the basement stairwell. I closed the door behind me.

'Sure,' I replied, 'go ahead.'

'I've gone over the numbers, the footfall from the past few months. I've been pushing Oscar to make a decision on this for a while but he's only just got back to me. He's also been going over the numbers and we – Roscree, I mean – qualifies for reclassification.'

There it was. Even after all our effort, the place wasn't meeting targets. We were being stripped of funding. The axe had fallen.

'Allie?'

'Yes?' I managed, struggling to conceal my disappointment.

'Allie, it's *good news*. They're upping the staff numbers. We're well clear of the mark and I want you to be the first to know that a part-time position has been opened. Now obviously you don't need to make any decisions now—'

Laughter bubbled through from the main library area. I glanced through the glass panel in the door just in time to see Adam stuff an entire cupcake into his mouth in one go.

'Yes,' I said abruptly.

'You want the position? I haven't told you the hours or—'

'I don't care. I'll do it. If that's what you're offering.'

'I was hoping you'd say that. I'll cmail you over the details. Oh, and by the way, a little birdie told me that a local community group has taken an interest in the library. One of them is the head librarian's cousin. She thought the Bake-Off was fabulous. Can't say too much more but big things are coming! I'm so excited!'

I laughed as Emily caught me staring through the glass panel and pulled a face.

'Thank you, Linda. I really appreciate it.'

I hoped that in those few words I had also conveyed some sense of forgiveness and apology. I knew that she hadn't been the one to cut my contract the first time around. I also suspected that she'd been badgering Oscar Coates on my behalf for some time. Reclassification normally happened at the end of a financial year.

I hung up and returned to the public area.

'Everything all right?' Adam asked.

'Better than all right.' I grinned. 'You might even say *mission accomplished.*'

*

'Hi, is this Allie Morgan? I'm calling from the BBC again. We're looking for someone to speak about libraries again for the PM show. Are you free tomorrow?'

My phone had experienced a flurry of notifications overnight.

There's no guide for what might happen when something you write goes viral. If I were to write that guide, I would make sure to mention that it often doesn't just go viral once. Sometimes you'll get picked up by another publication, or a celebrity will retweet the original thread and share it with their followers.

Sometimes, your thread is translated and mentioned on the news in other countries. An Indian TV station had featured my thread on their website. A French publication had also picked up on it.

The magic of libraries, it seems, transcends language and cultural barriers. The bookworms and artists and lovers of community spaces had come together again, rallied by a few notes I'd rattled out one dinner time about my own experiences of that Other Kind of Magic.

A newspaper fell into my lap.

'Oi, daydreamer,' Adam said. 'Check out that front page.'

The *Roscree Post*. I picked it up and laughed.

The front page featured a large photo of the queue outside the library on the day of the Bake-Off. The headline read, 'Library Draws a Crowd of Cake Lovers for Cancer Cause'.

'Looks like we're famous,' Adam said. 'Don't let it go to your head, eh?'

'Who, me? Nah. Just wait until we're fending off the rest of the press.' I flicked through the paper, pleased to note that we'd managed to generate an entire feature. 'I don't know about you but I reckon we should make some posters with this on it. Maybe the total, too. Nice and colourful.'

'Yeah, the place could do with sprucing up a bit. Back to the grind, eh?'

'Back to the grind.'

*

A few weeks later, a crowd of a different kind had gathered outside the library, or, rather, outside the empty building across the road from the library.

Moira had summoned an impressively large gathering of locals outside the abandoned care home to make a point about the place. As I'd suspected, she'd decided that the building would make the ideal home for the new Miners' Welfare centre and she and her associates now stood holding signs and handing out leaflets to all who passed the place.

'She'll scare off the public,' Adam remarked wryly, though I had already spotted one of the leaflets poking out of his trouser pocket.

'What public?' I said. 'She's got half the town out there. The retired ones, anyway.'

'She's mad,' Adam commented admiringly. 'Bonkers. If the council had any sense, they'd give her what she wants just to get her onside.'

I could already see a photographer approaching her. She was speaking animatedly with him. I recognised him as one of the staff from the *Roscree Post*. Two of the Friends of Roscree Miners' Welfare were unfurling a handmade banner, though from this angle I couldn't quite read what it said.

'Bonkers ...' Adam repeated, taking a sip of tea from his enormous travel mug.

*

'I'm really pleased, Allie. Really pleased.'

Graham continued to flick through his latest notes on me. I had a sudden, intense flashback to my school years, watching a parent thumb through my report card.

My cheeks flushed.

'You've come a long way,' he continued. 'I'd say we're looking at maybe three, four weeks.'

261

'Four weeks for …?'

'Four weeks until discharge.'

I swallowed. The earth seemed to open beneath me. The colour drained from my face.

'How do you feel about that?'

I'd been coming to Graham on and off (mostly on) for four years. We'd done grounding work, scent association and then a whole damn lot of EMDR together. He was a regular staple of my life now. I even found myself mentally noting events through-out the week to bring up at our sessions.

The idea of simply facing each day without a therapy session in my future was like finding myself treading water in the deep end of the pool for the first time. I tried not to panic.

'Uh … I hadn't thought of it,' I found myself saying hesitantly.

'Well,' he replied, 'we can stretch it out. Go from two weeks to three between sessions. Maybe four. I honestly think you're ready.'

I bit my lip. Perhaps an incline instead of a drop would be less extreme. I should have thought about this before now but the truth was that, until a year or two ago, I hadn't been able to conceive of a future at all, of an *after* with me in it.

'I'd … like to stretch it out. Do you really think I'm ready?' I asked.

'Allie, look at you! You're a different person from when I met you. You're out there, working, organising, campaigning. You're doing more than half of the people I've worked with. You're writing, you're not just standing up for yourself but your entire profession. Remember when we first met and you couldn't take a bus alone?'

I nodded. I didn't like to think about it but he was right. The panic attacks had been too common and too debilitating. The flashbacks left me confused and afraid.

Now? I still had the odd flashback, but I maintained control. I knew who and where I was. I had a purpose, too. Hell, I'd gotten the train into the city on my own, to speak to a presenter in a radio studio live on air!

'I think you have a lot to be proud of.'

The heat rose in my cheeks.

'Besides,' Graham said, 'we can't let all of these appointments get in the way of your goals. Sounds like you're pretty busy these days.'

I scratched my nose, but I found myself smiling.

'I do have a lot of things going on.'

'Just remember me when you're famous, eh?' he joked, getting to his feet. 'Same time in two weeks? Mull it over.'

I stood and nodded.

'Can I still call you?' I asked. 'If things … if things get bad again. Can I be uh … un-discharged?'

Graham's tone became sincere. 'If it comes to that, yes.'

'Then it's all good, right?'

'It's all good. You've got this.'

For once, my goblins seemed to be in quiet agreement.

*

A final rule – **Celebrate the little victories. Celebrate the big ones, too.**

Chapter 12

The Future of Libraries

In 2019, a study by the National Literacy Trust found that less than a quarter of children in the UK read regularly for pleasure. This generation of British children read less than any generation before them. Over 380,000 have never owned a single book.

I refuse to believe that this generation of children is somehow defective, somehow less capable of experiencing the joy of reading.

My love affair with books began in my little primary school library but I was recently shocked to discover that not every school has a library these days, so where are children supposed to catch the reading bug?

It seems common sense to me that bringing a child up in an environment where reading is only ever a chore, or a duty, will cause the child to associate reading with schoolwork, assignments, responsibility and seriousness.

Where is the magic in that?

When I was a child, the school maths curriculum was based around an American series of textbooks called Heinemann Mathematics. Having developed the habit of firing through my schoolwork as fast as my little hands and mind could manage, I succeeded in working through the entire set long before I was due to move into high school. It wasn't so much that I *enjoyed* maths any more than I particularly enjoyed any other subject. It was just that I'd developed a compulsive need to acquire as much knowledge and skill as possible. I hungered for it.

I had read somewhere that our ability to learn new things lessened with age and the thought terrified me. Suddenly there seemed a real urgency to my studies. I didn't know what I wanted to be, but I knew that I wanted to *know*.

Finishing textbook number 7 two full years before I was due to move on to anything new was an outrage to me.

My poor teacher tried to explain that, even though she'd asked, there was very little chance of the school acquiring textbook number 8. It was designed for high school students and therefore wouldn't be allocated for in the school's book budget.

So we studied textbook number 7 again. We filled out the workbooks again.

I began to act out, frustrated and bored. I do not doubt that, at times, my poor Primary 7 teacher put up with some truly awful behaviour from me. I also do not doubt that this behaviour was quickly made known to my parents.

When it comes to my upbringing, I have much to be thankful for. My parents, who no doubt took turns switching my bedroom light off every time I fell asleep with my face in a book, took me to the Big Library.

I already knew that the Big Library was a magical place but I was reintroduced to the children's reference section and there, nestled amongst past exam papers and workbooks, was a glossy, slightly worn copy of Heinemann Mathematics number 8. The '8' itself was a great, swooping infinity sign, which, to my childish eyes, seemed futuristic and exciting and bursting with potential.

I ended up spending many a day off and a summer holiday flipping through that textbook, in between readings of the works of Tolkien or Roald Dahl.

When I moved to secondary school, one of the first things my new mathematics teacher did was hold that textbook aloft, turning it to show that infinity-8 to each of us and ask, 'Have you seen this? Have you read it?' Our answer, along with one or two quick tests, helped determine the level at which we began our secondary mathematics studies.

The library's magic had saved me from slipping behind at a time when ploughing ahead meant the world to me. It had served the primary purpose of all libraries: it levelled the playing field. It didn't matter that I was working class or that my little school had struggled for books that other children might have found readily available to them. The library had made that information and knowledge available to any who asked.

The key is knowing and being able to ask.

It's no secret that decades of austerity along with a shift in the way society functions has led to library closures all over the country. The tale is always the same: those who use and need the library are the vulnerable, the poor and the voiceless. They are the ones hit hardest by the closures. Too late, the rest of the community picks up on the story and there might even be protests. Too late. The damage is done.

Then there are the stealth cuts. Staff numbers are cut, opening hours reduced. Qualified and knowledgeable library workers are replaced by volunteers (not that volunteers don't have their place but they cannot be expected to run a branch alone) and lo and behold, the service suffers, the usage drops and the bigger cuts begin.

If I have learned one thing from my time working in libraries, it is this: *it doesn't have to be this way.*

During one of my radio interviews, I was asked what I thought about the future of libraries. It was a very brief slot and

I didn't get to say as much as I'd have liked. This is what I would have liked to have said:

Libraries, as we see and use them now, will only have a future if we take a real, serious look at the way we fund them. If we continue to look at them in abstract, capitalist terms of 'productivity' (cash generated, feet through doors), we will be seriously undervaluing them. The true value of a library is not in the immediate cash and people-flow. It is far, far more complex than that.

How does one measure the money saved by providing a space for children and adults to learn for free? How does one measure the value of a worker who stays behind and helps a couple of elderly users set up their new phones so that they can stay in touch with their grown-up children who have moved abroad?

How do we count the cost of removing a space where anyone can go, without judgement or charge, and simply exist? What does it cost to deprive a community of a friendly face who can help those in real trouble apply for a crisis loan, fill out a form they can't read or just sort the mail they can't see into important and junk mail?

As long as library funding is decided by footfall, libraries will only continue to exist if people come through the door, but who wants to come to a place where it's not nice to be? Who wants to sit on broken, soiled chairs under broken windows covered in graffiti? Who wants to bring their children to a place where anti-social behaviour runs rampant because the only member of staff present is alone and traumatised by the violence they've experienced?

Walking through the door is only the first step.

So how do we ensure that this generation and the next have the same access to the same magic that we have been so blessed with?

I am no politician or economics expert but I have worked on the front line of the service that I love so very much for several years now. Thanks to my viral thread, I've been in touch with library staff and library lovers all over the world. I've interviewed exhausted librarians, had coffee with desperate reference staff, even chatted online with academic library staff, social workers, care workers, psychologists, mental health nurses, book club chairpeople, authors, publishers and those from every walk of life imaginable. We are all bound by a passion for saving the sector and a shared sense that something needs to change.

From my experience and research, I've concluded that there are three key ways we can save these beautiful, magical places:

1. Investment

    It's not sexy. It's not digital services and 3D printers and iPad rental. (Though greater investment means we can diversify what the library has to offer.) It's simple: the more we put into libraries, the more we get out. Invest in the people and the community and the rest will follow.

    While monetary investment is sorely needed, it's not the only investment that our libraries are in dire need of. We need the investment of time, of expertise. We need the investment of interest from the community. That might mean local businesses putting a little bit back into the community by donating towards events, or it might mean Tom from the local wildlife sanctuary popping in every few months to do a couple of talks on birdwatching. Maybe the local college could team up with the library to provide some simple classes together.

    We need the investment of local knowledge and not just the academic kind. Perhaps local pensioners' groups could team up with the library to share photographs and memories of the area for a display or a memory group session. Perhaps some of the residents of the local care homes could pop over for an afternoon and we could watch old football matches on the library projector.

Some days we hold Bookbug sessions in a care home for people with dementia. The children sing old nursery rhymes and many of the residents join in too. It's collaborations like these that can make all the difference to a community and we couldn't make it happen without the investment of time and work by care home staff, local parents and our children's librarians.

2. Public Awareness

If I had a pound for every person who, upon discovering what I do for a living, has said, 'Oh, I didn't know we had a public library', I would be able to afford my own, personal library.

The most vulnerable users know that we exist. The fact of the matter is that it's those who *don't* need the place to survive that we now need to make aware. Libraries *must* expand beyond bare-bones services that only help the poorest.

We'll continue to lose users to cafés, coffee shops, book shops, nurseries, Amazon, private childcare, pubs and every other private sector service unless we make libraries accessible, useful and attractive.

3. Autonomy/Democracy

The one-size-fits-all approach just doesn't work. Branches become so tied up in petty bureaucracy that staff and users alike lose sight of the core purposes of the library. The service suffers and the community suffers.

I often remind people that use of the library is free but it's not! You've paid for it! You pay for it every time you pay your council tax. It's *your* service, so don't you think that you should be entitled to a say in how it works?

Simply put, individual libraries need more control of their budgets at a community level. We need less red tape and more grassroots initiatives.

Here's an example of the kind of waste that occurs when policies are blindly applied across an entire sector:

In my local authority area, libraries, gyms, swimming pools and museums come under the same management structure. Staff are assigned a 'band', which is basically a level of pay and authority, whether they're a janitor, a children's library assistant or a lifeguard. Because of this, I have been forced to go through training on swimming pool maintenance and PH balance. Multiple times.

Does that infuriate you? It's your money that was used for these training sessions. Your money paid for me to sit and listen to an expert explain how to decontaminate a public pool.

Needless to say, I have never had to use any of this training in my role as a library assistant. In fact, I can't swim and tend to avoid the pool at the best of times.

This kind of idiotic waste wouldn't happen in the private sector. I know we don't exist to make a profit but this kind of bone-headed stupidity is commonplace at local authority level.

It doesn't have to be like this.

Doesn't it strike you as strange that you're already paying for a service that the majority of people are not currently using, many of whom aren't even aware that such services exist?

Now let's try something. Imagine going down to your local library and viewing manifestos with library-specific policies.

Imagine voting for the events that your library held. Imagine having input on what should be prioritised in the budget.

You know your area and you know which services you would use. Again, even if you don't use the library, imagine being able to have a say on what it would take to make you become a regular. What would help you in your day-to-day life? What services would you make use of? Why aren't you a member of the book club? Is it only available when you're at work? Are the genres chosen not to your taste? Are the library opening hours themselves too restrictive?

Imagine a truly community-run library. How might that look?

What we need is right there in front of us: we need to make our voices heard and we need to be listened to. *You* need to be listened to.

We need managers and staff to be held to account when the service *you* are paying for doesn't work for you. We need our investments of time and passion to be repaid in kind. We who are experts in our community need that expertise to be acknowledged!

Make complaints. Make suggestions. Make a noise! Kick up a fuss on social media. Offer your time when it suits you. Demand the right to make your *own* book club that suits *you*! Demand more books, better books! Demand facilities that work, printers that work, staff who are empowered to help instead of restricted by operating procedures written by bureaucrats who have often never even visited the branch!

I guarantee that the staff at a local level might be burnt out, but they started with the same passions and ideas as you. Push for a service that allows those ideas to flourish instead of being smothered in paperwork and red tape.

It's *your* library. What you put in, you should get out. Never forget that.

Oh, and for goodness' sake, please be kind to the staff on the front line. We want the same things, too, even if our hands are often tied. Some biscuits for the staffroom wouldn't go amiss, either. I personally like Hobnobs, just for the record.

*

Somewhere in the children's section, a woman sighed and said, 'No, you can't have THAT many books. Look at how many you have! How many is that?'

A child's voice replied, 'A MILLION!'

'You can have six,' the woman said.

There was a soft 'aww' of childish disappointment and the familiar flop of plastic-covered children's books falling from hands too small to carry the full pile.

'Just six?'

'Yes.'

'Really?'

'*Yes.*'

'But Mum, I LOVE books. I want them all! How will I choose SIX?'

Over at the reception desk, Adam had printed out a map of the local area. He held it up to show it to Mr Lewis.

'Now, see this bit I've circled?' Adam said.

Mr Lewis grunted and nodded.

'That's the old post office. You want to go up this street. That's us here, see? I've highlighted the way. It's round the corner there,' he continued.

He handed the map to Mr Lewis, who studied it at great length before concluding, 'Aye, I see what you mean now, son. How much will this cost me?'

Adam shook his head. 'No charge. I've put our number on the back. Just give us a call if you get lost.'

Mr Lewis grunted, though it was a jovial sort of grunt, and folded the map to put it in his coat pocket.

Laughter bubbled up from the corner where our knitting and crochet club were enjoying tea, a good gab and very little actual crafting. Since we'd started advertising the group on social media, the numbers had swelled. We went through two urns of tea every session. Newcomers were welcomed into the circle with needles and wool donated from members of the community. Sophie brought home-made biscuits every week. Cameron, now toddler-sized, babbled happily and scribbled with a crayon on the colouring sheets we printed off for him specially. (His favourite things to colour were unicorns.)

Emily was busy registering a small family, which consisted of one grandmother and three grandchildren. All had distinctive fiery red hair.

'So what date is *your* birthday?' she asked the youngest child, who blushed, stuffed a finger in his mouth and shrugged.

'It's August,' answered the grandmother.

'Noooooo, Gran!' the other two children chorused. 'That's Jessica's birthday!'

'Isn't she May?'

'Graaaaaan!' the eldest girl sighed. 'That's YOUR birthday!'

'Oh. Right. Yes.'

Emily smiled with all of the patience of a saint and slid three forms towards the group.

'Tell you what,' she said, 'why don't we let your gran have a seat and you can fill these joining forms out together? Bring them to me when you're finished.'

I was in the IT section with Mrs Collins, who had just thrust her phone into my hands.

'It's the new one, see?' she said. 'Tommy gave it to me before he and the kids went back to New Zealand. Says they can "Face-Space" with me.'

I nodded, smiling. Ever since Mrs Collins' son, Tommy, visited her for the holidays, the grandkids had been all she'd spoken about. I felt as though I knew this family as intimately as my own. I'd never seen her so enthusiastic about anything other than bowel movements or gritty crime novels until then.

'So you need me to turn the volume up?' I asked.

'Aye, hen. It doesn't seem to make a noise any more. I keep missing their calls.'

I spent the next ten minutes or so explaining the 'mute' function on her new phone and another fifteen explaining again as she retrieved a little leather-bound notepad from her handbag and licked the tip of her pen. She squinted at the notebook over her glasses, pen at the ready.

'Say that again, sweetheart. The volume is where?'

As always now, there was a queue at the front desk. All of our computers were booked out. Each library user got a one-hour slot for now, though there was talk of more machines being bought in, budget willing.

Susan emerged from the basement, which had been repurposed into a space for large groups and classes. Most of the storage boxes had been cleared away or moved aside to make room for tables and chairs in various adult and children sizes.

The after-school club decanted into the library, where they were met by parents and guardians, most of whom had clearly come from work.

'Remember, mums and dads, next week is a school holiday so no after-school club! We have lots of activities, though, so keep an eye on the posters because they book up fast!'

Our reclassification to a three-person branch had boosted our funding, though we'd been warned that the footfall would have to continue to rise if we wanted to comfortably ensure that we kept the money.

Already we had plans for more events.

A delivery driver shuffled around the children with a hand trolley stacked high with cardboard boxes. I waved off Mrs Collins as she left and darted over to sign for the delivery.

'More books, is it?' he said.

'Should be,' I replied as I helped him shift the boxes behind the desk.

'Can't believe how busy this place is. I thought nobody read books any more.'

'You'd be surprised.'

I waved the delivery driver off. He'd be spending the rest of the day delivering furniture and other items to the new Roscree Miners' Welfare centre across the road. I could just imagine Moira directing the steady flow of workmen and delivery drivers around the place. The thought made me smile.

I overheard Adam signing up another small family of new library users.

'All right, let's do this young lady first. What's your name and, more importantly, what's your favourite kind of dinosaur? Go!'

I laughed to myself as I wiped down a keyboard. If that interaction doesn't summarise library work, I don't know what does.

*

It's difficult to describe the reality of working in a library at times. The truth is that the only thing anyone can predict on any given day in the stacks is that *nothing is predictable.* If I could reach out and speak to the Allie who first started working in Colmuir, what would I tell her?

Allie, you will have plenty of days when you are leading the discussion at the reading group. You will have days when you're putting out tea and biscuits and cutting out crepe paper for a summer reading display. You will also have days when you will watch, helplessly, as an angry man drags a young woman and her toddler from a morning baby group because, it will turn out, she has skipped a day at school to give her child something resembling 'normal' playtime.

We can navel-gaze about the identity of a librarian (and by now you should know that I love a good navel-gaze) and we can debate the name and function of a library (is it a community centre? A local hub? An information depository? Who cares?!). None of that matters to the girl who has to choose between a day of high school education for herself or an hour or two of play and education for her baby.

A truly good, properly functioning library that is empowered and sufficiently-funded will find the place where skipping school to look after your baby need not mean missing out on an education or any other social opportunity. A good library will be the difference between poverty and success, surviving and actually living.

Call it what you like. Whatever shape it takes, a true library is not just a safety net but a beating heart of a community. A librarian is someone who does everything in their power to make that a reality.

Here comes the bad news: there is a battle going on, right now, in most developed (and many developing) countries around the world. As with the battle for Roscree, it's multi-faceted and often goes unnoticed by the general public until things become truly dire.

Libraries are not, by and large, very compatible with a capitalist culture and some of the biggest proponents of the culture also happen to be those with a lot of power politically. It's not good business to allow these little community safety nets to provide services for free that could, potentially, be run for profit.

You might have heard some politicians and businessmen say things like 'maybe we could pivot to a privatised model' (those are shops), 'libraries are not sustainable without income flow' (depends on your definition of 'sustainable' or, for that matter, income) or 'libraries are obsolete' (as though libraries are not needed now more than ever).

I honestly believe that statements like these come not from a place of malice, but of misinformation. Just as much of the general public could do with a bit of education on just what it is that libraries like Roscree *do*, these politicians and business-owners could do with a bit of education.

Let's give it to them. Let's use libraries. Let's *celebrate* our libraries. Let's demand more and better, and show with our money, actions and votes that value is measured in more than bottom-line profits!

I know I intend to.

Chapter 13

The Day the Plague Came to Roscree

It's easy to get complacent about our place in the world and the state of things. We see our life trajectories and we try to aim ourselves towards something better – mourning the failures, the falls and the losses – but we rarely consider the possibility of a great shift in the surrounding environment. We can be cynical about the government's policies, the state of capitalism, even the very nature of humankind, but very few of us are used to change in the states of these things in anything greater than tiny increments.

An election, even a referendum, does not change the world overnight.

COVID-19 came to Roscree in much the same way it came to the rest of the country – slowly, distantly and then suddenly up close and all at once.

I was working at Roscree when the official order came in: we were to close the building to the public as quickly as possible: the lockdown was coming. The Prime Minister would be making the announcement later.

I had spent the previous day in an antsy state of hyperawareness. Already the virus had reached UK shores. Already we had taped posters to the windows and walls reminding library users to stay two metres apart, to wash their hands for the time it took to sing 'Happy Birthday' twice.

I had watched in mounting horror as the library filled that day, Bookbug its usual anarchic mess, sticky little hands on every surface. I watched the queue at the desk grow and then bundle up, strangers huddled together or hunched around computer screens in the IT section.

I'd told Adam to go home. He has severe asthma and, no matter what we said or did, there was simply no way to enforce these sudden new social distancing rules. He'd refused to leave me alone and I'm not one for arguing with someone as stubborn as him.

The two of us stared in horror as one of our elderly regulars approached the desk, coughing and hacking and trembling. She hunched over her little tartan trolley, skin pale and glistening with sweat. The phrase 'patient zero' came to mind.

'Should you be here? Maybe you should get some rest at home,' I suggested as diplomatically as I could manage.

'No, hen,' she replied between coughs, hauling large-print books from her trolley and dropping them on the desk, 'I need my books. Got a touch of pneumonia. Need my books to pass the time.'

It would have been almost comical, had the danger not felt so real.

Without any guidance from management, I had procured my own rubber gloves and hand sanitiser. (I'd been lucky enough to have some sanitiser leftover from my camping kit.) I insisted on wiping down the books with cleaning spray myself, not wanting to put Adam at any greater risk.

After Bookbug, the only visitors that last day before lockdown were the elderly. I don't know if it's because our older users tend to rely on printed news and with the ever-changing situation they were perhaps slightly out of the loop but I suspect there was a generational difference in attitude towards the virus.

What I do know is that not one of those visitors seemed to share my anxiety. Many scoffed when I suggested that they stock up on extra books in case the library was closed down. Some referred to the virus as 'just another flu'. Most completely ignored our requests to maintain a safe distance from staff and other library users.

When the order to close came in, I all but cried with relief.

I'd spent the morning sanitising every surface I could manage. I'd heard that in places like Italy, where the lockdown was in full swing, people had hung pictures of rainbows in their windows to give each other – especially the children who would be most confused and frightened – some hope.

I quickly rattled off some rainbow posters, adorned them with slogans like 'stay safe, Roscree' and 'wash your hands' and covered our windows in them. I locked the place up and on the front door I left a sign with a few choice quotes from literature about resilience in times of difficulty.

I assumed that we would be closed for a month or two, just until the country had come to grips with this new situation.

My choice of quote would, over the coming months, become more poignant with each passing day.

*

For the next few days, Adam and I would continue to come to the library. We would clean the place and work on jobs that had been left by the wayside, like the weeding of old stock.

Meanwhile, the streets were empty. The car park contained only Adam's car. Nobody passed by on their way to the shops. It felt a little bit like the end of the world.

Greater writers than I will have the words to describe this time when civilisation seemed to silently teeter on the precipice of failure. I can only attest that there was a strange sense of mourning in that empty library as we went about our duties like we were carefully embalming an enormous corpse.

On the fourth day, the call came through from Linda: no more working in the library building. We were to go home for the foreseeable future.

That night, my husband and I watched Prime Minister Boris Johnson announce the lockdown proper. All citizens except vital workers must stay indoors. More instructions would be coming, he said, in a pre-recorded and carefully worded speech.

An eerie silence followed the announcement. The two of us looked at each other but what was there to say? It felt like there had been a declaration of war. An unspoken question hung between us: Now what?

*

After the initial shock, my thoughts turned to the library users and especially our regulars. How was Mrs Collins doing? Was she FaceTiming her family and explaining our new situation to them? What about Mr Lewis, or the poor Cheetos of the world? Who would explain the lockdown to our most vulnerable users, the regulars with learning difficulties and other disabilities?

What about the people living alone?

We library workers started receiving emails requesting volunteers. Some of us went to help local care home staff, others to help in schools where children of key workers were being looked after.

Over the days and weeks, Roscree was converted into a temporary call centre. Here, more library staff manned the council's new emergency line and helped coordinate services like food parcels for the most vulnerable, prescription collection and delivery. Others still, like Adam, took to delivering vital goods to those who needed them most.

My husband having asthma and being unable to drive, I opted to work from home, answering emails from our library users and helping establish remote library services such as virtual Bookbug streams and digital book lending.

Each morning, Linda would send out a cluster email to check on all of us. She'd ask where we were that day, what we were working on and just to confirm that we were still healthy. Emails began to include phrases like 'in these uncertain times' and later, 'as we approach the new normal'.

Nothing quite hammered home the peculiarity of the pandemic like answering the branch emails.

'I have forwarded you some documents. Can you print them off for me?'

Unfortunately, the branch is still closed to the public and so we cannot offer printing services at this time, apologies.

'I've been knocking on the front door but nobody has answered. I need to return my books.'

Unfortunately, the branch is still closed to the public and we cannot take returns in at present. All due dates have been pushed back to accommodate this. Apologies.

It's a plague, I wanted to say; we're living in plague times and I'm apologising in a customer service voice. The world ends not with a bang, but with a 'sorry for the inconvenience'.

Sometime in week eight of the lockdown, Graham got in touch with me to let me know that he'd tested positive for COVID-19.

Who does one seek therapy from regarding one's own therapist having the coronavirus?

I wished him well. He said the worst of it was over. He'd been a bit under the weather, no harm done.

Until that point, we'd been doing one or two sessions via phone but most had either been cut short or dwindled to nothing. The fact is that any sort of therapy is almost impossible when the world is out of kilter like this but it made me realise just how little I'd come to rely on our upcoming sessions. I was stressed as much as anybody amid a pandemic, but I was surviving, even thriving in some ways.

In my diary, I wrote:

There's probably a dark sort of joke to be made from the fact that my psychologist and therapist has COVID-19.

*Who do I talk to about **that**?*

He's in recovery now, thankfully, but it did make me think about my own mental health and that's the first thing I realised: I haven't been thinking about it. I've been so busy surviving and ensuring the survival of others that I haven't had a chance to analyse my own headspace.

Yes, the flashbacks crop up from time to time. They most likely always will. Yes, my compulsive hand-washing is normally not a great survival technique but in this particular pandemic, I feel oddly suited to survive.

I know anxiety. I know fear and I know the sense of despair at an uncertain future.

I am also bloody glad to be alive.

We've all lost people now. Everybody knows someone whose friend, cousin, aunt, even parent has succumbed to the virus. It's terrifying and we're all in survival mode but here's the thing: Some of us have been in survival mode our whole lives.

PTSD is an odd creature. We as a species are going through one of the most traumatic, wide-reaching events of a generation but it almost feels as though I've been preparing for it my whole life. When it comes to trauma, I've done my homework.

Now I find myself in a peculiar position where I'm advising my friends and loved ones. I'm parroting phrases Graham has used with me. I'm sharing the wisdom I gleaned from psychology textbooks and therapy sessions.

Perhaps I ought to start charging.

As lockdown began to lift, I was able to start answering calls for the library, though there wasn't much to say beyond 'Yes, we're still closed. No, I'm not sure when we'll be open.'

Still, as I wrote in my diary:

Some of our more vulnerable members don't seem to understand the pandemic at all but they perk up at the sound of our voices and we do our best to explain that even though nobody knows exactly what will come, we are still here for them. Their library will be here for them, in one form or another.

The library was still a hub, even closed off. Even as plexiglass screens were installed over the reception desk and the front door remained locked, people came to us, called us for advice and information. The people of Roscree trust their librarians. It's a genuine honour (and slightly anxiety-inducing) to be one of the people a community turns to in a crisis.

*

I could feel a bead of sweat forming behind the band of my plastic visor as I sat at my desk in the library. Unable to touch my face, I was helpless against the tickle-trickle of its progress down my forehead to rest on my eyebrow.

My glasses steamed up as I exhaled behind the home-made fabric mask until finally that infuriating little droplet slid beneath my glasses (thankfully missing my eyes) and completed its descent, adding to the moisture building up in the strips of fabric holding my mask on.

I tried to focus on the lecture, but Oscar Coates's voice was a monotonous drone. He'd joked at the beginning of the training session that they'd found 'the most boring man in libraries' to train us on our new decontamination procedures but that had been over an hour ago.

When we Roscree front-line staff arrived for our 'reopening procedures training' we'd shuffled awkwardly in front of the revolving door, each of us masked and squinting in the light. I'd moved to shake Emily's hand, having not seen her in months, only to have her recoil.

Wincing and apologising profusely, I'd shoved my gloved hands under my damp armpits. I had thought that social distancing had become second nature to me throughout lockdown but it seemed that the sight of my colleagues, even in their protective gear, had put me back into work mode.

Our laughs were muffled and awkward and she waved me off as Adam and the others arrived.

Heather was nowhere to be seen. Being in the highest risk category for contracting the virus, she'd been advised to remain at home for now.

Five of us in all gingerly made our way into the library, clumsily stepping and stopping each time we came close to coming within two metres of one another. I kept my hands firmly tucked in, lest I be overcome with the urge to embrace another colleague.

We must have looked like aliens freshly given human form, still working out the intricacies of human interaction and mobility.

Until that point, I'd been surviving lockdown by treating it like a sort of public holiday. I'd almost managed to convince myself that I was merely working from home on my own terms. Even while doing the dreaded shopping run, I'd found myself going into a sort of dissociative daze, keeping my head down and telling myself that things would be back to normal soon. This was a passing event, a spontaneous break from work for everyone in the country.

For months, I'd maintained my sanity in this way. Whenever the panic set in, I'd take a walk in the forest near my home. Who doesn't love a walk in the forest? I was simply enjoying the sun on my extra-long holiday. No need to overthink it.

Seeing Roscree transformed for our new plague times shattered my carefully crafted denial-cocoon and I gasped audibly – inhaling disinfectant fumes – at the sight of it.

All colour and decoration had been stripped from the walls and though the plexiglass barriers had been installed while we'd run the place as an emergency call centre, the place was now bedecked with truly dystopian signage. Hazard-tape marked the safe distance at which members of the public could stand. Signs, everywhere, at head-height, warned visitors to keep apart from each other, to stay away should they experience any symptoms of COVID-19.

Everywhere I looked, signs implored visitors to wear a mask and to use the hand sanitiser at the main doors both upon entering and leaving the library.

The post-apocalyptic feel was further emphasised by the new 'book drop bins' into which library users would place their returned books. These were plastered with biohazard warning symbols and lined with plastic bags.

Later, we'd learn that returned books and other items coming from outside the library would be quarantined in the basement for 72 hours. One member of staff each shift would be responsible purely for the movement and storage of these returns.

The entire building felt like walking into an oven.

Oscar informed us that though the air-conditioning was currently working, having been fixed during the lockdown, it was of a kind that moved the air around too much to be safe to run while there were people in the building. Electric fans of any kind were also verboten: these were a contamination risk as they would move droplets around that might harbour the virus.

As we sat for Oscar's lecture, I was no longer sure if my glasses were steamed due to my breath or the general humidity in the place.

We were given plastic visors, which we would also have to wear in the library at all times – apparently Scottish Government guidelines.

The combination of disinfectant fumes, alcohol smell from the hand-sanitiser (which we were instructed to use at every available opportunity) and stifling heat (compounded by the layers upon layers of Personal Protective Equipment) had me feeling slightly nauseous and sleepy.

Oscar's voice did nothing to alleviate the soporific atmosphere; neither did the content of the lecture itself.

We were each handed an entire stack of new SOP forms to read, each describing in painstaking detail the new procedures we'd be expected to memorise.

'. . . and of course, we will only be allowing one user per computer. As you can see in SOP 497-A, this conforms to . . .'

Emily's gloved hand darted up, which roused most of us from our drowsy reveries.

Oscar paused, clearly not expecting an interruption. He was a perfectly bald man in his fifties with coarse greying eyebrows that sprouted around his thick-rimmed glasses. He dressed like a stereotypical professor. Even today, he was in a three-piece suit, though the tweed had been ditched for black wool. I noted that he was the only person present not fully decked out in PPE. In fact, he wasn't wearing any kind of face-covering while we sweltered away in our masks and visors. The sunlight glinted off the sweat on his head.

'Er . . . yes?' he said.

'What about carers?' Emily asked. 'What about people with carers?'

His forehead wrinkled and he said, in a nasal, disbelieving tone that instantly grated on me, 'Is that likely to come up? Do those people use the computers often?'

'Yes,' I answered before Emily could reply.

I had remembered, as the man was droning on about various types of disinfectant, that his was the name that sat at the bottom of all of our SOP forms. This was the man who designed the library procedures and yet it was entirely likely that before the COVID crisis he hadn't set foot in a library in years. He had certainly never visited Roscree in all the time I had been there.

'We get that a lot,' I said.

'Well—' he produced an elegant engraved ballpoint from inside his suit and clicked it three times before scribbling down some notes '—we'll have to review that.'

Now that we were all more alert, it seemed as though a silent understanding had reached all of us. We all realised that this might be our only chance to bring Oscar back to reality. This was the one opportunity to criticise the procedures as they were created, instead of having them imposed upon us, no matter how impractical.

Adam's hand went up. 'What about browsing? You say you expect readers to put any books they've touched on a trolley. I don't know about anyone else here, but I've had plenty of days where just about every book in the place has been touched. How are we going to have time to disinfect all of these touched books?'

'Well, er … we can, of course, review … if that really is the case …'

'What about non-compliance?' I asked. 'If someone won't keep their distance from other library users, what can we do?'

'Well, I would hope that they would, er … you could, er … speak to them …'

We were on a roll. Emily was already rifling through the previously discussed SOPs.

'It says here that we have to wash our hands at least every half hour,' she said. 'Will there be cover at the desk while I head down to the basement? We don't have a sink on this floor.'

'Well, I suppose we could bend the rules a bit, depending on um ... circumstances.'

'It says here that only one person should be in the lift at a time,' Susan said. 'What about children? Will the activity rooms be off-limits to them?'

'We will, uh ... we will need to assess the, uh ... inherent risks ...'

And on it went. By the end, even the casual staff were picking up on gaps or flaws in the procedures: rules which were impossible to follow due to the layout of the building, procedures that would put visitors in danger were we to follow them to the letter, procedures which contradicted themselves more than once. The more we questioned, the more Oscar would 'hmm' and 'er' and scribble in his notes.

It was obvious that no one had ever pulled him up like this, at least not in a setting with front-line staff. It was also obvious that he'd never bothered to *ask* any of us, and so, for years, he'd gotten away with writing petty and nonsensical rules into standard procedure for libraries which had, by and large, made our jobs far more difficult than they needed to be.

It was cathartic at the time but, looking back now, I get angry. I'm angry because there's a real chance that my colleagues and I have been put in danger by this man. I'm angry because he typifies the pointless, out-of-touch and petty bureaucracy that is killing public libraries. I'm angry at the sheer chutzpah of a man paid four times what I make, sitting in front of me without the protective gear he insisted we wear, telling us how to do our jobs in a place in which he had rarely set foot.

The final straw came when we did a walk-round of the library so that he could demonstrate the placement of various tools and new signage to us. While the rest of us made an effort to remain at least two metres apart, Coates would gesture us to come closer, repeatedly leaning across or pushing around one of us until finally Adam, slightly muffled by his headgear, snapped, 'Back off, will you? For God's sake!'

Oscar recoiled to stare at him.

'You just leaned right across Emily! At least wear a bloody mask!'

'*Excuse—*'

'No, he's right,' I cut in. 'You stood on my foot earlier.'

Oscar's mouth opened and closed a few times. The wrinkles on his forehead deepened and he cleared his throat.

'Yes. Well. Apologies,' he said finally, backing away. 'I think we're done here for today. Please remember to take your information packs home.'

I could have sworn that I saw Adam wink at me, though he might have been blinking sweat out of his eye.

*

I have never been so grateful for an overcast sky as I was on my first day back at Roscree. The branch was stuffy and still but at least the smell of disinfectant had abated somewhat.

I finished logging into the staff computer and gave Adam a thumbs-up from behind the new Perspex screen.

He stood by the entrance, turning keys and flicking switches.

The rotating doors hummed into life as the first masked member of the public stepped inside.

Emily had just finished taping the laminated 'welcome back' sign to the front of the desk and she stepped away, allowing the elderly visitor to shuffle her way first to the hand-sanitising station, where Adam helped her fill out a track-and-trace form, and then over to the desk where I stood.

'Good morning, Mrs Collins!' I shouted through several layers of fabric and plastic. 'How are the grandkids?'

*

I can't quite pinpoint the moment when we settled into our old – yet new – roles. Over the course of the day, we went from being nervous sailors adrift in uncharted seas to experienced hands, navigating the waters with a degree of ease.

Every library has a rhythm, even in times like this. The beat of Roscree's heart may have slowed but once we settled into the new tempo it began to feel as though we'd never closed.

Of course, we couldn't run the activities and services that the community had come to expect from us. We could only have two computers running at once, with space between each booking for a thorough cleaning and disinfecting. We took names and numbers of visitors on the door for the government's track and trace programme, just in case a positive case came up.

I was surprised by quite how quickly the looming spectre of the virus became just another part of the background. Once we had real, live library users through our doors I was back in librarian mode. It was just another Monday, albeit with a few extra rules to follow.

The visitors themselves, for the most part, just seemed happy to be back through those rotating doors. Most were relieved to hear that all fines had been waived, others were anxious to let us know that they had purchased some books online but – not to worry! – now that the library was open again they'd go back to borrowing.

We joked about not being able to hear each other behind our masks and ended up resorting to writing questions and answers on sheets of paper.

When we switched positions – Emily at the front door, Adam at the desk and me cleaning and tidying as best I could – I took a few moments to make a chart with FAQs and symbols that users and staff alike could gesture to in order to get our points across.

As the days went on, we found new ways to get around various communication barriers. I downloaded a live transcription app onto my phone and displayed it at the reception desk so that anyone speaking to me would get a (rough) transcription of what I was saying.

Deliveries were, for now, suspended but this gave the visitors who had become accustomed to ordering books online a chance to properly browse our shelves, which led to new favourites and hidden gems being discovered.

I had expected visitors to be hesitant about actually touching the books on the shelves, especially with one of us dutifully following at a safe distance to collect and wipe down any unwanted titles as they were placed on the browsing trolley. While there was a bit of hesitant tiptoeing and squinting to begin with from our browsers, it soon became clear that we fully expected them to get stuck in, just like they always would.

The funny thing is, nobody had a bad word to say about our new procedures. We got the odd grumble about the track and trace procedure but everyone who visited understood that we were doing our best just to keep the place running and accessible to everyone.

I realise now that this is the true role of the librarian. Yes, we tidy books away and we explain Dewey Decimal numbers and we wipe down computers and we print off forms but, ultimately, it all boils down to one thing: keep the place running. Make it accessible to everyone.

Even in this reduced state, a library is first and foremost a place for all people. It's an equaliser, a safe space and the heart of a community.

We're glad to have you back.

*

I'd like to be able to end on that note, to say that Roscree will return to its previous glory once all this is over. I'd like to say that your local branch will make its steady recovery too.

I'd like to say that we've saved the library that saved me, but things aren't always that simple.

COVID-19 has taken an enormous toll on local authority budgets and the process of reopening is not only slow but very expensive. Sadly, this means that our libraries are in real danger right now, at a time when they're needed more than ever.

How this story ends depends on you: the library user, the reader and the community.

We have a fight on our hands and you should know by now that I love nothing more than a good fight.

The value of a library to a community cannot be easily measured, especially not monetarily. We need you, dear reader, dear lover of the magic of libraries, to make a noise! We need you to share what your library means to you. We need you to step through our doors if you can, to remind your friends and family of this precious community resource. We need you to keep that magic alive, whether by protest, petition, volunteering or a simple reminder to your local authority that you want to see what your taxes are being spent on.

In the meantime, we librarians will do what we do best: keep the place running, keep it accessible and keep the magic alive.

Of course, should you feel so inclined, now that you've finished this book, perhaps your local branch might be accepting book donations. Just a thought.

I also wouldn't say no to some Hobnobs.

The Rules

1. Never assume a level of familiarity with technology.
2. Patience is everything. You never know what someone is going through.
3. Get angry. You will use it.
4. Read what you love, not what you feel you '*should*' read.
5. The public is an unpredictable beast. Never turn your back on it.
6. Always fill out the paperwork.
7. The people within the library are as important a resource as the books.
8. Just because someone communicates differently doesn't mean they're communicating incorrectly. It's our job to try to bridge the gaps.
   a) Just because someone is swearing doesn't mean that they're swearing at YOU. Some people swear in everyday speech and it doesn't mean that they're being intentionally rude. Intent is everything.

9. Do no harm but take no shit.
   a) Sometimes the shit is literal. Sometimes you have no choice but to take it. Sorry.
10. Expect hardware and software to fail. Sometimes a note-pad can be a lifesaver.
11. Never lose your empathy, but learn to leave the anger at home.
12. Wash your hands. Wash them regularly.
13. Celebrate the little victories. Celebrate the big ones, too.